STUDIES IN ROMANCE LANGUAGES: 33
John E. Keller, Editor

LOVE AND REMEMBRANCE

The Poetry of
JORGE MANRIQUE

Frank A. Domínguez

THE UNIVERSITY PRESS OF KENTUCKY

Publication of this book has been assisted by a grant from
the Program for Cultural Cooperation between Spain's Ministry
of Culture and United States' Universities

Copyright © 1988 by The University Press of Kentucky

Scholarly publisher for the Commonwealth,
serving Bellarmine College, Berea College, Centre
College of Kentucky, Eastern Kentucky University,
The Filson Club, Georgetown College, Kentucky
Historical Society, Kentucky State University,
Morehead State University, Murray State University,
Northern Kentucky University, Transylvania University,
University of Kentucky, University of Louisville,
and Western Kentucky University.

Editorial and Sales Offices: Lexington, Kentucky 40506-0336

Library of Congress Cataloging-in-Publication Data

Domínguez, Frank, 1945-
Love and remembrance: the poetry of Jorge Manrique / Frank A.
Domínguez.

   p.   cm.—(Studies in Romance languages; 33)
Bibliography: p.
Includes index.
ISBN 0-8131-1651-1 (alk. paper)
   1. Manrique, Jorge, 1440?-1479—Criticism and interpretation.
I. Title. II. Series. III. Series: Studies in Romance languages
(Lexington, Ky.); 33.
PQ6412.M6D66 1988
861'.2—dc19   88-21627

This book is printed on acid-free paper meeting
the requirements of the American National Standard
for Permanence of Paper for Printed Library Materials
∞

To Katie and Charles

CONTENTS

FOREWORD

Each of the three centuries we think of as medieval—the thirteenth, fourteenth and fifteenth—produced at least two major writers in Spain. Gonzalo de Berceo and Alfonso el Sabio wrote great poetry in the thirteenth century; Juan Ruiz, archpriest of Hita, and don Juan Manuel composed their masterpieces in the fourteenth century; and in the fifteenth, the marquess of Santillana and Jorge Manrique stand out as the most famous. Two were clerics, Berceo and Juan Ruiz; one, Alfonso, was king of Castile and León; and three, don Juan Manuel, Santillana, and Manrique were nobles.

Jorge Manrique fought and died in battle for Isabel of Castile. He was a man of such worth that his contemporaries held him in high esteem. He wrote more than fifty poems, but the *Coplas que fizo por la muerte de su padre* (Verses Written on the Death of His Father) is the work that has made his name immortal. It is a long elegy, which allows his personal grief for his father to represent the collective sorrow of all humanity in the face of death. The *Coplas* describe the transitory quality of human existence and the rewards given to the good Christian on earth, through honorable repute, and in heaven. The

tone of the *Coplas* is noble, simple, and couched in a poetic meter that is pleasant, flowing, and conducive to memorization.

Spaniards are as familiar with the *Coplas* as are Americans
with *The Raven* or the English with *The Canterbury Tales*. But
few Spanish authors, aside from Cervantes, García Lorca, and
possibly Calderón, are even known by name to English speak-
ers. A century ago this ignorance did not exist. Educated
Americans read Manrique's *Coplas* in an English translation
from the pen of one of our best-known and most loved poets,
Henry Wadsworth Longfellow. Before becoming professor of
Spanish literature at Harvard University, Longfellow had
lived in Spain and read a great deal of Spanish literature. The
Coplas inspired him to produce a wonderful English rendition
that almost paralleled the original's meter and to bring most
of Manrique's sentiments into our language. Longfellow was
able to be as lofty, as noble, as lyrical (some think more lyrical), and as impassioned as Manrique. The American poet
achieved an originality of his own, utilizing much of the im-
agery, form, and sentiment of the Spanish poem. His trans-
lation-rendition is remarkable, and it is a pity that his *Song of
Hiawatha* and *Evangeline* seem to have drawn the attention of
American readers away from the *Coplas*. Probably the best
way to reveal Longfellow's debt to Manrique, and the excellence of his art as translator, is to compare the English and
the Spanish poems:

Oh let the soul her slumbers break,	Recuerde el alma dormida
Let thought be quickened, and awake,	abiue el seso y despierte
Awake to see	contemplando
How soon this life is past and gone	como se passa la vida,
And death comes softly stealing on,	como se viene la muerte
How silently!	tan callando.
Our lives are rivers gliding free	Nuestras vidas son los rios
To that unfathomed, boundless sea	que van a dar enla mar
The silent grave!	que es el morir:
Thither all earthly pomp and boast	alli van los señorios
Roll, to be swallowed up and lost	derechos a se acabar
In one dark wave.	y consumir.

In our own day Joseph Ricapito (1976) translated the *Coplas*
into English. His version of the same two stanzas is:

> Awaken, soul, remember:
> let the mind come alive
> and ponder
> how quickly life passes,
> how death comes upon us
> so stealthily
>
> Our lives are rivers
> which flow to the great sea
> that is death.
> There go the nobles
> directly to the end
> to be consumed and vanquished.

Even in translation, the majesty of Manrique's poetry and the
sentiments it expresses are clear.

Jorge Manrique, then, was one of Spain's greatest lyric
poets. Although there is a plethora of articles that treat his
work, there are only three important book-length studies
dedicated to the poet, and all appeared some time ago. Only
one is in English. It was written by Anna Krause, and was
published in 1937. Serrano de Haro's book is twenty-one years
old; the most respected study of all, that of Pedro Salinas,
goes back to 1947.

In this study, Frank Domínguez updates those works. He
also enriches and expands the criticism of the past by ana-
lyzing Manrique's minor poems, so often slighted. And he
treats with relevancy, sensitivity, perception, and common
sense the greatest of Manrique's creations, the immortal *Coplas*. It has been said that no book of criticism can stand un-
challenged for more than twenty years. In my opinion
Domínguez's work will last that long and will be considered
as close to a definitive study of Manrique's poetry as any book
can be.

Love and Remembrance: The Poetry of Jorge Manrique incor-
porates traditional methods of historical research with contemporary critical approaches to poetry. It not only includes

virtually everything important that has been written about Manrique, therefore serving as a reservoir of information, but is a modern presentation of a very great poet.

John Esten Keller
University of Kentucky

PREFACE

Jorge Manrique is currently considered to be one of the great poets of the fifteenth century. His place in the Spanish literary canon, however, has not always been so secure. Nineteenth-century literary historians considered the *Coplas por la muerte de su padre* to be an important work, but they did not necessarily regard it as a masterpiece. Editors often excised stanzas XXV-XL because they thought them inferior to the rest of the poem.[1] Even at the end of the last century, judgments about Manrique's work were colored by a general distaste for the "insincerities" and the "coldness" of fifteenth-century poetry. For Menéndez y Pelayo, Manrique's lyric was indistinguishable from that of other poets. He deemed it interesting only as a social document.[2] Another literary historian, Fitzmaurice-Kelly, considered Jorge Manrique's poetic accomplishment to be similar to that of his uncle. "Como su tío Gómez," he wrote, "su gracia es fría y desmayada, y sus estrofas satíricas contra su madrastra rayan en la vulgaridad. En sus acrósticos amatorios y en otras composiciones de carácter análogo, Jorge Manrique se muestra únicamente instruído en el artificioso estilo de muchos contemporáneos; es simplemente un escrupuloso artista a quien absorben los pormenores técnicos de su disciplina, y cuyo mérito, fuera esa habilidad formal, es bien escaso."[3]

Even though nineteenth-century critics rejected Manrique's lyric poetry, his fifteenth-century contemporaries considered him to be one of their most accomplished love poets. He is among the authors Sánchez de Badajoz, somewhat mockingly, put in his "Infierno de amor":

> Don Jorge Manrrique andaua
> con gran congoxa y tormento:
> de pensar no se hartaua
> pensando en el pensamiento
> que pensar mas le agradaua,
> diziendo entre si consigo:
> Siempre sere mi enemigo,
> pues en darme me perdi,
> mas si yo mismo me di,
> no se por que me fatigo
> pues con razon me venci.[4]

The Portuguese poet, Fernando de Silveira, included Manrique with Juan de Mena and Rodríguez del Padrón as examples of famous poets who sighed for love in a poem of the *Cancioneiro Geral de Garcia de Resende*.[5] Another poet, Urrea, used the *ubi sunt* questions that Manrique so effectively employed in the *Coplas* to ask for the whereabouts of the famous love poet:

> ¿Do tanto galan lucido,
> Las damas de gran primor,
> Tanto varon lindo,
> Don Jorge tan sabido,
> Manrique mantenedor?[6]

Toward the end of the fifteenth century, Juan del Encina placed Manrique among the poets who attend Fame in his "Triunfo de la Fama." There he appeared in the company of

Mena, Guevara, Cartajena, Santillana, Pérez de Guzmán, and his uncle, Gómez Manrique.[7] By then Manrique's reputation as a poet had been augmented by the publication of *Coplas por la muerte de su padre*.

Although the traditional Castilian lyric began to lose ground in the sixteenth century to Italianate poetic forms introduced by Garcilaso de la Vega and Boscán, the beauty of the *Coplas* assured Manrique a devoted following. More often than not, however, the poem was read in glossed editions that presented an incomplete and mangled text. Time also obscured the relation of the *Coplas* to the lyric, impeding the understanding of both. This book seeks to show why Manrique's contemporaries thought him to be a model love poet, how the love poetry is related to the *Coplas*, and how the *Coplas* justifies Manrique's reputation as one of Spain's greatest lyric poets.

Chapter 1 outlines the facts known about the Manrique family and discusses the historical events that shaped their destinies. Knowledge of the politics of the period is essential if the contemporary reader is to understand Manrique's major work, the *Coplas por la muerte de su padre*.

The second chapter is dedicated to the study of the poet's minor lyrics. These poems reflect the social concerns of the mid- to late fifteenth century. In addition, they illustrate the poetic craft of the period in their use of the formal and thematic resources available to poets at the time. Manrique excels in his control of the language of the lyric. His lexicon is drawn from semantic fields consecrated by tradition. At the same time, he is a master at using the substitution and opposition of lexical items in complex verse structures to express his thought. Manrique's use of parallel verse structures in his lyric poetry is most evident in the *copla de pie quebrado*, which he later employed in the *Coplas*.

The study of the *Coplas* is divided into two chapters. Chapter 3 includes a discussion of matters of text, genre, structure, meter, and style in order to present the vast body of often repetitive and contradictory commentary on the poem without distracting from the reading of it offered in chapter 4.

Toward the end of chapter 3, the question of the relationship between the minor lyric and the *Coplas* comes to the fore, suggesting that if one neglects to study the love lyric, one limits one's understanding of the verbal and formal resources of the elegy. Manrique built on the language and structures of the love lyrics when writing his elegy. The universality of the *Coplas* is rooted in that particularity.

Chapter 4 contains an explication of the poem and addresses two related questions. The first concerns the unity of the poem. Some of the better known images and topics associated with death appear in the *Coplas* in stanzas I-XXIV. Those of the panegyric appear in stanzas XXV-XL. Stanzas I-XXIV denigrate life, XXV-XL seem to extol it. Consequently, the sentiments expressed in the first section seem to be opposed to those expressed in the second. As the review of the critical literature on the poem in chapter 3 reveals, the temptation to see two major—and sometimes incompatible—units in the poem is great. Such an attitude, however, is based upon preconceptions the modern reader brings to the work. By insisting that the poem adhere to a certain model, the reader imposes expectations on a work that was not written to satisfy them. Chapter 4, therefore, analyzes the way Manrique uses the topics and images of the elegy in order to glorify his father. Special attention is given to the importance of parallelism in the poem and to the way the language gives the poem semantic cohesiveness.

The second problem posed in chapter 4 pertains to the relationship between the poem and its literary context. This chapter addresses only infrequently the question of Manrique's indebtedness to other texts. María Rosa Lida de Malkiel warned some years ago that Manrique's poetry is not an elaboration of the author's readings but "recuerdos de lecturas, asimiladas y transformadas ya en el propio pensamiento del artista."[8] Some of those "recuerdos" come from the poet's own love lyric, others from the doctrinal texts popular in his age. As Lida de Malkiel said, however, it is doubtful that the poet had any particular texts in mind when creating his masterpiece. Four poems of his uncle, Gómez, may be exceptions to this.

Critics have long regarded Gómez Manrique's "Dezir a la muerte de Garcilasso de la Vega," "Coplas a Diego Arias," "Aguilando al conde de Paredes," and "Planto de las virtudes" as models for some of the language and the topics of the *Coplas*. This reliance of Jorge Manrique on the work of his uncle is the key to the interpretation of the poem in chapter 4. The "Dezir a la muerte de Garcilasso de la Vega," the "Aguilando al conde de Paredes," and "El planto de las virtudes" were not only written by a close and respected relative—the poet's uncle and poetic mentor—they are also poems about family members (the marquess of Santillana, Garcilasso de la Vega, and don Rodrigo Manrique). These poems had great importance within the family context, and it is this factor, in all probability, that weighed heavily on the poet's mind when he came to make his own contribution to the family's evolving poetic history. Chapter 4, therefore, looks at the *Coplas* as a partisan statement uttered by Jorge Manrique on behalf of the Manrique clan and its allies in the face of a great personal loss and mounting political danger. Like the "Dezir" and the "Planto" before it, the *Coplas* inducts a clan leader into the pantheon of family heroes. It also allows the family to share in a portion of his personal glory as it holds up his achievements like a shield before the world. The *Coplas* is not a document that contains "una gran lección de desnudez espiritual" in which the poet "fatiga la figura de su padre con tanto ropaje encomiástico . . . para que la muerte . . . se los quite."[9] Instead, it is, above all, a panegyric. Don Rodrigo is not despoiled by Death, but enlarged by it. When Death comes to him, it comes to give, not to take away.

All quotations of Manrique's poetry are from A. Cortina's *Jorge Manrique: Cancionero* (4th edition [Madrid, 1960]). Several reasons led to the decision to use Cortina's text. First, Cortina used one of the best versions of the *Coplas*, the one contained in the *Cancionero de Llavía*, as the base for his edition. Second, over the years Cortina's work has proved to be the most widely available and frequently used edition of the poetry. It is the source of countless other editions published in Spain and Latin America. Finally, almost all studies of Manrique's

Preface

poetry quote Cortina's text.[10] Translations, unless otherwise noted, are my own.

I would like to thank Dr. María Salgado for proofreading parts of the manuscript, Dr. John E. Keller for making substantive suggestions, Dr. William Ilgen for his kind assistance with difficult bibliographical citations, and most of all, my wife Patricia, who patiently read through all the versions of the manuscript, invariably pointing out weaknesses and suggesting improvements. To her and to them, my heartfelt thanks.

ONE

The Historical Setting

The policies and behavior of Pedro I of Castile alienated many nobles who saw the king as a threat to both their lives and their prerogatives. The assassination of the ruler in 1369 threw the kingdom into social and political turbulence that lasted until the end of the fifteenth century.[1] The murderer, the king's half-brother, assumed the crown under the name of Enrique II (1369-79) and established the Trastámara dynasty.

THE TRASTÁMARAS

Enrique II owed his success to an alliance with disaffected minor nobles who eventually demanded a share of the spoils. The grants made by the crown in response to these demands (known as the *mercedes enriqueñas*) created a new nobility of the first rank, which replaced the families that had been annihilated, exiled, or were extinct by the time the new dynasty took power.[2] Later Trastámara kings endowed these nobles with ever more prestigious titles, donations of land, and revenues taken from the sequestered estates of those who supported Pedro I, and from the royal patrimony. Until Enrique's reign, the major estates of the crown provided a living for members of the royal family, or for important nobles, reverting to the crown at the death of the holder. The Trastámaras generalized the practice of founding *mayorazgos* (entailed estates) to which passed a good part of the royal domain. The *mayorazgos* were the source of the wealth and power of such families as the Mendozas, the Velascos, the Estúñigas, and others.

Enrique III (1393-1406) had some success in recuperating the lands and revenues alienated by his predecessor. In time the monarchy might have consolidated its position, had it not been for a royal minority that instead allowed the consolidation of noble power.

Enrique III died when his son, the future Juan II, was less than two years old. During his minority, Catherine of Lancaster, the queen mother, and the king's brother, Fernando de Antequera, divided the administration of the kingdom between themselves. While the queen sought to protect her son's patrimony, Fernando's own position was more ambivalent.

THE INFANTES OF ARAGÓN

Fernando (regent from 1406 to 1416) took steps to defend his nephew's inheritance from the interests of the nobility by increasing his own hold on Castilian politics. His first opportunity to secure his nephew's throne came with the death in 1408 of Fernán García de Villalobos, master of the Order of Alcántara. Fernando had his son Sancho hastily elected master of Alcántara. The following year he did the same for his son Enrique, when the mastership of the Order of Santiago became vacant.[3]

The advancement of the regent's sons guaranteed for the crown the wealth and power of two institutions that were almost independent states within the borders of Castile. The two military orders, Santiago and Alcántara, had standing armies and revenues derived from extensive landholdings. In addition they held the mountain passes used by the great herds of the Mesta, on which they exacted a levy.

Fernando de Antequera's attempt to consolidate his power followed well established precedents. Castilian kings had always tried to influence the election of the masters of the military orders to their advantage. However, the link forged by Fernando between the crown and the orders was fragile. As long as Fernando's interests coincided with those of the Castilian crown, his sons were willing to remain the crown's allies. But the unexpected happened. In 1410, King Martín of Aragón died without issue or determination of a clear successor. With a ready army and the coffers of Castile at his disposal, Fernando de Antequera was by far the most powerful contender for the Aragonese crown, which he acquired in 1412. The achievement precipitated a series of events in Castile that were still having repercussions fifty years later.

Though admired by the Castilians for his integrity, his military exploits, and his gallantry, Fernando de Antequera lost popularity amidst the deeply rooted antagonism between Castile and Aragón. It did not help matters that he did not give up the regency of Castile when he was crowned king of Aragón or that, although he removed his son Alfonso (the heir to the Aragonese crown) from the family's Castilian inheritance, the power that remained in his and his son's hands was enough to control the destiny of the kingdom. In addition to Lara, Peñafiel, and Mayorga, Fernando had received the towns of Cuéllar, San Esteban de Gormaz, Castrojeriz, and an annual income of 400,000 *maravedíes* from his father, Juan I of Castile. Fernando added to his estates by marrying the richest heiress in the land, doña Leonor de Alburquerque.[4] Her possessions brought Fernando the lands adjacent to the Portuguese and Navarrese borders, which were later to provide his sons sites from which to launch their invasions of Castile. Fernando's second son, Juan, duke of Peñafiel, lord of Lara, and count of Mayorga, married Blanche of Navarre in 1414, and was thus also heir to the Navarrese crown.[5] The third son, Enrique, the master of Santiago, inherited the county of Alburquerque. The fourth, Sancho, continued to be master of Alcántara until his death in 1416.[6] Through marriage, war, and intrigue, Fernando's sons secured a political and economic base that threatened the Castilian monarchy. Around them gathered those same disgruntled nobles whom Fernando, as regent, had opposed.

The sons of Fernando de Antequera, however, did not enjoy their father's popularity. Their very prominence outside the country made them seem like outsiders who meddled in the internal affairs of Castile. Unwittingly, they set in motion the machinery that was eventually to deprive them of their Castilian holdings. They became the *Infantes* (princes) of Aragón, so wistfully remembered in Jorge Manrique's *Coplas*.

When Fernando de Antequera died, his oldest son, Alfonso V of Aragón became the head of the family. Alfonso V received the loyalty of his brothers, who were now willing to act only in defense of their own interests, and no longer as extensions of Castilian royal power. This intolerable situation created an opportunity for three men of low birth to rise and oppose the Infantes. They were Alvaro de Luna (favorite of Juan II of Castile), Juan Pacheco, and Beltrán de la Cueva (favorites of Enrique IV of Castile). These men primarily sought their own advancement. Nevertheless, Alvaro de Luna managed to neutralize the power of the sons of Fernando de Antequera in Castile—though not their political legacy. The Infantes formed a faction within the Castilian nobility whose adherents put their own particular interests before the interests of the crown or of the nation. Even after the disappearance of the Infantes from the Castilian scene, that faction of the Castilian nobility generally retained its ties to the Aragonese monarchy (eventually inherited by the last of the Infantes, Juan II of Aragón). It was instrumental in bringing about the reunification of the two branches of the Trastámaras with the marriage of Fernando (son of Juan II of Aragón) and Isabel of Castile.

DON PEDRO MANRIQUE (1381-1440)

The Manrique family belonged to the old Castilian nobility, originating, it seems, as an offshoot of the Laras, the most powerful and prominent of the old families.[7] They adopted the given name of their ancestor, Manrique Pérez de Lara, lord of Molina, as a reminder of their origin.[8] Before its rise to prominence in the fifteenth century, the Manrique clan held the lordship of Amusco, and many of the family members were *ricos-hombres*, members of the nobility of the first rank. They were among the few clans to survive the social and political upheavals of the late fourteenth century and establish, through the children of Jorge Manrique's grandfather, Pedro Manrique, several families that were to play a significant role in Spanish history.

Pedro Manrique, eighth lord of Amusco and *adelantado mayor* (military governor) of the kingdom of León, married Leonor of Castile, granddaughter of Enrique II and daughter of the duke of Benavente.[9] According to the family histories, they had fifteen children. Through his sons, don Pedro established the power of the Manrique clan. Don Diego was the first count of Treviño; Rodrigo, first count of Paredes and father of the poet; Pedro, lord of Valdescaray; Gómez, lord of Velvimbre; Iñigo, archbishop of Seville; Juan, archdeacon of Valpuesta; Fadrique, lord of Baños; and García, lord of Las Amayuelas. The daughters married well and helped extend the clan's alliances. Beatriz became countess of Haro; Juana, countess of Castro; Leonor, duchess of Béjar; Inés, lady of Cañete; María, lady of Fuentidueña; and Isabel, countess of Oñate. Only one, Aldonza, did not marry but became, instead, abbess of Calabazanos, a family foundation.

Pedro Manrique supported the Infantes of Aragón throughout his life.[10] When the Infante don Enrique imprisoned Juan II of Castile in 1420, Pedro Manrique was one of don Enrique's closest advisors. He was also among those who followed in fruitless pursuit when the king escaped with the help of Alvaro de Luna.

The Manrique family fortunes waxed and waned with those of the Infante don Enrique, until the Infante's final expulsion from Castile in 1432. However, Pedro Manrique was not always estranged from the king or from his favorite. In 1431 Alvaro de Luna married Juana Pimentel, Pedro's niece, and—in a gesture that can only be seen as conciliatory—don

Alvaro allowed Pedro to partake of the sequestering of don Enrique's estates, with the grant in perpetuity of the town of Paredes de Nava.

A few years later, fear of the ever increasing power of Alvaro de Luna again brought Pedro Manrique to rebellion. In 1437, recognizing the danger that Pedro posed to his rule, Alvaro de Luna had him imprisoned in the castle of Fuentidueña. With his sons' aid, Pedro managed to escape through a window of the castle and soon after led a new revolt against Alvaro de Luna.

Pedro Manrique died in 1440. He did not live to see the defeat of his party in the battle of Olmedo (1445). For Alvaro de Luna Olmedo was a pyrrhic victory. The fractious nobles soon reemerged with greater strength than before, having found a willing ally in the person of the crown prince, the future Enrique IV. Alvaro de Luna was finally seized and beheaded in 1453.

By the time of Pedro Manrique's death, his progeny was well entrenched in the Castilian landscape. Diego Manrique, the eldest, became the head of the family, but the second son, don Rodrigo Manrique was the most active member of the family in the events of his generation.

DON RODRIGO MANRIQUE (1406-1476)

Don Rodrigo Manrique, from the very beginning, seemed destined to make history. When he was twelve, the Infante don Enrique made him a knight of Santiago. Later, the same prince entrusted him with the commandery of Segura de la Sierra, a dangerous and important frontier post.[11] At twenty-eight he established his reputation as a warrior by forcibly taking the city of Huesca from the Moors. He was so highly esteemed that when Alvaro de Luna imprisoned Pedro Manrique in Fuentidueña, don Rodrigo's brothers turned to him for direction. It was under his leadership that Pedro escaped. Don Rodrigo also served as liaison between the family and the Infantes. In 1439, the Infante don Enrique asked him to attempt to recover the administration of the Order of Santiago, usurped by Alvaro de Luna.

Don Rodrigo married doña Mencía de Figueroa. The fertile marriage produced six sons (Pedro, Diego, Rodrigo, Fadrique, Jorge, and Enrique) and two daughters (Leonor and Elvira). Through Doña Mencía de Figueroa's mother, Elvira Lasso de Mendoza (a sister of don Iñigo López de Mendoza, first marquess of Santillana), the children were related to the most distinguished poet of the previous generation.[12] Rodrigo Manrique, who was, as second son, not exceedingly wealthy, procured commanderies of the Order of Santiago for his sons.[13]

The Order of Santiago, founded in the twelfth century, was composed of lay and clerical *freyles* (brothers) who came together for the purpose of serving God and aiding in the reconquest of Moorish lands. All members were under the supervision of a *maestre* (master), whose immediate superior was the Pope. The master gave out the lands of the order as *encomiendas* (commanderies) to knights, who were then known as *comendadores* (commanders). Included in the grants were the people, lands, rights, goods, and rents of the territory, to be held as a nonhereditary estate until the death of the recipient. In practice, and especially in the fifteenth century, sons often followed fathers in the tenancy of commanderies. Santiago was a major source of livelihood for Manrique children and clients.

After the death of doña Mencía, Rodrigo Manrique married Beatriz de Guzmán (with whom he seems not to have had issue), and after Beatriz's death, Elvira de Castañeda. Doña Elvira was a daughter of Pero López de Ayala, first count of Fuensalida, and a great-granddaughter of the last great poet and writer of the fourteenth century, Pero López de Ayala, chancellor of Castile. The marriages brought don Rodrigo money and alliances with other clans.[14] With the young doña Elvira, don Rodrigo had three more sons: Enrique, Rodrigo, and Alonso.[15]

In 1440 (possibly the year of Jorge Manrique's birth), Rodrigo Manrique was in the entourage that accompanied the crown prince of Castile to Valladolid to celebrate his marriage to Blanche of Navarre. Pedro Manrique died a few days before the princely wedding, leaving Rodrigo the town of Paredes de Nava. That same year, Rodrigo joined the Trece, the thirteen senior members of the Order of Santiago that formed its ruling council.[16] He was, therefore, sufficiently secure in the order's hierarchy to maintain an independent stance when, after the death of the Infante don Enrique of Aragón, Juan II moved to make don Alvaro de Luna *de jure* head of Santiago.[17] Rodrigo refused to participate in the favorite's election and contested the new master's rights by taking several commanderies by force and proclaiming himself master. To resolve the conflict, the king returned the town of Paredes de Nava, expropriated after the battle of Olmedo, to Rodrigo. The latter, in order to reestablish himself peacefully in his patrimony, to return to the grace of his sovereign, and to leave his descendants a perpetual dignity in exchange for another that was not inheritable, recognized Alvaro de Luna as master of Santiago in 1452.[18] Rodrigo Manrique received the title of count of Paredes de Nava, to be held in perpetuity by him and his descendants. But not even a title was enough to effect a reconciliation. Rodrigo soon opposed the favorite again and continued to oppose him until the latter's death.

Juan II of Castile died in 1454. The new king, Enrique IV, at first favored the Manrique family, but the advancement of two other favorites, Juan Pacheco and Beltrán de la Cueva, and the king's desire to curb the power of the nobility, soon revived the struggle. Factions began to form around the question of succession. Enrique IV's only daughter, Juana, was rumored to be in reality the daughter of Beltrán de la Cueva, the king's—and the queen's—favorite. In 1460 a confederation of noblemen demanded that the king recognize his brother Alfonso as heir, until he had a direct male successor. When their demands were ignored, the nobles appealed to Juan II of Aragón for help and prepared for war. A confrontation seemed inevitable when the king capitulated.

In 1464 Enrique IV had his brother Alfonso proclaimed prince of Asturias. But the move came too late to close the gulf that separated the king from the nobles.[19] In 1465, a federation of nobles placed a throne with a statue of the king on scaffolding erected outside the walls of the city of Avila. In an unprecedented ritual, the master of Alcántara and the counts of Paredes and Benavente undressed the statue, the archbishop of Toledo removed its crown, the marquess of Villena its scepter, and the count of Placencia its sword. Prince Alfonso was then invested with the regalia and was proclaimed king (twelfth of that name) at the age of eleven.[20] On that day Rodrigo Manrique became constable of Castile and prepared to champion the prince's rights against the king.

A long civil war seemed inevitable. When Alfonso died prematurely in 1468, his sister, Princess Isabel, inherited the allegiance of the rebellious nobles. A reconciliation between the two factions again seemed possible when, during a parley at Guisando that same year, the rebels agreed to recognize the authority of the king in exchange for his recognition of Isabel as crown princess.

The princess's marriage then became the most pressing problem confronting both sides. The king favored an alliance with Alfonso V of Portugal. Rodrigo Manrique and his confederates preferred Prince Fernando of Aragón, the son of Rodrigo Manrique's first cousin, Juana Enríquez, and of Juan II of Aragón, the last of the Infantes. Rodrigo's brother, Gómez, secretly negotiated the alliance with Aragón. In spite of the opposition of the king to a union that threatened his power, the marriage of Fernando and Isabel took place in 1469.

Juan Pacheco, marquess of Villena and master of Santiago, died in 1474. Immediately several candidates claimed the office, but Rodrigo Manrique emerged as the most potent contender in Castile.[21] Acclaimed by several of the Trece (among them, possibly, his sons Jorge and Rodrigo), he finally became master in a disputed election.

Enrique IV's death that same year presented Castilians with a difficult choice: Juana and an alliance with Portugal, or Isabel and an alliance with Aragón. Either choice meant war. Rodrigo Manrique's stance was clear. He championed the cause of Isabel against those who favored the rights of Enrique IV's daughter. To him fell the task of reducing the lands of Juana's main partisans to obedience. Rodrigo Manrique's field of action was in the south and east: the lands and fortresses of the Order of Calatrava, and the marquisate of Villena; in particular, the fortresses of Almagro, Calatrava la Vieja, Almodóvar del Campo, Villarrubia de los Ojos, and Daimiel—all very close to Uclés and Ocaña, both then occupied by Pacheco. After conquering Ciudad Real and Alcaraz, Rodrigo divided his forces. His son Jorge took half and continued to subdue the commanderies of Calatrava; don Rodrigo concentrated on the marquisate of Villena. Uclés, the principal seat of Santiago in Castile, urgently required recapturing; the siege took two months. It proved easy to take the city, but the castle resisted. There was a danger that Rodrigo Manrique's troops would find themselves besieged in the town by forces outside its walls and have to fight on two fronts.

The marquess of Villena and the archbishop of Santiago gathered their men and came to battle Rodrigo. But Jorge Manrique, who had since rejoined his father, foiled their attempt. He attacked Villena's train and inflicted heavy casualties. Villena's other attempts to relieve Rodrigo Manrique's siege proved fruitless, and Uclés capitulated. By 1475 Pacheco's lands were in Rodrigo Manrique's hands. This was don Rodrigo's last military campaign. He died in his town of Ocaña in 1476.[22]

JORGE MANRIQUE (CA. 1440–1479)

Rodrigo Manrique's life overshadows that of his son, Jorge. When Jorge Manrique appears in the chronicles, he is more often than not acting as his father's surrogate in a military engagement. No one knows where he was born or when, though traditionally 1440 is given as the most likely date. The place of birth may have been either Segura de la Sierra or Paredes de Nava, both towns in which Rodrigo Manrique and his first wife, doña Mencía de Figueroa, spent considerable time. However, the traditional claim of Paredes de Nava to be the birthplace of the poet probably has more to do with

Rodrigo Manrique's title than with anything else. Don Rodrigo inherited the town in 1440, but did not secure it until 1452, when he became count of Paredes and reacquired the town, which had been occupied by the forces of the king since the battle of Olmedo. On the other hand, don Rodrigo was involved with Segura de la Sierra in the province of Jaén from 1428 on. His marriage to doña Mencía and their settlement in that town took place on or shortly after 1432.[23] Doña Mencía and her sons were also buried close to Segura, until their remains were moved to Uclés.[24] Because commanders were expected to spend at least four months out of the year in their commanderies, circumstantial evidence seems to favor Segura as the probable birthplace of Jorge, or the place where he spent most of his youth.[25]

Ecija and Valladolid have also been suggested as possible birthplaces of the poet, but evidence is even more tenuous. José Martín Jiménez, on no evidence, proposed that doña Mencía may have gone to Ecija, the seat of the Figueroas, during her pregnancy.[26] Another possibility is Valladolid. Juan, Diego, Pedro, Gómez, and Rodrigo Manrique participated in the Valladolid festivities that preceded and followed Enrique IV's marriage to Blanche of Navarre on September 15, 1440. On Wednesday the twenty-first of the same month Pedro Manrique died. The following day the family came before Juan II to witness the confirmation of don Pedro's eldest son, Diego, as Adelantado de León.[27] The family probably stayed in Valladolid at least through the end of October, when Rodrigo took part in a joust organized by the Infante don Enrique of Aragón in honor of the newlyweds. Unfortunately for these theories, the presence of don Rodrigo in Valladolid does not guarantee the presence of doña Mencía.[28]

About the early period of Jorge Manrique's life one can do little more than conjecture.[29] Rodrigo Manrique's household, under doña Mencía must have been bustling with activity, especially because the commandery of Segura de la Sierra and his household in Toledo were rallying points for the Manriques who held posts in the Order. Though almost all family members wrote poetry, Gómez Manrique, Rodrigo Manrique's brother and one of the great poets and statesmen of the age, was probably Jorge Manrique's poetic mentor.

Toward 1465, the pretender Alfonso confirmed the grant of an annuity from state revenues to Jorge Manrique, in repayment for military service.[30] The same prince's donation of the commandery of Montizón to Jorge Manrique also dates from this time.

Several years earlier Montizón had belonged to Doña Mencía's brother, Garcilasso de la Vega, who died during an ill-fated expedition to Granada captained by Enrique IV.[31] The relatives of Garcilasso de la Vega, including his brother-in-law Rodrigo Manrique and the sons of the marquess of Santillana, implored the king to give Montizón to Garcilasso's son. But that same day, Enrique IV gave the post to Nicolás Lucas, the brother of Miguel Lucas de Iranzo, constable of Castile. The appointment must have enraged don Rodrigo and the Manrique family, who had been instrumental in forcing Enrique IV to surrender the direction of the order to Prince Alfonso.[32]

The renewed meddling of Enrique IV in the affairs of Santiago was galling to the Manrique family, but possession of Montizón was not just of symbolic importance. Montizón was deep in Manrique territory. It controlled one of the most viable routes from Castile to Andalusia and, in the hands of an unfriendly person, could jeopardize nearby Segura. The danger prompted Rodrigo Manrique to secure the commandery for one of his sons. From 1465 to 1467 (when it finally capitulated) Jorge Manrique and his brother Pedro besieged the castle with the permission of Prince Alfonso and in defiance of the Enrique IV's wishes. Pedro began the hostilities with a campaign against the town of Alcaraz, during which their brother Diego Manrique was killed.[33] Montizón capitulated because Lucas de Iranzo was unable to lift the siege and because the troops the constable sent to relieve the siege were routed by Sánchez de Benavides, an ally of don Rodrigo.[34] The very reason that Montizón was an important prize, its strategic location in Manrique territory, made assistance difficult.[35]

The documents by which Jorge Manrique promised to

swear allegiance for Montizón to Pacheco, then acting master of Santiago, and the instrument by which he empowered one of his vassals to do so are extant, both bearing his signature.[36] In spite of its formulaic nature, the first of these documents is fraught with irony in light of the Manriques's feelings about Juan Pacheco, who at that point was their ally:

> Conoçida cosa sea cómo yo, don Jorge Manrique, fijo de don Rodrigo Manrique, condestable de Castilla e conde de Paredes, por quanto a mi notiçia es venido quel señor prior de Uclés e trezes eletores de la Horden e Cauallería de Santiago al ylustre señor don Juan Pacheco, maestre de Santiago que agora es; por ende, conozco que yo, el dicho don Jorge, como comendador que só de Montizón, e freyle e cauallero de la dicha Horden de Santiago, e le conozco e reçibo por mi señor e maestre al dicho señor don Juan Pacheco, maestre de Santiago, e en señal de obediençia [e] reberençia que deuo al dicho señor maestre, que beso una crus qués de la dicha Horden, que tiene puesta en las ropas de sus pechos el comendador Juan d'Ajofrín.[37]

In his biography of Jorge Manrique, Serrano described Montizón based on a deposition made by a *visitador* (inspector) of the order shortly before the poet's death.[38] Another description, written by Francisco de León, commander of the Bastimentos de León when Alonso de Cárdenas was master, came to light more recently. It is based on an older document, and gives an appraisal of the commandery done shortly after the fortress surrendered to Jorge Manrique:

> Es comendador de ella don Jorge Manrique, dio el habito el prior de Ucles, la provision de la encomienda aun no gela habia dado el maestre don Juan Pacheco; no se si gela dio el o despues su padre. Tiene esta encomienda alli en Montison una muy buena fortaleza, que no esta llegado ningun lugar en ella, y señorea gran parte del campo de [   ] de la una parte e de la otra, esta frontero

de la Orden de Calatrava e [   ] la torre del homenaje, que es muy buena, y ansi mesmo gran parte del muro del cuerpo de la fortaleza y de las barreras esto era de haser del maestre don Juan Pacheco que [   ] era, non sabemos si se fiso asimismo el cimiento de dentro de la fortaleza, esta muy mal reparado en algunos logares que se malparo cuando el cerco del dicho castillo. Esto es de faser al comendador. Mandamos gelo haser. Tiene esta encomienda otra fortaleza en otra villa de vuestra orden que se llama Chiclana, y es muy bonita fortaleza, y esta de reparar el muro della en algunos logares y Petrilar y Almenar, y señorea mucho la villa. Habra en la villa fasta doscientos vesinos, y es cercada, y esta cerca de Veas. Tiene esta encomienda grandes terminos y pastos e dehesas. Rendio el año de nuestra vegitasion doscientos e veinte mil maravedis poco mas o menos, e rendira agora mucho mas segun han sobido las rentas. Ha de servir esta encomienda con cinco lanzas.[39]

In 1470 Jorge Manrique married doña Guiomar de Meneses, daughter of Pero López de Ayala and sister of doña Elvira de Castañeda, his stepmother.[40] Jorge Manrique's marriage was in the interest of both father and son. Doña Guiomar had a large dowry, part of which she had inherited from her grandmother.[41] She also further cemented the Manrique family's relations with the powerful Ayala family of Toledo.

A favorite seat of the Castilian kings, fifteenth-century Toledo witnessed the arrival of many noble families who, like the Manriques, established households in the city and contended for public office. Rodrigo Manrique held the *alcaidía* (governorship) of the fortresses, gates, and bridges of the city. The post was later held by his brother Gómez, who was also *corregidor* (mayor or highest civil official of a city in charge of administering justice) of Toledo under Fernando and Isabel. Gómez enjoyed the complete trust of the king and queen, who placed one of the most ungovernable cities of Castile under his care for thirteen years. By the next century the Manriques were part of the ruling oligarchy of Toledo. The

Relaciones de los pueblos de España ordenadas por Felipe II lists among the principal "ancient" noble houses of the city the "Silvas y Ayalas, Guzmanes y Mendozas, Rojas y Riberas, Manrriques y Toledos, Lasos y Carrillos."[42]

Relations between doña Elvira and Jorge Manrique were probably never good, perhaps because of the deep-rooted Spanish antipathy toward stepmothers. They deteriorated quickly after Rodrigo Manrique's death. Rodrigo Manrique had disposed of some of the properties held in security for doña Elvira's dowry to pay for the siege of Uclés. His will stipulated that she be repaid, given all of his movable goods, and some moneys owed to him by Fernando and Isabel. With three young sons to care for, the countess of Paredes was anxious that Rodrigo Manrique's will be executed without delay. The children of doña Mencía apparently did not look very favorably upon this action, for the estate was not settled for nine years.[43] It is in light of this clash of interests that critics account for Jorge Manrique's bitter satire against his stepmother in the *Combite*.[44]

Jorge Manrique's next appearance in the chronicles involves an episode very similar to the taking of Montizón. Enrique IV had restored Juan de Valenzuela to the Priorship of the Order of San Juan, to the detriment of Jorge Manrique's cousin, don Alvaro de Zúñiga, son of the duke of Arévalo.[45] But Montizón was close to Consuegra, where the Prior resided. When Valenzuela attempted to dispossess don Alvaro, in 1470, Jorge Manrique assembled a fighting force composed of his brothers and vassals. He attacked Valenzuela's forces, routed them, and once again frustrated the plans of Enrique IV.[46]

In 1474, as mentioned earlier, Jorge Manrique may have participated in the election of his father as master of Santiago for the province of Castile.[47] He took part in Rodrigo Manrique's campaign to reduce the towns of Alcaraz and Uclés to the obedience of Fernando and Isabel, and his help was not strictly military. The siege of Uclés was so costly that Rodrigo Manrique was forced to sell part of Jorge Manrique's marriage settlement.[48]

After the death of don Rodrigo, Jorge Manrique continued to serve Fernando and Isabel in their efforts to put an end to the civil war—though on occasion taking up arms in defense of family interests.[49] In 1477 he went to the aid of Juan de Benavides, whose children Jorge's son and daughter, Luis and Luisa Manrique, were to marry. The marshall of Baena had exiled Juan de Benavides from Baeza. Together with Juan de Benavides Jorge Manrique forcibly entered the city in search of the marshall, but did not find him. Forces quickly gathered to repel the invaders, who could not maintain their positions. Those who could, fled. Jorge Manrique and Juan de Benavides, among others, were captured. Manrique was accused of disobedience against Fernando and Isabel, a charge he vehemently denied.

Near the end of his life Jorge Manrique became a captain of the Santa Hermandad of Toledo (Holy Brotherhood or provincial constabulary of Toledo), and in that capacity saw his last military action in the marquisate of Villena.[50] Fittingly, thanks to Pedro de Baeza, Manrique's death is one of the best known moments of his life.

Pedro de Baeza was one of the chief lieutenants of Diego López Pacheco, second marquess of Villena. Baeza was in charge of protecting Villena's lands, while the latter looked for a propitious moment to negotiate a peaceful and advantageous capitulation to Fernando and Isabel. Baeza revealed, in a deposition addressed to Villena years later, that he commanded the defenses of the castle of Garcimuñoz when the poet started his incursions into the marquisate:

> muchas veces me hallé sin vos en lo del Cañavate, donde peleé con Don Xorxe Manrrique, é le desbaraté é tomé la cabalgada que llevaba de la Motilla, y entré en Almodovar del Campo por fuerça, é hiçe coxer el pan que estaba sembrado en tierra de Alarcon, estando las capitanias de la Reina tan çerca, donde me ví con ellos en muchas afrentas é peleé muchas vezes, tantas que yo ternia mala memoria de ellas, porque me pareçe que pocos dias passaron despues que me dexaste, señor, en

el castillo, donde no obiese menester las manos; y á la
postre la noche que Vuestra Señoria sabe que peleé con
don Jorxe, como vuestro capitan, él salió herido de una
herida de que murió, é yo saqué otra de un enquentro
por la boca en que me derrocaron algunas muelas, é me
passaron la quixada, é fué tan peligrosa la herida, que
vuestro çirujano aquella misma noche me dixo que me
confesasse y ordenase mi alma.[51]

Jorge Manrique was less fortunate than Pedro de Baeza.
He died on April 24, 1479 as a result of his wounds.[52] A
century later, the villagers of Garcimuñoz still remembered
the incident, and maintained that he was killed by a lance
thrust that entered his side at the level of the kidneys. The
people of the village of Santa María del Campo Rus, where
Jorge Manrique had his encampment, could point to a house
where they claimed he died.[53] The poet's body was taken to
Uclés, where it was laid to rest close to those of his father
and his mother.

Don Rodrigo Manrique had been buried in front of the main
altar of the convent church. Later, a chapel with an alabaster
monument depicting him had been erected on the spot. On
the pillows on which his sculpted figure lay could be read the
inscription "Aqui yaze muerto un hombre que vivo dexo su
nombre." Jorge Manrique was buried nearby, without any
monument to distinguish his grave. Eventually his remains
may have been moved to a chapel built by the second count
of Paredes for members of his family. All trace of the tombs
disappeared in the sixteenth century, when the old church
was pulled down to build a new one. The remains in the old
church were moved to the new one and reinterred without
identifying markers.[54]

Little more factual information is known about Jorge Manrique. The poetry confirms his respect for his father and his
uncle Gómez. It reveals that he probably did not get along
with his second stepmother, and that, like all the Manrique
family, he was faithful to the cause of Fernando and Isabel,
as long as family interests coincided with those of the crown.

Poetry was an occasional pastime. Jorge Manrique was a warrior like his father, yet not as prominent. He was a poet like
his uncle, but not as prolific or as respected in his lifetime.
Yet he is the only member of the family to achieve the lasting
fame for which they all quested.

TWO

The Minor Lyrics

Fifteenth-century poetry survives in numerous manuscript *cancioneros*, which contain short lyric compositions and longer poems meant to be read or recited rather than sung.[1] The *cancioneros* document the appearance in Castile of the courtly lyric, which developed in southern France in the late eleventh, twelfth, and thirteenth centuries.

The influence of the courtly lyric in the peninsula was first felt in Galicia, in Portugal, and in Aragón. With a few notable exceptions, until the end of the fourteenth century, Castilians used Galician to express themselves in song.[2] In the fifteenth century, however, a significant number of Castilians began to write lyrics in their native language. The Castilian court's move away from Galicia to the south, the creation of a new nobility of great power and wealth, and closer ties with Aragón fostered by the Trastámaras contributed to the change.[3]

The Aragonese Trastámaras put the Castilian nobles who followed their banner in more immediate contact with the culture of Provence and its traditional patronage of letters. In turn, these nobles influenced their fellow compatriots. The prefaces and dedications of late fourteenth- and fifteenth-century manuscripts bear witness to the fact that the titled nobility newly created by the Trastámaras sought to increase their prestige by commissioning translations and original works, by composing poetry, by engaging lettered men in poetic exchanges, and by promoting poetry as a means of instruction in those desired forms of social behavior that tended to differentiate them as a class.[4]

GÓMEZ MANRIQUE
AND THE TOLEDAN POETS

Castilian courtly poetry was destined for a noble audience. On occasion it reached the public during a festivity, but its normal context was the household of a great lord or the court of the king. Invariably it was directed to a close circle of friends.

Though it is not known where, when, or for whom Jorge Manrique wrote most of his poetry, actual and circumstantial evidence points to Toledo, and to a circle of people that included Gómez Manrique and the friends, family members, and associates who frequented the household of archbishop Alfonso Carrillo in the 1460s and 1470s. Don Rodrigo Manrique, Gómez Manrique, and Alfonso Carrillo were among the leaders of the faction that supported Prince Alfonso, and later Princess Isabel, against Enrique IV. Don Rodrigo's eldest son married a niece of the archbishop in 1465; in 1469 don Rodrigo himself married Elvira de Castañeda, daughter of the count of Fuensalida, the most important nobleman of Toledo; and in 1470 Rodrigo arranged Jorge's marriage to Elvira's sister. In addition, Gómez Manrique was *mayordomo* (chief steward) of the household of Alfonso Carrillo and commander of his forces. Toledo is therefore the logical place for Jorge to have developed as a poet. The few known recipients of his poems were residents of the city.

Manrique exchanged poetry with his uncle Gómez, with Guevara, and with Alvarez Gato, whom John G. Cummins identified as members of Gómez's literary circle. Other poets included were Bocanegra, Diego del Castillo, Rodrigo Cota,

Rodrigo and Fadrique Manrique, Juan de Mazuela, Francisco de Miranda, Juan Poeta, Diego de Rojas, Sancho de Rojas, Diego de Saldaña, the count of Treviño, and, of course, Pero Guillén. Given Gómez's connections with the household of Carrillo, Cummins believes that the literary circle of Gómez may have been the same as that surrounding the archbishop of Toledo.[5]

The only known object of Jorge's love lyric was the Toledan doña Guiomar de Meneses, who became his wife. Two of Jorge's compositions name her and probably belong to the period of courtship. The rubric that precedes the first of these in the *Cancionero general* reveals the composition to be a common poetic courtly game: "Otras suyas en que pone el nombre de su dama; y comienza y acaba en las letras primeras de todas las coplas y versos." Read acrostically, the initial letters of each verse of each octosyllabic octave spell out GVYOMAR:

I	Guay d'aquél que nunca atiende	1
II	Verdadero amor y pena	9
III	Y estos males qu'e contado	17
IV	O, si aquestas mis passiones	25
V	Mostrara vna triste vida	33
VI	Agora que soy ya suelto	41
VII	Rauia terrible m'aquexa	49

The other poem ("Otra obra suya en que puso el nombre de su esposa, y asimismo nombrados los linajes de los cuatro costados de ella, que son: Castañeda, Ayala, Silva, Meneses") similarly hides the name and lineage of his wife in the octaves:

I	Según el mal me si*GUIO*	1
	*MAR*auíllome de mí	
	como assí me despedí	
	que jamás no me mudó.	
	Cáusame aquesta firmeza	5
	que, siendo de vos ausente	
	ante mi estaua presente	

contino vuestra belleza.[6]
(*Cancionero* 56)

The subsequent stanzas conceal Guiomar's last names: II: "pues que las congoxas mías de muchas tornases po*CAS* / *TANED A*gora, pues, vos, / en cuerdas de gûalardón;" III: "*VAYA LA* vida passada / que por amores sufrí;" IV: "*SI'LÛ-A*ler vuestro querra / —pues que me quiso valer;" V: "Lo que me causa más a*MEN* / *ES ES*perança de ver / buen galardón de querer." These games sharpen the poet's skill at finding phonological parallels, and focus attention on the importance of the beginnings and endings of verses.

Poetry was an inherent part of court life: a discipline studied by young nobles seeking to improve their social graces. Manrique's extant poetry conforms to this picture. His poems can be classified by length into two types—shorter lyric compositions called *preguntas, canciones, esparsas,* and *glosas de mote,* and longer poems that treat the casuistry of love from a somewhat more impersonal stance: "De don Jorge Manrique quexándose del Dios de amor," "Castillo de amor," "A la Fortuna," "Diziendo qué cosa es amor," and "De la profesión que hizo en la orden del Amor."[7] The shorter lyrics, which are more indicative of the courtly function of much of fifteenth-century poetry and of the virtuosity of the poet, will be treated first. The longer poems are better for studying Manrique's use of the conventions of courtly love.

The *pregunta* is a form of poetic debate popular from the beginning of the fifteenth century. Though there are three types of poetic debates in medieval Spanish poetry (the fictitious, the narrative, and the *pregunta*), only the *pregunta* and its concomitant *respuesta* constitute a real exchange between poets.[8] The person interrogated in the *pregunta* replies in the *respuesta* with a composition that uses the same verse form and rhyme scheme employed in the *pregunta*. Although most *preguntas* and *respuestas* are paired poems by the late fifteenth century, it was not unusual for more than one poet to reply, initiating a poetic debate that would continue over several compositions.

A late fifteenth-century *pregunta* frequently begins as a question about love. It asks for suggestions about a course of action to follow, or advice on a choice to be made. Often the question is phrased as a paradox.[9] Jorge Manrique's "Entre dos fuegos lançado" is typical:

> Entre dos fuegos lançado   1
> donde amor es repartido,
> del uno soy encendido,
> del otro cerca quemado;
>   y no sé yo bien pensar   5
> quál será mejor hazer:
> dexarme más encender
> o acabarme de quemar:
> dezid qué deuo tomar.
> (*Cancionero* 73)

The *pregunta*, openly directed to another man, often does not take the sentimental tone of the love lyric. Indeed, it can be quite ironic and contravene some of the basic tenets of courtly love. It does so here, when it argues that love and desire can go in two directions at the same time. Manrique requests advice in choosing between an old and a new love. The old love has almost consumed him, the new affection is just beginning to burn. The question, then, is whether the lover should continue to burn until consumed by the old fire, or should he stoke the new?

In a *pregunta* he directs to the poet Guevara, Manrique uses a similar idea to express sentiments that are more in accord with courtly tenets:

> Entre bien y mal dobl*ado*   1
> pasa vn gran río caud*al*;
> yo estó en cabo del m*al*
> y el río no tiene v*ado*.
>   Galardón, que era la pu*ente*,   5
> es ya quebrada por m*edio*;
> ¿qué me daréis por rem*edio*,

qu'el nadar no lo consi*ente*
la fuerạ de la cresci*ente*?
(*Cancionero* 74)

The poem's main theme is forced separation. The obstacle dividing the narrator from his desire is a great river whose rushing waters are too strong to swim (1-2). The river has a "good" and an "evil" bank. The narrator is condemned to the evil bank; all good resides on the opposite shore. Manrique asks Guevara to advise him on how to attain the object of his desires when all avenues to it seem blocked.

Serrano de Haro believes this poem to be an expression of Manrique's doubt about joining forces with Prince Alfonso against Enrique IV.[10] He bases his interpretation partly on a rubric that introduces the poem in some of the manuscripts ("Pregunta que fizo don Jorge sobre los hechos de Castilla"), and which intimates a political theme, and partly on Guevara's answer to the question:

Sea, señor, arris*cado*,   1
vuestro pequeño caud*al*,
do puede el bien desigu*al*
con aquel ser alcanç*ado*;
    y armad de importuna *gente*   5
una barca por rem*edio*,
ca deligencia es vn m*edio*
que del pobre y más doli*ente*
haze sano y muy prud*ente*.
(*Cancionero castellano* 1: 252)

Serrano de Haro believes that Guevara's answer exhorts Jorge to abandon his indecision and join forces with Prince Alfonso. If one ignored the rubric of the poem or read it in the *Cancionero general*, where it is only designated as a *pregunta*, however, the poem would more likely be considered a typical love question.[11] The language and images support this interpretation.

Guevara and Manrique use martial metaphors to describe

love's war, not civil war. The poem's subject is the *mal de ausencia* (pain of absence), a common courtly theme.[12] Jorge's question is posed by a lover who is separated from his beloved by "un gran río caudal." The river may be a real obstacle, as Serrano claims, but *caudal* can also refer to fortune and be an allusion to the superior status of the lady—one of the most common clichés of courtly poetry. It may also refer to memory. Elsewhere, Manrique uses a river metaphor to represent separation and remembrance. In "Castillo de amor," he describes his fortress as surrounded by "vn río mucho crescido, / qu'es membrar" (*Cancionero* 22). The river in "Entre bien y mal doblado" can be considered a similar metaphor. The lady's superior social standing and her absolute beauty separate the lover from her. Withdrawal of her favor condemns the lover to the evil shore of the river and provokes his feelings of alienation and sorrow.

The existence of the bridge called *galardón* (reward) which, though now broken, must have been whole, implies that the beloved had once allowed the lover's service. Without the bridge—i.e., the lady's favor—the lover feels inadequate to span the river that separates them. The distance between them is expressed metaphorically in the value attached to the banks, *bien* and *mal*. Guevara advises Manrique that fortune helps those who help themselves (7), and that persistence and ingenuity can win the day, even when the lady is uncooperative. Love, says Guevara, is a game in which one can risk a *pequeño caudal* (a small fortune) in order to win a great one.

The *esparsas* (from Provençal *coblas esparsas*) are one-stanza lyric compositions of variable verse length and rhyme scheme in which a thought is wittily expressed.[13] Though they can be found in the Castilian *cancioneros* from the early fifteenth century, during the time of the Manriques they come into greater vogue. Jorge and Gómez Manrique are among the most accomplished practitioners of the form.[14] Typical of the *esparsas* is the lyric which begins "Pensando, señora, en vos:

Pensando, señora, en vos　　　　　1
vi en el cielo vna *cometa*

es señal que manda Dios
que pierda el miedo y *cometa*
    a declarar el *desseo*   5
que mi voluntad *dessea*,
porque jamás no me *vea*
vencido como me *veo*
en esta fuerte *pelea*
que yo comigo *peleo*.   10
(*Cancionero* 66-67)

As in the previous poem, the encounter with the lady is projected inward as an internal struggle between Reason and Will. The lover's Will is not strong enough to approach the lady with his desires, yet it hopes, with the help of a portent, to overcome Reason's objections. Reason's challenge is based on unalterable truths that are not stated but understood. The beloved is desirable, but cannot be possessed, because she represents transcendent beauty. Only an upheaval in the natural world can change such truths. Comets are portents, of course, of such upheavals (1-3).

The use of homonyms (*cometa*: noun, "comet"; verb, "to undertake"), of the same word used as a noun and as a verb (*desseo/dessea, pelea/peleo*), or of a verb in different tenses (*vea/veo*), is a common feature of the *esparsas* and was probably considered a virtue, rather than a fault. In "Pensando, señora, en vos," the repetition of a word in different cases (polyptoton) always appears at the end of paired verses with the exception of verse 3.

The *canción* is one of the most popular fifteenth-century fixed forms and the preferred poetic vehicle of the courtly love lyric.[15] It is a short lyric composed of a three-, four-, or five-line refrain and a stanza divided into a *mudanza* elaborating the themes of the refrain in a *redondilla* with a different rhyme and a *vuelta* that in some degree reproduces the refrain.[16]

Manrique's *canciones* are fairly typical of the genre. Seven of them have four-line refrains and seven use five. The *mudanza* always has four lines. All repeat the rhymes of the refrain in the *vuelta* except the lyric, "Quien no estuviere en presencia," which reorders it ABBA CDDC BABA:

I	Quien no'stuviere en presencia	1
	no tenga fe en confiança,	
	pues son oluido y mudança	
	las condiciones d'ausencia.	

II	Quien quisiere ser amado	5
	trabaje por ser presente,	
	que quan presto fuere ausente,	
	tan presto será oluidado:	
	y pierda toda esperança	
	quien no'stuuiere en presencia,	10
	pues son oluido y mudança	
	las condiciones d'ausencia.	
	(*Cancionero* 59)	

Apart from its rhyme scheme, "Quien no'stuviere en presencia" is fairly typical of the *canción*. The first four lines establish the theme: a warning to lovers to remain near to their beloved, because absence leads to forgetfulness. This thought is expanded in the *mudanza*, where it includes some practical advice and a restatement of the warning (6-8). The rhyme change (CDDC) makes the *mudanza* distinct from the other two parts of the lyric structure. The *vuelta*, as the name implies, returns to the rhyme of the first stanza by restating part or all of the original text. Like the other *canciones*, the lyric comes full circle to end where it began, warning of the *males de ausencia*.

The freedom to use the *vuelta* to achieve different effects is one of the charms of the *canción*. It is the feature that relieves the genre of rigidity. Manrique never restates all of the refrain. Instead, he uses the first part of the *vuelta* to link the refrain to the *mudanza*.

Though the last line of the refrain tends to be faithfully repeated in the *vuelta*, there are exceptions. The poet could repeat only the rhyme scheme of the refrain (as in "No sé

por qué me fatigo"), or one or more of the rhyming words of
the refrain in any combination.[17] It was also acceptable to
repeat a verse of the refrain, changing only the tense of the
verb to accommodate to the thought being developed.[18]

Manrique's two *glosas de mote* are a variety of the *glosa*, a
composition, which like the *canción*, expands upon a text. The
text of the *glosa* is borrowed from another poet and divided
among the stanzas of the new poem, where it must be per-
fectly integrated into the new poem in sense, syntax, meaning, and rhyme.[19] The *glosa de mote* expands upon a single
verse that served as someone's motto.

The motto, a form akin to the proverb, was widely used
in the late middle ages. But while the proverb was a maxim
of general application, the motto made an enigmatic pronouncement that encapsulized an attitude or a commitment.
To adopt a motto was, in Huizinga's words, "to choose a text
for the sermon of one's life."[20] The *glosa de mote* either extends
or explains the enigmatic pronouncement of the motto.

Most fifteenth-century mottoes, including the two glossed
by Manrique ("Siempre amar y amor seguir; and "Sin Dios y
sin vos y mí") are about love. The latter poem is one of the
most admired and imitated of Manrique's short lyrics:

I   Yo soy quien libre me vi,   1
           yo, quien pudiera oluidaros;
           yo so el que por amaros
           estoy, desque os conoscí
           sin Dios y sin vos y mí.   5

II   *Sin Dios*, porqu'en vos adoro;
           sin vos, pues no me queréys
           pues *sin mí* ya está de coro
           que vos soys quien me tenéys.
              Assí que triste nascí,   10
           pues que pudiera oluidaros;
           yo so el que por amaros
           estó, desque os conoscí
           sin Dios y sin vos y mí.
           (*Cancionero* 71)

The refrain is partially the work of the poet (1-4) and partially the motto to be glossed (5). The text glossed by the poem is therefore longer than the motto, "sin Dios y sin vos y mí." As in the *canción*, the second stanza develops the themes and provides the answers: the lover is without God because he is a heretic (6), he is without his lady because she does not consent to his love (7), and he is without himself because his soul is captive to her beauty (8-9).

Two other compositions that Manrique's *cancionero* also labels *motes* do not follow the normal *glosa* pattern. The first glosses Manrique's own motto, "Ni miento ni m'arrepiento." The nine-line stanza extends the motto's ambiguity in a series of parallel statements that are followed by a *fin*, or explanatory stanza, in which the ambiguity is dispelled:[21]

I	*Ni miento ni m'arrepiento,*	1
	ni digo ni me desdigo,	
	ni estó triste ni contento,	
	ni reclamo ni consiento,	
	ni fío ni desconfío;	5
	ni bien biuo ni bien muero,	
	ni soy ageno ni mío,	
	ni me venço ni porfío,	
	ni espero ni desespero.	

	Fin	
II	Comigo sólo *contiendo*	10
	en vna fuerte *contienda,*	
	y no hallo quien m'*entienda,*	
	ni yo tampoco m'*entiendo;*	
	entiendo y sé lo que *quiero,*	
	mas no *entiendo* lo que *quiera*	15
	quien quiere siempre que *muera*	
	sin querer creer que *muero.*	
	(*Cancionero* 69-70)	

The motto is one element in a parallel series of contrasting verbs introduced by the negative *ni*. Normally, verbs provide the dynamics of a poem. In this poem, however, all movement

is undermined by the sequence of syntactically parallel verses
that set two terms in opposition line by line and neutralize
their meaning. The verbal oppositions express the paralysis
of a lover who does none of the things mentioned. The meaning of the motto is revealed in the last stanza, where the
polyptoton and the repetition of the last word of a line at the
beginning of the next (anadiplosis) express the lover's puz-
zlement, while the alliteration (17-18) accents his grief over
the lady's unpitying neglect.

The last motto written by Manrique is a four-line stanza
akin to a *letra* or *cartel*, an explanatory text that accompanies
an image or a representation. The rubric of the poem reveals
the occasion of its composition: "Don Jorge Manrique sacó
por cimera una annoria con sus alcaduces llenos, y dixo:"

> Aquestos y mis enojos
> tienen esta condición:
> que suben del coraçón
> las lágrimas a los ojos.
> (*Cancionero* 69)

Manrique's *mote* belongs to a minor lyric genre that precedes the explosion of emblematic literature in the sixteenth
and seventeenth centuries. The stanza is not properly speak-
ing a *mote* but an *impresa*, which the *Cancioneiro Geral de García
de Resende* and the *Cancionero general* call *invenciones* or *letras
de justadores*: verses composed on the occasion of a tournament
to explain the symbolic meaning of the jouster's choice of
headgear or of something in his apparel (the color of the cape,
the meaning of a particular embroidery or of a painted
cloth).[22] Unlike the *mote*, the *letra de justador* is almost invariably about love. *Letras* characteristically explain a metaphoric
relation between a concrete image and an emotional state or
another condition. In Manrique's composition the *alcaduces*'s
likeness to the poet's *enojos* ("tienen esta condición") is that
they both lift water. The *alcaduces* lift it to the surface of the
earth, the *enojos* to the windows of the soul, the eyes.

JORGE MANRIQUE AND
THE COURTLY LOVE TRADITION

As in twelfth-century France, the adoption of a lyric circumscribed by a narrow set of redundant rhetorical, thematic, and formal conventions coincided with the transformation of the loosely configured Castilian aristocracy into a closed social caste for which nobility was not the result of deeds, but a corollary of being.[23] To be noble was to be a person endowed by birth with special qualities. These traits resulted in an aggregate of behavioral patterns that could be refined by nurture, especially by the practice of poetry. According to Juan Alfonso de Baena, for example, poetry is created by the grace of God, and only the most discreet and learned men, knowledgeable of books and languages, men who have had courtly correspondence with other great men and who have seen the world can be poets. Above all, says Baena, the poet must be "noble fidalgo e cortes e mesurado e gentil e graçioso e polido e donoso e que tenga miel e açucar e sal e ayre e donayre en su rrasonar, e otrosy que sea amador, e que siempre se preçie e se finja de ser enamorado, conuiene a saber, que ame a quien deue e como deue e donde deue . . . "[24] This last instruction summarizes the nature of the medieval lyric. The poet must love "a quien deue" (a member of his own class), "como deue" (according to rules prescribed by tradition), and "donde deue" (in the court and in his poetry).

The characteristic circumspection of the medieval lyric reflects other aspects of medieval aristocratic culture. The noble functioned within society according to strictly prescribed rules that determined his relationships with all others. From childhood he was brought up with the idea that he was a being set apart by nature. His separateness established him as a member of an elite and inculcated in him a belief in his own superiority. Such a person did not seek to create or modify a role, but to fulfill it. The king had to be a good king, the knight a good knight, the poet a good poet. The only way that a poet could achieve greatness within this ideology was through imitation of other poets. Such imitation was not limited to the

form and content of his poetry, but included also his role as
author.

Like most medieval lyric traditions, fifteenth-century love
poetry is characterized by its use of the lexicon of feudalism
and Christian devotion.[25] Castilian poets, like their counterparts beyond the Pyrenees, used feudal metaphors to pro-
claim their devotion to a beloved. The women they celebrated
were *damas*, who exercised (at least in poetic convention) a
lord's prerogatives over their *vasallos* (vassals), the poets. The
bond uniting poets to their ladies was the *pleito homenaje* (the
hommage lige of French feudal terminology), a fealty oath that
took precedence over all other oaths and allegiances, and
served to express the poet's complete submission to the lady
he served. In Manrique's "Memorial," for example, the lover
sends a messenger to tell his lady that he is "presto a toda
ora / a su mandar y obidiente; / y que es buelto a mi servicio /
un público vasallage / y mi fe en pleito omenaje" (*Cancionero*
53).

Manrique's lover is sensitive, obedient, constant, and ob-
servant of the rules of love. No other special characteristics
can be ascribed to him. He cannot be identified as an individual. The lady is not specifically described either. We intuit
the usual paragon of perfection: blond hair, blue or green
eyes, delicate and well proportioned features, good color,
white teeth, and sweet breath. She is learned in courtly virtues. She is invariably inaccessible.

The lady is always superior to the lover. Men praise her
beauty, and her repute is enough to engender desire and force
the lover to seek her out:

III	Y diré que me llamaron	21
	por los primeros mensajes,	
	cienmil que vos alabaron	
	y alabando no negaron	
	recebidos mil vltrajes.	25
	(*Cancionero* 29)	

I	Quien tanto veros dessea,	1
	señora, sin conosceros,	

¿qué hará, después que os vea,
quando no pudiere veros?

II   Gran temor tiene mi vida   5
de mirar vuestra presencia,
pues amor en vuestra ausencia
me hirió de tal herida;
aunque peligrosa sea,
delibro de conosceros,   10
y si muero porque os vea,
la victoria será veros.
(*Cancionero* 60)

The lady's dwelling is a castle or a great house, guarded
by a *vela* (watchman):

II   No que mi dezir s'asconda
mas no hallo que aproueche,
ca puesto que me responda
vuestra vela o vuestra ronda,
responderá que yo peche;   15
dirá luego: —¿Quién te puso
en contienda ni quistión?
(*Cancionero* 28f)

Beauty, however, is not benign. There is no sweetness in
the lady's disposition. Her beauty overpowers and enthralls.
A banner flies over the lady's dwelling, but the lover does
not see it, nor is he aware of his stumbling gait as he ascends
to her dwelling:

IV   Enprendí, pues, noramala   31
ya de veros por mi mal,
y en subiendo por la'scala,
no sé quál pie me resuala,
no curé de la señal;   35
(*Cancionero* 29)

The nearer he gets to his goal, the more the lover enters into a contemplative state that saps his will and deprives his body of strength.

Once in the presence of the lady the onset of love is not subtle or gradual. The image of the lady's beauty charges suddenly through the eyes and pierces the heart with a *llaga mortal*, an *herida*, or more simply, a wound that is incurable, because of the continuing presence of the wounding agent (the image of the lady) in the lover's heart. In one of his poems to Guiomar, Manrique mentions how perfect beauty, once seen, can never be forgotten:

I   Cáusame aquesta firmeza   5
     que, siendo de vos ausente,
     ante mí estaua presente
     contino vuestra belleza.
     (*Cancionero* 56)

In "Estando ausente de su amiga, a un mensagero que alla embiava," Manrique describes how the lady shines with her own light, and warns the messenger to approach her with averted eyes:

I   y mira quando llegares
     a su esmerada presencia
     que resplandesce,
     do quiera que la hallares   10
     tú le hagas reuerencia
     qual meresce.
     (*Cancionero* 47)

Manrique's favorite metaphor for the onset of love compares it to the breaching of a castle's defenses. In the "Escala de amor" the lover says: "A'scala vista subieron / vuestra beldad y mesura / y tan de recio hirieron / que vencieron mi cordura" (*Cancionero* 26).[26] The lover's body (i.e., the castle manned by Cordura, Voluntad, Sentidos, Ojos, and Coraçón) confronts Beldad, Mesura, and Amores. Beldad and Mesura lead an assault. While Voluntad nods, they attack Cordura, rout the Sentidos and, with the help of the traitorous Ojos, throw open the doors of the fortress. Amores enter and imprison Coraçón:

III   Mis ojos fueron traydores,
           ellos fueron consintientes,
           ellos fueron causadores
           qu'entrassen aquestas gentes   20
             qu'el atalaya tenían,
           y nunca dixeron nada
           de la batalla que vían
           ni hizieron ahumada.

IV   Después que ouieron entrado,   25
           aquestos escaladores
           abrieron el mi costado
           y entraron vuestros amores;
             y mi firmeza tomaron,
           y mi coraçón prendiero   30
           y mis sentidos robaron,
           y a mí sólo no quisieron.
           (*Cancionero* 27)

The conventions of siege warfare allowed the defenders of castles either to negotiate a capitulation and retain certain rights and privileges, or to fight on and let the outcome of the battle determine their fate. In the latter circumstance, the final surrender was unconditional. The weak, like the lover, surrendered at once or were forcibly taken.

The description of the lover's body as a castle is common in medieval poetry and prose and reflects the importance of fortifications to medieval society. Manrique himself participated in sieges of castles, both as defender and attacker. He was familiar with their defense during a siege, and with their repair after it. He had also undoubtedly encountered the comparison of cities and castles to human bodies in doctrinal treatises and in love poems. "Mirrors of princes" often compared cities or castles to the body, and the citadel (or donjon) to the heart. Organs and structures are associated by analogy based on centrality and importance. Just as the heart is the most important organ of the body, the citadel and its keep are the most important structures of city and castle. Citadels, and castles as well, are also the abode of the ruler, as the heart is the most important organ of the body.[27] A strong citadel, moralists were fond of saying, is like the heart of a prudent man. It must follow good, flee evil, and defend itself against those who would give offense. The analogy extends to the provisions the ruler of city and castle must make to prepare for war, even when no war is imminent. He must maintain a unified citizenry, knights who are knowledgeable in the exercise of arms and virtue, and have good horsemen, abundant weapons, treasure, and victuals. Above all, he must know war and be of stout heart himself.[28] This advice advances a standard of reasonable behavior for rulers of cities and castles that is in stark contrast to the behavior of the lover. The lover's heart is not an ideal ruler of his own body. When Beldad attacks, the castle's principal defenders are unprepared. Reason is easily routed, Will is caught napping, and Heart hides in the strongest tower.[29]

The allegory presents a spiritual struggle in the guise of an actual conflict and explains, in abbreviated form, the psychological reasons for the lover's surrender of self. Its personifications reflect Scholastic ideas about the nature of the soul. Scholastic psychology considered Reason and Will the most important, though not the most stable, of the Soul's distinct potencies. For some writers the Will was an active agency in its own right, able to function independently of the Intellect. Others saw it as subject to causal influence from the Intellect or from the natural world, though still capable of independent action.[30] The poets, however, preferred to demonstrate how Will and Reason were both enslaved by Beauty, and how their collapse transformed the lover into a captive.

In the "Castillo de Amor" there is no indication that the lover is happy as a result of his defeat. The castle, once taken, becomes an impregnable fortress, manned by the lover for his suzerain. The lover says:

I   Hame tan bien defendido,   1
            señora, vuestra memoria
            de mudança,
            que jamás nunca ha podido
            alcançar de mi victor   5
            oluidança:
              porqu'estáys apoderada
            vos de toda mi firmeza
            en tal són,
            que no puede ser tomada   10
            a fuerça mi fortaleza
            ni a trayción.
            (*Cancionero* 21)

The eyes, always the potential traitors, can no longer do harm, because every time they look at others, a vision of the lady appears before them (*Cancionero* 23 and 26-28). But it is not only the eyes that succumb to the lady. All the other senses are equally under her sway:

I   Allá verás mis sentidos,   1
            coraçón, si los buscares,
            pienso que harto perdidos,
            con gran sobra de pesares.
            (*Cancionero* 52)

Nothing goes well for the lover after he is taken. In the "Escala de Amor," after Amores take the heart, the lover in anguish exclaims: "y a mí sólo no quisieron" (*Cancionero* 27). The surrender of the lover's body does not result in his acceptance into the lady's favor. Even in the "Castillo de Amor," where the fortress is not under attack but long held, all is not well. Parts of the fortress are ruined:

VII   Otra torre, qu'es ventura
            está del todo cayda
            a todas partes,   75
            l'a muy recio combatida

con mil artes.
(*Cancionero* 24)

Ventura (fortune) is the happiness of the lover, which has fled. Though he is possessed, he does not possess. His senses desire the lady, but they are not satisfied. In the "Escala de Amor," the senses flee "con sendas llagas de muerte" (*Cancionero* 26). In the "Memorial" she imprisons them (*Cancionero* 52). Only the treacherous Ojos are satisfied: "los ojos enbeuecidos / fueron tan bien acogidos, / que del todo m'alegraron" (*Cancionero* 31).

The sight of the lady is the only tangible recompense for the lover. It is termed a *galardón, merced,* or simply a *gozo*—all indicating the enjoyment of the lady's presence. From the time of surrender, the lover's well-being is dependent on the presence or absence of the lady. Because his service is a way of staying near to her, it begins at the moment of surrender. In the "Castillo de Amor" he voices his pledge:

X   A tal postura vos salgo   110
con muy firme juramento
y fuerte jura,
como vassallo hidalgo
que por pesar ni tormento
ni tristura,
    a otri no lo entregar   115
aunque la muerte esperasse
por beuir,
ni aunque lo venga a cercar
el Dios d'amor y llegasse
a lo pedir.   120
(*Cancionero* 25)

As a vassal entrusted with a fortress, the lover must serve by keeping his fealty oath. The lady's nearness and the hope of favor compensate for the loss of freedom implied by the binding oath. When the lady withdraws her favor, the lover becomes more conscious of his unhappiness.

"De la professión que hizo en la Orden del amor" ennu-
merates the toils of the lover as if they were the rule of a
monastic or a chivalric order. Love's rule consists of lack of
happiness and pleasure, eternal obedience, constancy, and
secrecy.[31] In other words, a hopeless, yet paradoxically hope-
ful service. The same theme is taken up in a lyric called "Diziendo qué cosa es amor":

II	Es plazer en c'ay dolores,	11
	dolor en c'ay alegría,	
	vn pesar en c'ay dulçores,	
	vn esfuerço en c'ay temores,	
	temor en c'ay osadía;	15
	vn plazer en c'ay enojos,	
	vna gloria en c'ay passión,	
	vna fe en c'ay antojos,	
	fuerça que hazen los ojos	
	al seso y al coraçón.	20
	(*Cancionero* 17)	

The chiasmus of the first two lines is not repeated. At the
conceptual level, however, the structure is maintained so that
the terms expressing pleasure or pain alternate from verse to
verse and describe the lover's turmoil. Courtly love is rooted
in a basic denial of satisfaction or possession. The lover never,
or nearly never, sings about attaining the object of his desires.
He therefore never attains true happiness. He does acquire,
however, an exquisite sensitivity to his condition. Out of his
distress he creates a song of praise and complaint through
which he solicits the lady's favor.

Though the pursuit of earthly love is at variance with the
teachings of the church, the love poetry defines itself by
analogy to the Christian conception of service, based on the
absence and idealization of the lady. The lady is an alternative
to God. She is the *summum bonum* of the poet, and her description is indebted to the language of the Scholastic's metaphysics of Beauty.[32] The service of love is a form of religious

devotion in which Beauty assumes the place of God, and the god Amor acts as arbiter and intercessor.

In "Quexándose del Dios de amor" the despairing lover recognizes that he has wandered from the path of righteousness when don Amor tells him to take his complaint to God. "¿Cómo," he says, "paresceré / ante'l Dios a quien erré /quexando del que serví?" (*Cancionero* 6). The question is not a prelude to a confession of mistakes or sins, but a playful reference to the fundamental distance between the two value systems.

The tension of the lyric arises from a conflict between the ideal of service borrowed from religion (embodied in the language of the metaphysics of Beauty) and the feudal metaphor it uses to express that service. The lover is a vassal subject to the rule of his lady. The feudal bond, however, is a contractual arrangement. The *pleito homenaje* binds vassal to lord and lord to vassal with corresponding duties. When either fails to fulfill those duties, the bond is broken. But because the compulsion to love Beauty cannot be broken, the lover's bond (his *pleito omenaje*) is a chain that binds him to a tyrant.

Other connections with religion are also apparent. The true Christian sacrifices even his life in a token of faith and hope. The lover, on the other hand, believes in a wayward, unjust god, whose only promise is the satisfaction of an imposible desire.[33] Therefore, where the Christian martyr finds fulfillment in his passion, the martyr of love only finds pain and sorrow. In "Diziendo qué cosa es amor", the lover describes love as a "gloria en c'ay passión," and a "fe en c'ay antojos." In "De la professión que hizo en la Orden del amor" he calls the love service a "religión," and considers himself confirmed in an "orden d'enamorado." In "En una llaga mortal," the lover, like Christ, is mortally wounded on his left side:

I	En vna llaga mortal,	1
	desigual,	
	qu'está en el siniestro lado,	
	conoscerés luego qual	
	es el leal	5

seruidor y enamorado
(*Cancionero* 33)

The suffering may also be compared with the martyrdom of a saint:

XI   Qual aquel cuerpo sagrado   101
de San Vicente bendito,
después de martirizado,
a las fieras fué lançado
por cruel mando maldito;   105
  mas otro mando mayor
de Dios, por quien padesció,
l'embió por defensor
vn lobo muy sin temor
y vn cuervo que l'ayudó.   110

XII   Fin
  Assí aguardan mi persona,
por milagro, desqu'e muerto,
un león con su corona
y vn cuervo que no abandona
mi sér hasta ser despierto.   115
(*Cancionero* 32)[34]

Love's martyrdom, however, has no transcendence:[35]

XII   Venga, pues, vuestra venida   116
en fin de toda mi cuenta;
venga ya y verá mi vida
que se fué con vuestra yda,
mas deue quedar contenta.   120
(*Cancionero* 33)

At times, the lover hopes for a *galardón* after death:

VI   Si en esta regla estouiere   51
con justa y buena intención,

y en ella permanesciere,
quiero saber, si muriere
qué será mi galardón;   55
(*Cancionero* 20)

In "De don Jorge Manrique quexándose del Dios de amor," Manrique addresses precisely the tension between the language of love and feudal service:

I   ¡O, muy alto Dios de amor,
          por quien mi vida se guía!
          ¿Cómo sufres tú, señor,
          siendo justo juzgador,
          en tu ley tal erejía?   5
             ¿Que se pierda el que serbió,
          que s'olvide lo servido,
          que viva quien engañó,
          que muera quien bien amó,
          que valga el amor fengido?   10
          (*Cancionero* 3)

The poem is cast as a *pleito*, in which the lover is the plaintiff and Amor is both judge and defendant. The argument moves back and forth between the two. The lover threatens apostasy, because he has found he serves an unjust God. Don Amor, however, argues that it is not injustice that has condemned the lover, but rather his own neglect. The lover was absent from the Court of Love and therefore he received an unjust sentence. The debate quickly degenerates into an unseemly squabble. The lover questions Don Amor's power over him, but Don Amor dismisses the lover and tells him that he will respond with violence to a man who presumes to be what he is not. The despairing lover in the end casts himself on his knees and swears service if he can have his lady back. Don Amor then reveals that he has been testing the mettle of the lover, and having found him constant, is willing to restore his lady to him.[36]

The poem recalls the story of Job. Where Job is patient,

however, the lover is impatient. Where God's test proves the mettle of Job, Don Amor's test proves the lover's conclusive submission to the world. No fault in Job's character prompts God's test, but the lover is guilty of transgressing one of Love's rules: he lost sight of his beloved. In the end, Don Amor and the lover may reconcile, but the lover will not find happiness. At best he will find contentment.

The lover's need to satisfy his desire gives him agony. He accepts his condition as proper and natural, because reason tells him that he must love perfection. Reason also makes him acknowledge the impossibility of his love and accept as his due a lesser good—contemplation of the lady—as sufficient *galardón* for his services. This compromise, however, is not always viewed as satisfactory. In "Quanto más pienso seruiros," for example, the lover recognizes that he is blinded by love, and that there will not likely be a reward for his service:

I	Quanto más pienso seruiros,	1
	tanto queréys más causar	
	que gaste mi fe en sospiros	
	y mi vida en dessear	
	lo que no puedo alcançar.	5
II	Bien conosco qu'estóy ciego	
	y que mi gran fe me ciega,	
	y que esperando me niega	
	que n'os vencerés de ruego;	
	y que, por mucho seruiros,	10
	no dexarés de causar	
	que gaste mi fe en sospiros,	
	y mi vida en dessear	
	lo que no puedo alcançar.	
	(*Cancionero* 63)	

Even on a first reading, many of Manrique's minor lyrics impress one with their somberness and violence. Poem after poem equates love with death, and the process of love with war. It is not unusual to find this desperate tone expressed in the *cancionero*. Manrique's lyric, however, is particularly consistent in the way it portrays love as war, and the lover as a man who has lost or is losing an engagement with a vastly superior enemy. In those lyrics addressed to personifications like don Amor or Fortuna, woman is always the enemy, and she is almost invariably associated with Death.

The martyrdom of love is a common topic in courtly poetry. Manrique's use of the concept is considered by critics like Pedro Salinas to be of a completely traditional expression. More recently, however, María del Rosario Fernández Alonso has attributed great originality to Manrique's conception of death in the love lyric. According to her, Manrique's poetry marks the beginning of the conception of Death as the beloved ("la muerte como amada").[37] The composition in which Manrique's fascination with death can be recognized most clearly is "No tardes, Muerte, que muero:"

I	No tardes, Muerte, que muero	1
	ven, porque biua contigo;	
	quiéreme, pues que te quiero,	
	que con tu venida espero	
	no tener guerra comigo.	5
II	Remedio de alegre vida	
	no lo hay por ningún medio,	
	porque mi graue herida	
	es de tal parte venida,	
	qu'eres tu sola remedio.	10
	Ven aquí, pues, ya que muero;	
	búscame, pues que te sigo;	
	quiéreme, pues [que] te quiero,	
	e con tu venida espero	
	no tener vida conmigo.	15
	(*Cancionero* 65)	

Though devoid of its doctrinal dress, there is an image of death in this poem that is very similar to that found at the end of the *Coplas*, and radically different from that found in the "Razonamiento con la muerte" of Juan de Mena, to take one example. In Manrique's lyric poetry death is not an unanticipated accident or a hideous adversary, but a longed-for lover, whose presence provides a desired release. As in the *Coplas*, Death can also be considered a lady who comes calling at the door, bringing, not anguish or surprise, but fulfillment.[38]

THE LANGUAGE OF
JORGE MANRIQUE'S LOVE LYRIC

The best love lyrics can be found among the shorter pieces, the very poetry that Menéndez Pelayo called "artificiosa y amanerada," "insípida," and "trivial."[39] These poems make use of a highly stylized poetic language that deviates from the norm in its restriction of vocabulary.[40] It has few special lexical forms, and its ungrammaticalities are those common to a poetic based on rhetorical tradition. The love lyrics are based on a canon that functions as a source of materials and as an obstacle against which poets struggled to create something novel.

Paul Zumthor characterizes tradition in the medieval lyric as a continuum on which the trace of past texts is embossed.[41] This trace, in turn, determines the production of new texts by imposing its paradigms and linguistic, syntactical, and prosodic models. Tradition teaches the poet his skill and provides his readers and listeners with an interpretive competence which, because it is based on knowledge of previous texts, increases the associative power of the poetry in an almost inverse relation to its lexical limitations.

In a study of the *canciones* of the *Cancionero general* of 1511, Keith Whinnom found that of a total of 297 nouns used in the poems, twenty-five are used fifty percent of the time a noun is employed. In their order of frequency these nouns are: *vida, mal, dolor, muerte, amor, pena, razón, passión, gloria, esperança, coraçón, fe, ventura, alma, desseo, placer, tormento, bien, remedio, memoria, temor, tristura/tristeça, morir, causa,* and *pensamiento.*[42]

seven of the "Castillo de amor," for example, the equivalent
terms *matar* and *herir* are opposed to *guarir* and *defensar*. In
stanza eight the series of nouns characterized as the *provisiones*
of the castle (85-90) are an example of substitution:

VII	antes *matar* y *herir*	80
	y desamar	
	vn tal seruidor, a quien	
	siempre deuiera *guarir*	
	y *defensar*.	
VIII	Tiene muchas prouisiones,	85
	que son *cuydados* y *males*	
	y *dolores*,	
	angustias, fuertes passiones,	
	y *penas* muy desiguales	
	y *temores*	
	(*Cancionero* 24)	

Though nouns are the most common equivalent substitutes,
verbs may be employed in the same manner:

XIV	No cures d'*amenazarme*	131
	ni estar mucho brabacando,	
	que tú no puedes *dañarme*	
	en nada más qu'en *matarme*,	
	(*Cancionero* 8)	
VI	Que ya las armas proué	61
	para mejor *defenderme*	
	y más *guardarme*,	
	y la fe sola hallé	
	que de ti puede *valerme*	65
	y *defensarme*;	
	(*Cancionero* 12)	

The verbs can be set in one-to-one opposition as above, or
lead to a climactic opposition:

VIII   y si no quiere *valerme*,   91
                 pues yo no sé *remediarme*
                 en tal modo,
                 para nunca *socorrerme*,
                 muy mejor será *matarme*   95
                 ya del todo.
                 (*Cancionero* 51)

IV   Después que ouieron entrado,   25
                 aquestos escaladores
                 abrieron el mi costado
                 y entraron vuestros amores;
                    y mi firmeza *tomaron*,
                 y mi coraçón *prendieron*,   30
                 y mis sentidos *robaron*,
                 y a mí sólo *no quisieron*.[44]
                 (*Cancionero* 27)

Opposites are maximally separated along one dimension of meaning (for example, "que tus guerras y tus pazes" (*Cancionero* 10), yet they are also related.[45] In the hands of the poet this perceptual ambiguity gives rise to a paradox, which usually is resolved at the end of the poem. In the stanza quoted from "Diziendo qué cosa es amor," for example, the paradoxical inclusion of pain in pleasure and fear in boldness is resolved in the last two verses. *Plazer* and *dolor, esfuerço* and *temor* result from the "fuerça que hazen los ojos / al seso y al coraçón." Because the eyes are the conduits of Beauty into the heart, it is the image of the beloved reflected in the mind that is responsible both for the lover's joy and for his pain.

Oppositions are easily recognized, because they usually come in familiar pairs. To read courtly poetry well, however, one must also be sensitive to their respective semantic fields, to the way these fields oppose each other, and to the manner in which that opposition can be resolved. *Presencia* and *ausencia*, for example, are paired in several of Manrique's poems not mentioned previously:

III   Prometo más: obediencia   21
             que nunca será quebrada
             en presencia ni *en ausencia*
             (*Cancionero* 19)

             Quien no'stuviere en *presencia*   1
             no tenga *fe en confiança*
             pues son oluido y mudança
             las condiciones d'*ausencia*.
             Quien quisiere ser *amado*   5
             trabaje por ser *presente*,
             que quan presto fuere *ausente*,
             tan presto será *oluidado*:
             y pierda toda esperança
             quien no'stuuiere en presencia,   10
             pues son oluido y mudança
             las condiciones d'ausencia.
             (*Cancionero* 59)

Presencia guarantees the minimal reward of the lover: the *galardón de los ojos*. *Presencia* also fosters *esperança*. Absence denies both. It results in *olvido* and *mudança*, which in turn cause *dolor*. Conversely, *olvido* and *mudança*, and their cause, *ausencia*, are presupposed by *dolor*, as *bien*, *dicha*, and *plazer* presuppose *presencia*. *Presencia* and *ausencia* therefore respectively denote *alegría* and *dolor*, the two archilexemes that subsume the affective lexicon of the lyric.[46] However, the opposition can be overcome by the lover. Although *ausencia* represents the lover's exile from his beloved, when the lover steadfastly holds on to his love he paradoxically overcomes the "normal" effects of absence ("olvido y mudança") by continually keeping an image of the lady *in praesentia* in his heart:

I   Cáusame aquesta firmeza   5
             que, siendo de vos *ausente*,
             ante mí estaua *presente*
             contino vuestra belleza.
             (*Cancionero* 56)

I   Hame tan bien defendido,   1
         señora, vuestra memoria
         de mudança,
         que jamás nunca ha podido
         alcançar de mi victoria   5
         oluidança.
         (*Cancionero* 21)

Like *presencia/ausencia*, the most common pairs of antonyms
(*vivir/morir, vivo/muerto, vida/muerte; ventura/desventura; placer/
tormento; bien/mal; tristeza/alegría*) totally divide a conceptual
domain, yet can be reconciled in the poetry. What is not alive
is dead, what is not dead is alive; what is not present is absent,
what is absent is not present. The poet struggles to minimize
this opposition through paradox, lexical and grammatical
symmetries, balanced structures, and the accumulation of
forms.

The artificiality sensed by Menéndez Pelayo and others
results in part from the elaborate repetition of parallel structures. For example, the composition that carries the rubric
"Otras suyas en que pone el nombre de vna dama" conceals
the name of doña Guiomar in an acrostic that repeats a letter
taken from the name at the beginning of each verse in each
of the seven stanzas (I: G, II: U, III: I, IV: O, V: M, VI: A, VII:
R). The acrostic forces the poet to begin each verse with a
word that contains the appropriate letter. Stanza seven is typical:

VII   Rauia terrible m'aquexa,   A
           rauia mortal me destruye,   B   50
           rauia que jamás me dexa,   A
           rauia que nunca concluye;   B
              remedio siempre me huye,   B
           reparo se me desuía,   C
           rebuelue por otra vía   C   55
           rebuelta y siempre rehuye.   B
           (*Cancionero* 56)

The poet could begin each verse with a different word but repetition is one of his preferred emphatic devices. The first four verses are therefore introduced with the same word: *rauia*. In spite of the anaphora, however, the substitutions reveal that the verses can actually be divided into two-verse sequences that link synonyms or synonymous expressions: *Rauia terrible m'aquexa* and *rauia mortal me destruye, rauia que jamás me dexa* and *rauia que nunca concluye*. The first pair refers to the nature of the affliction (*terrible, mortal*) and to its effect on the lover (*me destruye, m'aquexa*), the second to its persistence (jamás me dexa, *nunca concluye*). The next two verses begin and end with different words that have the same semantic content: *remedio* and *reparo*, *me huye* and *se desvía*. Only in the last two verses is the pattern modified by the placement of the opposites *rebuelve* and *rehuye* at the beginning and end of their respective verses, where their position emphasizes their meaning. Like many other stanzas, this one balances between two semantic poles, *rauia* and *reparo/remedio*, without ever resolving the lover's condition.

The repetition and contrast of nouns and verbs and the modification of the parallel syntactic structures in which they are contained is one of the chief characteristics of the fifteenth-century love lyric. Far from being a defect, the ability to control the distribution of the lexicon over suceeding verses was considered a virtue by its practitioners.[47]

Even in verses that are not completely parallel, related words occupy parallel positions in their respective verses.[48] In so doing, they emphasize the contrastive relationship between the verses. The positional relationship expressed may be one similarity, as it is in the following refrain, where all A-rhymes are verbs in the present tense and all B-rhymes are prepositional pronouns:

I	No tardes, Muerte, que *muero*;	A	1
	ven, porque biua *contigo*;	B	
	quiéreme, pues que te *quiero*,	A	
	que con tu venida *espero*	A	

no tener guerra *comigo*.   B   5
(*Cancionero* 65)

Or it can express contrast:

II   y tiene dos baluartes
          hazia el cabo c'a sentido   20
          ell *oluidar*,
          y cerca a las otras partes,
          vn río mucho crescido,
          qu'es *membrar*.
          (*Cancionero* 22)

Finally, it may simply relate one verse to another by mentioning an associated feature:

IV   Las cauas están *cauadas*
          en medio d'un *coraçón*
          muy leal,
          y después todas *chapadas*   40
          de seruicios y *afición*
          muy desigual;
          (*Cancionero* 23)

In this example, there are correspondances in meaning that notionally link *cauas* (*cauadas*) with *chapadas*, *coraçón* with *afición*, and *muy leal* with *muy desigual*. This tendency to place words that are conceptually related in end-line positions is a particularly important, though not exclusive, feature of the *copla de pie quebrado*.[49]

Grammatical figures (the *figurae verborum* of medieval rhetorics) are the preferred rhetorical devices of a poetry that proclaims a conscious and sophisticated approach to art. Anaphora, antithesis, and polyptoton express the tormented obsession of a lover by turning the poetry in upon itself, revealing that what is said is less important than how it is said. This attention to language patterning is present at all levels of the poetry, from the individual verses, substanzas, and stanzas, to stanza groupings, to entire poems. The courtly poet's verbal legerdemain, however, works best when limited by a short poetic form. Perhaps one of the best examples of the ability to compress meaning into minimal verse structures can be found in one of Manrique's *esparsas*, a form that, like the *canción*, amplifies verbal play:

Hallo que ningún poder	A	1
ni libertad en mí tengo,	B	
pues ni'*stó* ni *vo* ni *vengo*	B	
donde quiere mi querer:	A	
que si'*stó*, vos me *tenéys*;	C	5
[y] si *vo*, vos me *llev* áys*;	D	
si *vengo*, vos me *traéys*;	C	
assi que no me *dexáys*,	D	
señora, ni me *queréys*.	C	
(*Cancionero* 66)		

In this *esparsa*, the five-line stanza that rhymes CDCDC, explains a riddle expressed in verses 3 and 4, by using three parallel verses divided into two half-lines (5-7), and a two-line coda (8-9). All the verses reveal some kind of parallelism. Except for verses one and four, which end in nouns formed from infinitives, all end words are verbs. Verses 5-7 can be divided into two parts, each with a different subject (*Yo/vos*) and verb (*stó*, *vó*, *vengo/tenéys*, *llev* áys*, *traéys*). All the verbs, except one, are verbs of motion set in a causal relation to the first-person verbs (*stó*, *vo*, *vengo*) by the if-clause. The pattern that sets first-person verbs in contrast with second-person, plural verbs disappears in the last two verses, where the lover becomes the object of the verbs (*dexáys*, *queréys*). To the reader or listener is left the important task of deciphering the linguistic play based on the verbs. The piquancy of the lines lies in the evocation of a lady who seems to pull her lover willfully here and there when, in reality, she is disdainful and uncaring of him. The secret hidden by the poem—though not too deeply—is that the mistress does not move the lover. Rather, it is his love of her that makes his will subject to her will. Only in that sense is everything he does, paradoxically, done by her.

A similar condensation of thought characterizes "Yo callé males sufriendo:"

> Yo *callé* males *sufriendo*   1
>   A   B
> y *sufrí* penas *callando*,
>   B   A
> *padescí* no *meresciendo*
>   C   D
> y *merescí padesciendo*
>   D   C
> los bienes que no demando.   5
> (*Cancionero* 66)

Half of the nineteen words in these verses are verbs. *Callar, sufrir, padecer,* and *merecer* are each used once in the past tense and once as present participles. *Demando* is the only verb in the present. All verbs depend on the same subject (*Yo*), which is only stated once. The stanza sets up a situation ("Yo callé males sufriendo") that is amplified over the next three verses and resolved in the last. The chiasmus sorts verses 1-4 into two groups (*callé/sufriendo, sufrí/callando* 1-2; *padecí/mereciendo, merescí/padesciendo* 3-4).[50] Except for subject and connectors, the verses are composed mostly of verbs. The direct objects (*penas/males*) of the first two verses are set in apposition to the other direct object in the stanza (*bienes*). The poem therefore operates between two opposites represented by the antonyms *bienes* and *males*. The preterite verbs are brought forth in sequence as the poet itemizes his suffering. They reveal a gradation of the love experience (*callé, sufrí, padecí* = *males*), that ends in a climax: *merecí* = *bienes*. The past tense of the verbs is in tension with the indefinite time reference of the gerunds, where the progression of successive states loses its concreteness. Finally, what seems a past grief is revealed to be a present grief by the last verb, *demando*. Paradox is again at the core of the passage. The poet compresses the entire courtly love experience in the space of five lines: constant suffering, introversion, the superiority of his lady, and a stubborn, yet acquiescent, plea for relief.

Another stanza, excerpted from "Los fuegos qu'en mi encendieron," shows a similar gradation of sentiments, this time by using nouns:

VI   Sobró mi *amor* en *amor*   51
            all *amor* más desigual,
            y mi *dolor* en *dolor*
            al *dolor* que fué mayor
            en el mundo, y más mortal;   55
                y mi *firmeza* en *firmeza*
            sobró todas las *firmezas*,
            y mi *tristeza* en *tristeza*
            por perder vna *belleza*
            que sobró todas *bellezas*.   60
            (*Cancionero* 47)

The poem compares the poet's experiences with those of unnamed others reputed to have been great lovers. In comparison with them, his love is greater than the greatest love, his pain greater than the greatest pain, and his constancy greater than the greatest constancy. The verses carrying these repetitions are arranged in pairs. The figure used is diaphora, where the term repeated (the nouns *amor, dolor, firmeza, tristeza,* and *belleza*) is first designated, and then qualified. The diaphora extends over several verses dependent on the same verb.[51] At the same time, positive and negative terms alternate: *amor/dolor, firmeza/tristeza.* The cumulative effect is similar to that of the outdoing comparison used in the panegyric, except that the comparisons refer to experiences or qualities instead of people.[52] The oscillation between positive and negative terms ends with a characteristic turn: the poet's love is greater than the greatest love; his sorrow greater than the greatest sorrow, and his constancy greater than all constancies. His greatness, however, is a by-product of the loss of a beauty greater than all beauties.

Manrique's longer poems are, in reality, no more than a collection of smaller ones. Language patterning through figures of repetition remains their principal characteristic. In "Ved qué congoxa la mía," for example, every *quebrado* is repeated at the beginning of the following octosyllable:

I   Ved qué congoxa la mía,   1
ved qué *quexa* desigual
que m'*aquexa*,
que me cresce cada día
vn *mal* teniendo otro *mal*   5
que *no me dexa*;
   no me dexa ni me mata,
ni me libra ni me suelta,
ni m'oluida,
mas de tal guisa me tracta,   10
que la muerte anda rebuelta
con mi vida.

II   *Con mi vida no me hallo*,
porqu'estó ya tan vsado
del morir,   15
que lo sufro, *muero* y callo,
pensando ver acabado
mi beuir;
   mi beuir que presto muera
muera porque *biua* yo;   20
y *muriendo*
fenezca el mal, como quiera
que jamás no *fenesció*
yo *biuiendo*.

III   *Biuiendo* nunca podía   25
conoscer si era *beuir*
yo por cierto,
sino ell alma que *sentía*
que no pudiera *sentir*

siendo *muerto*;   30
  muerto pero de tal mano
que, aun teniendo buena vida,
era razón
perdella, y estando sano
buscar alguna herida   35
al coraçón.

IV   *Al coraçón* qu'es herido
de mil dolencias mortales,
es d'escusar
pensar de velle guarido;   40
mas de dalle otras mil tales
y *acabar*,
  acabar porque será
menor trabajo la *muerte*
que tal pena,   45
y acabando escapará
de vida c'aun era fuerte
para agena.

V   *Para agena* es congoxosa
de vella y tanbién de oylla   50
al que la tiene,
pues ved si será enojosa
al que forçado sufrilla
le conuiene;
  le conuiene aunque no *quiera*,   55
pues no tiene libertad
de no *querer*;
y si *mueriere*, que *muera*,
quanto más que ha voluntad
de fenescer.   60

VI   *De fenescer* he desseo
por el mucho dessear
que me fatiga,
y por el daño que veo
que me sabe acrescentar   65
vn enemiga;

vn enemiga tan fuerte,
qu'en ell arte del penar
tanto sabe,
que me da siempre la muerte   70
y jamás me da lugar
que m'acabe.

FIN

VII   Ya mi vida os he contado
por estos renglones tristes
que veréys,   75
y quedo con el cuydado
que vos, señora, me distes
y daréys.
    N'os pido que me sanéys,
que, según el mal que tengo,   80
no's possible;
mas pido's que me matéys,
pues la culpa que sostengo
es tan terrible.
(Cancionero 39-42)

The poem's anaphoras—*Ved que* (1-2), *que* (3, 4, 6), *ni* (8, 9)—chain stanzas and substanzas. Such is the case in lines 6-7, 12-13, 18-19, 24-25, 30-31, 36-37, 42-43, 48-49, 54-55, 60-61, and 66-67. The anadiplosis is expressed in a complete or an incomplete chiasmus, or a duplication of the thought, which expresses an antithesis or a paradox: "no me dexa [vivir] ni me mata, / ni me libra ni me suelta" (7-8), "mi beuir que presto muera / muera porque biua yo" (19-20). The linked repetitions create a sense of strong emotional excitement. The poem also makes liberal use of polyptoton (*queja* [2], *aqueja* [3]; or *muerte* [11, 44, 70], *morir* [15], *muero* [16], *muera* [19, 20, 58], *muriendo* [21], *muerto* [30, 31], *mueriere* [58]; *fenezca* [22], *feneció* [23], *fenecer* [60, 61]; *acabar* [42, 43], *acabando* [46], *acabe* [72]; *vivir* [18, 19, 26], *viva* [20], *viviendo* [24, 25]), which is coupled occasionally to internal repetitions of sounds to convey an emotional state. In the first four lines of the poem, for example, alliteration (*qué congoxa, qué quexa, que me aquexa, que me crece*) halts the reading of the verse, by its repetition of *que*, before stressing the despair of the lover with a sequence of six negatives (6-9).

The reiteration of elements serves a concrete function in this poem. As the introductory apostrophe discloses, the poem is an invitation to witness the distress of the lover. That distress is a malady that continually rebegets itself. Its major symptom is self-absorption. The poem is therefore a clinical exposition of the disease, a spiritual biography that the lover puts before the lady ("Ya mi vida os he contado / por estos renglones tristes," 73-74).

The structure of the work reflects the inward thrust of the lover's revelations. Each half stanza flows into the next in a chained movement that gives concrete shape to the idea that sorrow begets sorrow. The speaker suffers from two afflictions, one of which is the result of the other (4-5). The underlying *mal* is desire (6-8) the resulting *mal* is the longing for death engendered by frustration. Desire is created by an outside force over which the poet has no control. A slave to love, he can only escape through death. But he cannot die. Instead his *vida* becomes a living death.

If it were not for its reasoned art, the poem could be considered a form of stream of consciousness. It is not, however, an outpouring of the unconscious, but a highly structured and organized manifestation of a collective literary experience. The artfulness of the poem lies in the inventiveness with which it treats the essential contradictions of love. Its language manipulations create paradoxes, and through paradox it captures the attention and engages the intelligence of the audience.

With the exception of satiric poetry, the weight of poetic tradition in the lyric does not allow much room for individualized expression. The charm of the fifteenth-century lyric is in its technical and linguistic virtuosity. Each song is an expression of received elements reworked by an individual. The poet is free to choose from among the inherited elements those which his talent and inventiveness tell him best express his feelings. But both the tradition and the author mold and shape the artifact.[53] This interchange must be kept in mind when approaching the work of any fifteenth-century poet. Salinas, Manrique's best known critic, says that what is missing from Manrique's minor poetry is "la incorporación total del autor, la adhesión de su ser entero a la obra que está escribiendo." He adds that "nos hallamos frente a un caso obvio de tradición poética pasivamente restaurada."[54] Such a view misses the point.

What Salinas says about Manrique's poems is true about practically all poetry of the fifteenth-century. The lyric of that period is not the place to look for personal sentiment couched in an individualized language. Indeed, courtly poetry has few themes and uses a limited vocabulary. It is not formally creative. It may lack sincerity. But these limitations are imposed by the poet and the traditions he used. The presumed object of the lyric poem is a pretext.[55] The real object is the poem itself. In it the poet seeks to show his virtuosity.[56]

Keith Whinnom, in a recent book, calls fifteenth-century poetry "intellectual," and even "metaphysical."[57] When read with attention, the linguistic games, the forced ambiguities, and the seemingly simple, yet complex rhetorical and metrical structures of the short lyrics reveal a circumscribed, yet tremendously dense thoughtfulness.

THREE

Coplas por la muerte de su padre
The Background

No holograph of the poetry of Jorge Manrique survives. Editors generally rely on the *Cancionero general* of Hernando del Castillo for the texts of the minor lyrics, and on early manuscripts and prints, and occasionally on the glosses of the poem (particularly those of the early sixteenth century) to establish a text of the *Coplas*.[1] The two best known modern editions are R. Foulché-Delbosc's *Coplas que fizo don Jorge Manrique por la muerte de su padre*, printed several times in the early part of the century, and A. Cortina's edition for Clásicos Castellanos, *Jorge Manrique: cancionero*, which has gone through several reprints and revisions.[2]

Foulché-Delbosc used three manuscripts and four prints to establish a text of the *Coplas*, but without indicating the text used as base. Cortina based his version on the *Cancionero de Ramón de Llabía* and noted the variants in the gloss of Diego de Barahona (1512). Because the differences between the two editions are not substantial, critics of the *Coplas* subsequently assumed that the text of either editor was sound and proceeded to explicate the poem printed by them. Neither editor knew or paid much attention to the radically different stanza order of the earliest edition of the *Coplas* (Zaragoza, 1482) that—if well known—would at the very least have resulted in more cautious pronouncements about the structure of the work. Compared with the Foulché-Delbosc edition, the Palermo print has the following stanza order: 1-2-3-4-5-6 / 25 / 7-8-9-10-11-12 / 26-27-28-29-30-31-32-33-34-35-36 / 13-14-15-16-17-18-19-20-21-22-23-24 / 37-38-39-40.[3] The commonly accepted text of the *Coplas*, however, may reflect the form in which Manrique left it if, as Ricardo Senabre thinks, the printer either received an unsewn or poorly sewn manuscript, or took the manuscript apart to set the type and transposed two folios. It is not an uncommon mistake. As Senabre reconstructs the accident, the manuscript probably contained the *Coplas* foliated in the following manner: fols 1r (I-VI), 1v (VII-XII); 2r (XIII-XVIII), 2v (XIX-XXIV); 3r (XXV-XXX), 3v (XXXI-XXXVI); 4r (XXXVII-XL). In Senabre's opinion, the printer transposed folios 2 and 3.[4] The resulting poem would reflect the structure of the early Zaragoza edition. Senabre, however, does not mention the dislocation of stanza XXV, which does not appear after XII, but after VI.

There is also disagreement about the authenticity of the stanzas that begin "Oh mundo pues que nos matas" and "Es tu comienzo lloroso," first published in Alonso de Cervantes's 1501 gloss of the poem, and which, tradition says, were found on the body of Jorge Manrique.[5] Editors have not generally included them in the work.[6] Recently, J. Labrador, A. Zorita, and R.A. Difranco argued they should be inserted right after stanza XXIV. They based their conclusions on a close reading of Alfonso de Palencia's *Cuarta Década*, supported by a careful study of manuscript 617 of the Biblioteca de Palacio, and by the fact that the earliest glossers accepted them as part of the work.[7]

This study quotes the texts of the poems of Manrique from Cortina's edition. Of the numerous editions of Manrique's complete works made since Cortina published his, only Serrano de Haro's *Jorge Manrique: obras* makes a significant attempt at establishing a critical text. Serrano's edition, however, does not indicate which text was used as base text for the *Coplas,* or the criteria used to select among the variants in the many manuscripts and prints. The text itself does not significantly differ from Cortina's although it does represent an advance in the amount of textual commentary made available to the reader.

GENRE

The *Coplas* is a lyric poem, but of what type? Quintana called it a funeral sermon, Burkart, an exhortation to man to lead an exemplary life. Anna Krause and A. Cortina preferred to describe it as an heroic elegy or a Renaissance ode. Petriconi and Salinas saw the existence of two sections: an elegiac meditation and a panegyric of don Rodrigo. Prieto, noting that the elegiac element was of secondary importance, called the *Coplas* a work that, because of its sobriety and decorum, transcended the elegy. And Gilman described it as neither an elegy nor a meditation about death, but a "dance of life."[8]

One could go on documenting the variety of ways in which readers of the *Coplas* have categorized the poem. Some see the work as the orthodox and sententious epitome of a medieval tradition. Others regard it as one of the first manifestations of the Renaissance in Spain, still other critics think it a transitional work. Their disagreements reflect the inherent difficulty in calling the *Coplas* an elegy, when it differs in so many ways from the classical elegy.[9]

The classical elegy was not so much characterized by its themes as by its poetic form and tone. Its subject matter could be the death of a man, but it could also be any event or psychological state that called for a somber, formal approach. In late classical times it even included mythological narratives and love poetry. The meter was its distinguishing feature: an hexameter followed by a pentameter line.

Jorge Manrique probably knew little, if anything, about the classical elegy. The first known edition of the *Coplas* carries the rubric: *Dezir de don Jorge Manrique por la muerte de su padre.*[10] In other words, the poem's first known title (*Dezir*), and that by which it has been most commonly known, *Coplas,* point to the poem's origin in the vernacular Castilian poetic tradition. The meter Manrique used was also indigenous: two octosyllable lines followed by a four- syllable half-line. Obviously, in spite of the similarities that may exist between the *Coplas* and the classical or the renaissance elegy, the work's immediate sources of inspiration are fifteenth-century Castilian poems; more particularly, poetry about death.

Whatever the difficulties encountered in calling the *Coplas* an elegy, one is loath to abandon a term that so aptly conveys the mood of the poem. This study, therefore uses the term elegy and considers it to mean a lyric poem that laments the death of a person and the impermanence of life. It will not be identified with any particular metric form, but rather by its sentiments, themes, and relationship to the medieval literature about death. Such a definition aptly describes most of the poem. What remains outside the elegy, though not completely outside of it, is the final dialogue with Death, which arises out of its own tradition in medieval poetry.

DEATH IN MEDIEVAL LITERATURE

The admonitions of the church fathers and their commentators to be contemptuous of the world, and their insistent call to contemplate the fragility and corruptibility of the flesh conditioned medieval beliefs about life and death.[11] Although these ideas were at the core of the church's teachings to men, the late Middle Ages saw an important change in human attitudes toward death.[12]

Until the thirteenth century death was thought to be a doorway that led the good Christian from this life to the next. It was the last phase in the return of the soul to God, or in its fall to eternal damnation. In the thirteenth century works like Pope Innocent III's *De Miseria Condicionis Humane* (1195) began to emphasize the impact of death on human life, rather than its transitional role.[13] Innocent's work dwelt on the physical aspect of human misery, particularly the decay of the body, creating images of extraordinary literary resonance.

In the fourteenth century the awareness of the finality of

life introduced by the *De Miseria*, and fostered by the Franciscans and Dominicans, intensified. Work after work considered its horror, its power, its physical decay, building on the examples of the *De Miseria*, and perhaps on a stratum of folk belief not evident before this time. Death emerged as a personality whose dominion over the world seemed to rival God's, and whose very conception was at variance with traditional Christian values.

Late medieval man despaired of the fragility of the tangible world, of human flesh, of human fortune, and of human hopes. These attitudes are reflected in such poems as the thirteenth-century *Vado mori* and the fourteenth-century *Dit des trois vifs et trois morts*.[14] In the latter composition, three men encounter three dead counterparts in varying degrees of decomposition and hear the ominous warning: "We have been as you are, you shall be as we are." Faced with such prospects, medieval man clung dearly to life, while reminding himself of what was in store for him.

The earliest literary expressions about the death of an individual underwent a similar evolution toward the macabre. In medieval Spain, elegiac sentiments first appear in the epic or in Latin works. They are invariably short expressions of grief. The first (also the earliest appearance of the *ubi sunt* motif in a secular work) is a *planctus* attributed to Alfonso VI upon the disappearance of his son Sancho during the Battle of Uclés (1108): "Ubi est filius meus, jucunditae vitae meae, solatium senectutis, unicus haeres meus?"[15] A deeply felt death evoked the *planctus* but, typically, the sorrow was overcome in the course of the composition by the recognition that the dead man had achieved salvation.[16] The *planctus* led to the *consolatio* and placed death within the larger Christian framework. In the thirteenth and fourteenth centuries, however, Spanish writers also grew more concerned with the discrete events that made up a human life, and with the phenomenon that ends it. They sought to understand death, but inveighed bitterly against its finality.

Castilian poetry about death, however, is not as copious or as macabre as it is in other literatures. Many Castilian poetic texts evoke the evanescence of life and the vanity of the world, but relatively few are extensive laments over the death of a dear one, over death's power, or over the corruptibility of the body. Before the fifteenth century there is only one major exception: the Archpriest's lament for Trotaconventos in *El libro de buen amor.* In this work, the Archpriest dedicates two hundred and thirty-two verses to a satiric lament over the death of his go-between, forty-eight of which assess death's power over men, and dwell on the horror of the decaying body.[17]

Even in the fifteenth century, when texts dealing with death in the abstract or with the death of an individual multiply, poets are characteristically circumspect about the phenomenon of death.[18] Instead they prefer to expose earthly vanity through the topics of the *memento mori* and the *ubi sunt qui ante nos fuerunt?*, a subtopic, or—better yet—one of the expressions of the *memento mori* that examines the destiny of men. The *ubi sunt* reveals how everything is subject to death. A series of parallel rhetorical questions ask for the whereabouts of individuals, classes, things, or qualities that have disappeared. The questions may or may not be answered, although an answer is always implied. Fifteenth-century Castilian poets frequently used the formula, rendering *ubi?* as *¿ó?, ¿dó?, ¿ónde?, ¿dónde?, ¿adó?, ¿en dónde?,* or as *¿qué es de?, ¿qué fue de?, ¿qué se fizo de?* They also mixed biblical, classical, and contemporary figures in their questions.

The reluctance of Castilian writers to describe the decay of the body diminishes during the fifteenth century, with the appearance of the "Dança de la muerte" and of the elegy— a form well suited to attracting the favor of noble patrons.

It is not known when or where the Dance of Death originated, or whether its first expression was literary or pictorial. The earliest known depiction was a fresco painted on the wall of the cemetery of the Holy Innocents in Paris (1424). It is thought that the text of the French *Danse macabre* is a commentary on that fresco.[19]

Normally, the Dance of Death takes two forms, the *Todestanz* (Dance of Death) and the *Totentanz* (Dance of the Dead).

In the *Totentanz* a live person alternates with his dead double in a series of figures. In the *Todestanz* Death leads a line of men, ordered according to their earthly rank, in a procession or a dance. The Dance of Death is the more successful of the two treatments. It has the advantage of depicting Death's equalizing power and its absolute sway over man graphically.

Two Castilian texts treat the Dance of Death, the "Dança general de la muerte" (ca. 1400), and the "Danza de la muerte," a reworking of the "Dança general" published in 1520.[20] The "Dança general" is a seventy-nine stanza poem in which forty characters come before Death to hear its sentence. The Dance of Death is also an incidental topic in many fifteenth-century poems, including the *Coplas*.

Fifteenth century elegies have no fixed form. They may be short lyrics destined to be sung, or poems to be read or declaimed. They may contain allegories. They always, however, invoke certain themes and give evidence of some rhetorical homogeneity to evoke pathos through the use of amplification, repetition, apostrophe, periphrasis, and the topics of the panegyric.

In a study of the elegy in Spanish literature, Camacho Guisado divides fifteenth-century Castilian elegies into two groups: 1) poetry about death, and 2) poetry about the dead.[21] Though both groups use the same motifs and images, they can be distinguished from one another by their approach. The poems about death treat it in a general manner, using as topics the brevity of life, the equalizing power of death, and the corruptibility of the body. Poems about the dead are more like the classical elegy in that they include a lamentation, a praise of the dead, imprecations against death, and a consolatory passage.

Poems like Pérez de Guzmán's "Dezir quando muryo Don Diego Furtado de Mendoza," Villasandino's "Dezir para la tumba del Rrey Don Enrrique el Viejo," Santillana's *Doctrinal de privados*, and Gómez Manrique's "Coplas para el señor Diego Arias de Avila" belong to the first group. Although they seem to have a particular death as subject, in reality they are meditations on the brevity of life. To the first group also belong poems that personify and establish a dialogue with death, like the "Dança general de la muerte," and Mena's "Razonamiento que hizo con la muerte."

The second group established by Camacho Guisado, the poetry about the dead, is made up of a large number of compositions generally called *defunziones.* They begin, almost always, by mentioning the date of the death of the individual whose passing is poetically commemorated. A good example, because of its relation to the *Coplas,* is Gómez Manrique's "Defunzion del noble cauallero Garcilasso dela Vega."[22] The poem begins:

> I A veynte e un dias del noueno mes,
> el año de cinco, despues de cincuenta,
> e quatro dezenas poniendo en la cuenta,
> nueve centenas e una despues
> (*Cancionero castellano,* 2: 28)

In spite of the trite beginning, there follows some memorable poetry in which the poet tells how he witnessed the lament of the Castilian troops for a fallen relative, Garcilasso de la Vega, whose military prowess was greater than that of Hector, Achilles, and Troilus. The poet, distressed and saddened, participates in the funeral rites, while a messenger is sent to the fallen hero's mother with the news (stanzas I-XIV).

The messenger is struck dumb with grief when he comes before the lady, who slowly draws the story out of him. He finally reveals that Garcilasso died in battle (stanzas XV-XXVI), but declares that there should be no mourning for the man because, though he lost his life, he won eternal glory and left behind the memory of his deeds:

> XXVI >>Por ende, señora, pues perdió la vida,
> ganando por siempre la celeste gloria,
> dexando de sí perpetua memoria,
> non deve ser su muerte plañida;
> por ende vos noble, maguer dolorida,
> tomad su fazienda e bienes amargos,

> e descargadle de todos sus cargos
> porque reçiba la gloria conplida.>>
> (*Cancionero castellano* 2: 31)

Garcilasso's sister, doña Elvira, and the other women of the household cry out and tear their clothes in sign of mourning, but the mother receives the news stoically (stanzas XXVII-XXXVII) and prepares to go for the body and bury it in the family convent.

Garcilasso, a brother of doña Mencía de Figueroa, Jorge Manrique's mother, was a close ally of the Manrique family. Gómez deeply felt his passing.[23] Garcilasso died from a poisonous arrow wound received during a battle against the Moors.[24] As was customary, the family urged the king to bestow the dignities of the dying Garcilasso on his son. Enrique IV gave an equivocal reply and immediately thereafter gave Nicolás Lucas the commandery of Montizón. It must therefore have given don Rodrigo Manrique great satisfaction to challenge Enrique IV over the tenancy of the commandery. Gómez Manrique's poem, though full of rhetorical artifice, lacks the solemn, elevated, and often impersonal tone of many *defunziones*. It is a more personal poem than many of the courtly elegies of the fifteenth century. Nevertheless, the usual topics are present. The grief is so strong that the poet doubts that words can express it. The dead man is compared to mythological and historical figures and finally some sort of religious and secular consolation is rendered.

Comparison of Manrique's *Coplas por la muerte de su padre* with the *defunziones* and with the poems about death cited above shows that the *Coplas* is an amalgam of both. The poem begins with general admonitions about life and its value, such as might be found in a sermon or in a poem condemning the vanity of life. There are echoes of the Dance of Death, but they are followed by an evocation of a particular life that shares some characteristics with the *defunzión*. The poem ends with an allegorical dialogue that again has some relation to the Dance of Death.[25]

THE STRUCTURE OF THE *COPLAS*

It is impossible to know with certainty whether any of the surviving versions of the *Coplas* is a final version. Three years elapsed between the death of Jorge Manrique (1479) and the earliest known edition (1482), so Manrique did not have a hand in the publication of his poetry. Like his contemporaries, Manrique left no indication of how he approached the creative process, nor did he give any idea of the elements he considered appropriate to an elegy. Moreover, though certain topics appear consistently in the poetry of death (and as with the *defunziones,* a recurring element may serve to differentiate a particular kind of composition), lengthy works of the time tend not to adhere strictly to predetermined forms.

Notwithstanding, the *Coplas* is considered to be either a model of unity and coherence, or a work of uneven excellence. Serrano de Haro writes: "Es rasgo sobresaliente de las Coplas la uniformidad y unidad del poema. La obra de arte debe comunicarse entera, cerrada en sí como un orbe propio. Dentro de él destellan tales o cuales bellezas particulares, pero en función de un conjunto. Si esta integridad no se logra la obra falla en un requisito esencial. Las Coplas son un modelo de estructura y coherencia . . . ."[26]

This view, held by a majority of modern critics, assumes that the normally printed version of the *Coplas* reflects the correct order of the stanzas. The earliest available text of the *Coplas,* however, has a different stanza order, and sixteenth-century readers often read the *Coplas* in versions that intercalated two additional stanzas after number XXIV. In addition, if—as Francisco Caravaca thinks—the stanza order of the first print is not Manrique's but an "improvement" made by the person who provided the manuscript to the printer, then an early reader of the poem found the work's structure deficient.[27]

The late appearance of don Rodrigo (stanzas XXIV-XL) in a poem ostensibly dedicated to him is an important reason for the recurring criticisms of the poem. Nineteenth-century editors like Quintana accused Manrique of a lack of filial devotion and dismissed the section that praises don Rodrigo as inferior, thinking that Manrique's poetic gift waned when he reached the part about his father.[28] G. Ticknor divided the *Coplas* into two parts: a general meditation on Death, of high poetic quality, and a less gracious section devoted to don Rodrigo, which one could wish away.[29] Blanco White, in his edition of the poem, concurred, saying that in Manrique's poem one feels the lack of grace, especially toward the end.[30] Menéndez Pelayo, however, recognized the worth of the second half of the poem. He took Quintana to task for suppressing the very stanzas in which Manrique expresses his filial love.[31] Others explained the poem's changes of tone and approach as a consequence of the fact that parts of the *Coplas* were composed at different times, and under different circumstances.[32] Senabre, for example, says that the order of the stanzas in the *Cancionero de Llavía* "produce la sensación de que nos hallamos ante dos obras distintas, meramente yuxtapuestas."[33] Even if the canonical order is correct, without a reliable text, no interpretation is totally secure.

Those who plead the case for structural coherence divide the work into two, three, or four subsections. Rosemarie Burkart was the first to make a serious effort to come to grips with the structure of the poem.[34] Burkart divided the *Coplas* into three parts: 1) stanzas I-XIII, which exhort the reader to examine the realities of life; 2) stanzas XIV-XXIV, which introduce the *ubi sunt* motif; and, 3) stanzas XXV-XL, which glorify Manrique's father. Burkart revealed a poem that moves from the general to the specific; from contemplation of the transitoriness of worldly things and of historical figures, both ancient and modern, to the specific transit of don Rodrigo. This analysis has come to be accepted as outlining the fundamental structure of the *Coplas*, although there has been room for refinements.

Anna Krause, for example, argued that there are two distinct subunits in the third section: stanzas XXV-XXXIII (which eulogize don Rodrigo), and stanzas XXXIV-XL (which describe his passing). Manrique's editor, A. Cortina, concurred, although he distinguished two different moments in the middle section: the *ubi sunt* proper and stanzas XVIII-XXIV, which portray both the hardships and the people Manrique and his father knew.[35]

Pedro Salinas, in his book on Jorge Manrique, was even more conscious of distinct units of meaning within the poem.[36] In the first section (stanzas I-XIV) Salinas saw an exposition of the transitoriness of life (stanzas I-III), and an evaluation of the world and its goods (stanzas IV-XIV). In the second section (stanzas XV-XXIV) he distinguished the *ubi sunt* (stanzas XV-XXII) from stanzas XXIII-XXIV, which he considered a poem within a poem summarizing the effects of death. The third section (stanzas XXV-XL) he divided into a praise of don Rodrigo (stanzas XXV-XXXII), followed by a transitional stanza (XXXIII), which leads to the appearance of Death on stage (stanzas XXXIV-XXXVII). Stanzas XXXVIII-XXXIX contain don Rodrigo's reply to Death's challenge, and with stanza XL the reader witnesses the very moment of his death.[37]

Regardless of other refinements, most critics accept Burkart's basic division of the *Coplas* into three parts. One must explain, however, why early readers and glossers thought that the poem naturally divides into a general and a specific section, and judged the former to be better than the latter. The first half of the *Coplas* is well suited to moralizing. It contains the poem's most moving and evocative lines and an imposing treatment of death. The second is an expression of theosis in the figure of a knight. Given the peculiar religiosity of early glossers of the poem, this may have been unpalatable. It may explain why few glossers ever bothered to go beyond the first half of the poem.[38] Furthermore, a dimly remembered historical figure was the subject of the second half. When literary critics and historians restored don Rodrigo to his proper prominence in the work, readers became aware again of the fact that, within a religious context, the rejection of all earthly glory is not complete. The treatment of death in stanzas I-XXIV leads to certain expectations that are not be fulfilled in stanzas XXV-XL by the measure of sixteenth-century religiosity. They are, however, fulfilled from the point of view of Jorge Manrique's own religiosity, and in a manner that is in keeping with the ideology of his class.

METER

The elegy has forty stanzas of twelve verses each. These stanzas divide into two six-verse substanzas with the rhyme scheme ABc ABc CDe CDe. The basic unit of the substanza is a tercet composed of two octosyllables, followed by a four-syllable line rhyming ABc, where -c and -e represent the rhyme of the *pie quebrado* (half-line or limping foot). The rhyme is consonant. Everything rhymes from the last stress of the line on. Seventy-five percent of the verses stress the second syllable from the end. The recurrent stress pattern gives the poem a regularity that makes those verses stressed on the last syllable more emphatic. The stanza form, though not invented by Manrique, has come to be known as the *estrofa manri-queña.*[39]

Quintana criticized the poet for choosing so trite a meter for a composition of such an elevated nature. Quintana maintained that the *pie quebrado* stanzas were opposed to all harmony and enjoyment, and that the meter of the *Coplas* was so tiresome, inharmonious, and given to sharpening thought in the form of concepts or epigrams, that it interfered with the pleasure of reading the poem.[40] Few critics have concurred with Quintana. Dorothy Clotelle Clarke characterized the octosyllable as a meter that had "the lightness desirable for expression of joyful exultation, of bantering mood, or of swift narrative," and yet had "sufficient volume and depth to give the required weight for a serious poem on Death." The meter "could be extended or combined with a staccato effect by means of its *quebrado*, or it could be held smoothly within its own bounds. It was short enough to flow freely and yet long enough to allow for resonance and tone variation."[41]

Manrique's fine poetic sense led him to choose a meter that in its versatility approximated the classical elegiac couplet. Both the *copla de pie quebrado* and the elegiac couplet alternate long and short verses. Though the effect of the octosyllable in Manrique's stanza is perhaps more intimate than that of the heroic hexameter, the alternating lines provide the poet with rhythmic resources that suggest those of the classical couplet.[42] This similarity was obvious to sixteenth-century Spanish theorists of poetry, who, especially in light of the Italian elegists' use of *terza rima*, saw no difficulty in writing elegies in three-line stanzas. López Pinciano, for example, considered Manrique's stanza to be the equivalent of latin elegiac meter: "si buscamos algú[n] metro que responda al elegíaco latino, exámetro y pentámetro, no estoy mal en la copla castellana de ocho, con su quebrado, la qual parece quebrar de la manera que el exámetro y pentámetro, aunque no es tan sonoro. Exemplo sean las coplas de don Iorge Manrique."[43]

The possible rhythmical permutations of the octosyllable provided Manrique with a very adequate means of expression. Navarro Tomás studied the rhythmic patterns of Manrique's verse and found that 43 percent of the octosyllables are trochaic, 16.7 percent are dactyls, and 38.1 percent are mixed.[44] The half-line (composed of four syllables in sixty of the eighty sextets) is generally trochaic in rhythm. In those stanzas where the half-line is more or less than four syllables, Manrique followed the standard poetic practice of his time by adding an extra syllable to the *pie quebrado* when the last syllable of the octosyllable was stressed, or subtracting one when there was a final vowel in the octosyllable that could elide with an initial vowel in the *pie quebrado*. The verses stressed on the second syllable from the end (seventy-five percent), give the composition a serene quality that is reinforced by a preference for the use of open rather than closed vowels in the rhyme.

With a polyrhythmic verse at his disposal Manrique attained striking effects by careful patterning. In the first stanza, for example, he suggested reflection by delaying the stress in the first two octosyllables and delaying it even more in the *pie quebrado,* where the three initial closed syllables suggest a gradual inward movement. He then chose two dactyls to

quicken the pace and call to the attention of the reflective soul
its most immediate concerns:

I   Recuerde el alma dormida,   1
        abiue el seso e despierte
        contemplando
        cómo se passa la vida,
        cómo se viene la muerte   5
        tan callando
        (*Cancionero* 89)

The octosyllables of the first substanza can also be replicated in the second substanza, giving the sestet a rhythmic
unity which, in the third stanza acoustically parallels the flow
of the waters of life. They reach their destination as the substanza reaches its end in the final stress of the *pie quebrado*:

III   Nuestras vidas son los ríos   25
        que van a dar en la mar,
        qu'es el morir;
        allí van los señoríos
        derechos a se acabar
        e consumir;   30
        (*Cancionero* 89)

The replication can also allow questions expressed in the dactyl to predominate:

XVII   ¿Qué se hyzieron las damas,
        sus tocados e vestidos,
        sus olores?   195
        ¿Qué se hizieron las llamas
        de los fuegos encendidos
        d'amadores?
        (*Cancionero* 97)

The rhythmic patterns can be replicated in inverted fashion:

> mas los buenos religiosos
> gánanlo con oraciones
> e con lloros;
> los caualleros famosos, 430
> con trabajos e afflictiones
> contra moros.
> (*Cancionero* 107)

They can even be the same:

> partimos quando nascemos, 55
> andamos mientra viuimos,
> y llegamos
> al tiempo que feneçemos;
> assí que quando morimos
> descansamos. 60
> (*Cancionero* 91)

The last example captures the regularity of man's life on earth, cut short by death. The reader moves through the octosyllables expecting continuance of the regular rhythm in the third line only to be surprised and stopped by the single verb of the *pie quebrado,* and by the continued flow of the syntactic structure into the next verse.

As mentioned earlier, a tally of the occurrence of the different rhythms reveals that the trochaic rhythm is the backbone of the poem, but only in combination with others.[45] Though the dactyl appears in only 16 percent of the cases, its appearance usually marks an important passage that requires a more emphatic stress; for example, the invocation to Christ:

> XXXIX   Tú que, por nuestra maldad, 457
> tomaste forma seruil
> e baxo nombre;
> tú, que a tu diujnjdad 460
> juntaste cosa tan vil
> como es el hombre;
>   tú, que tan grandes tormentos

> sofriste sin resistencia
> en tu persona,   465
> non por mjs merescimjentos,
> mas por tu sola clemencia
> me perdona.
> (*Cancionero* 108-109)

Far from being a trite verse form as Quintana maintained, the *copla de pie quebrado* is a supple instrument, well suited to create the effects that Manrique sought. Much, if not most, of the excellence of the *Coplas* results from Manrique's mastery of this supposedly simple poetic meter.

STYLISTIC FEATURES

The small number of neologisms and latinisms makes the *Coplas* a work of simple majesty.[46] The parsimonious use of adjectives, the predominance of nouns and verbs, and even, in the latter case, of verbs often used as nouns, rivets the attention of the reader. Manrique developed his skill with language by writing love lyrics.

Even in the most famous lines of the *Coplas* there are echoes of the language of the love lyric. The two half-lines of the first stanza ("contemplando" 3, "tan callando" 6) are rhythmically identical and end with the same rhyme as the *quebrados* of a stanza of "Estando ausente su amiga, a un mensajero que allá enbiava:"

> Llegarás con tal concierto,   13
> los ojos en el sentido
> *reguardando*,   15
> no te mate quien ha muerto
> mi coraçón y vencido
> *bienamando*[47]
> (*Cancionero* 48)

A little later in the same poem Manrique associates remembrance and memory:

> *Recuerde* bien tu *memoria*   43
> de los trabajados días
> qu'e sofrido   45
> por más merescer la gloria
> de las altas alegrías
> de Cupido.
> (*Cancionero* 49)

In the concluding stanza he exhorts his messenger to return with his lady's answer using exactly the same word as the third verse of the *Coplas*:

> Remediador de mis quexas,   102
> no te tardes, ven temprano
> *contemplando*
> el peligro en que me dexas,   105
> con la candela en la mano
> ya penando;
> (*Cancionero* 51)

The love poet refers to the power of the lady's beauty to overcome the will through the eyes, and therefore warns his messenger to avert them. He also considers the experiences brought by memory before reason to be under the shadow of the image of the beloved. *Reguardar* (15) suggests the same inward movement that begins the *Coplas*. It points to the fact that the suffering of the lover is, in part, a consequence of a malfunction of memory, which allows only one image—that of the beloved—to be contemplated.[48]

In the love poetry, memory is the faculty that provokes the lover's pain by reminding him of past joys, or simply by bringing up before his mind's eye the image of the lady. In the *Coplas*, on the other hand, the association of memory and contemplation is characteristic of the process of self-illumination related to a religious experience. The exhortation to remembrance (*recuerde*) and its natural and immediate combination with *memoria* and *contemplando* are part of a poetic language that is common to both genres, but the elegy actualizes a different set of associations. The similarity of the language shows how the poet chose from the code he knew elements capable of carrying the message he wished to convey. He linked these elements into a temporal chain that is the message itself. Jakobson's processes of selection and combination are at work, but each within its own context.[49]

Manrique's use of the *copla de pie quebrado* to express thought in parallel verse structures also owes a debt to the love lyric. If parallelism is a formal resemblance between two or more units of surface structure, resemblance can occur at any one or more surface structure levels (syntactic, positional, lexical, morphological, phonological, metrical, and numerical).[50] The following verse pairs of the *Coplas*, for example, show resemblances that are syntactic (there is complete identification of the syntax), positional (all the elements in each line appear in the same place), morphologic (two or three words repeat in each line), metric (each verse pair is metrically identical), and numeric (each contains the same number of components):

cómo se passa la vida,	4
cómo se viene la muerte	5
(*Cancionero* 89)	
allí los ríos caudales,	31
allí los otros medianos	32
(*Cancionero* 90)	

At least twenty-seven of the poem's forty stanzas contain verses that display some or all of these parallelisms.

As in the minor lyric, parallel structures perform certain rhetorical functions in the *Coplas*. They lend clarity and symmetry to the verse, provide emphasis, tie together groups of stanzas, and build to a climax. The syntactic, lexical, and positional parallelisms of the *Coplas* establish notional relationships between different verses or parts of verses, either by drawing equivalences or contrasts between them:[51]

II   Pues si vemos *lo presente*   13
        cómo en vn punto s'es *ido*
        e *acabado*,   15
        si juzgamos sabiamente,
        daremos *lo non venido*
        por *passado*.
        (*Cancionero* 89-90)

In stanza II the syntactic parallelism of verses 13 and 16 emphasizes the contrast set up by the poet between *presente* and
pasado. The notional equation established in the participles *ido*
and *acabado* (14-15) is paralleled in verses 17-18, where the
future, represented by the negated opposite of the verb *ir*,
venir: lo non venido (17), undermines the semantic contrast by
an equation (present = "es ido / e acabado" = "lo non venido" = future). The present and the future are the same as
the past, and *ir* equals *venir* from the narrator's judgmental
position.

As discussed in chapter 2, the *copla de pie quebrado* readily
lends itself to the replication of parallel structures and shows
a special affinity to positional parallelisms. In the *Coplas*, positional parallels are so common that they can often be antici-
pated. The second *pie quebrado* of a six-verse substanza will
often contain a synonym or antonym of the word that appears
in the first *pie quebrado*. Both *acabado* and *passado* in the stanza
cited above refer to the past, and *passado* is no more than
amplification of the thought introduced with *acabado*. Though
some of the parallels are not totally clear when taken out of
context, other examples of amplification through substitution
are: *morir/consumir* (III); *oradores/sabores, verdad/deidad* (IV); *sin
pesar/sin errar, llegamos/descansamos* (V); *descendió/murió* (VI);
corremos/perdemos (VII); *gloria/memoria* (XL). Oppositions are
just as common: *chicos/ricos* (III), *juuentud/senectud* (IX), *tem-
porales/eternales* (XI), *corporal/angelical* (XIII), *jouentud/senectud*
(XXXI), *mundanales/infernales* (XXXVI). Often, however, parallelism extends to the octosyllables. In the posthumous
verses that are normally printed after the *Coplas* there are
oppositions in each of the octosyllables and in the *quebrados*:

I   De tu vida, *tan cubierta*   7
           de males y de dolores
           tan poblada;
           de los bienes *tan desierta*   10
           de plazeres y dulçores
           despoblada.

The list parallels can be extended to include a high per-
centage of the poem's verses, particularly in the *quebrados.*
These examples, however, represent only a sampling of the
richly varied parallel texture of the poem.

Normally, as in the last example, the *Coplas* tends to de-
velop in increments of two three-verse units, the second of
which usually parallels the first. It is not uncommon, however, to find stanzas where the whole is carefully patterned
so that almost all of its elements show some form of parallelism. In XV, for example, verses 169 and 172 are immediately
perceived to be perfect mirrors of each other:

           Dexemos a los troyanos,   169
           dexemos a los romanos,   172

A closer look, however, reveals other extraordinary corre-
spondences:

XV   Dexemos a los troyanos,
           que sus males non los *vjmos,*   170
           nj sus *glorias;*
           dexemos a los romanos,
           haunque *oymos e leymos*
           sus *estorias,*
               non curemos de *saber*   175
           lo d'aquel siglo *passado*
           qué fué d'*ello;*
           vengamos a lo d'*ayer,*
           que tan bien es *oluidado*

como *aquello*. 180
(*Cancionero* 96)

The rejection of the Trojans and the Romans each covers a three-verse substanza beginning with two octosyllables that show obvious syntactic, positional, lexical, and morphologic parallels. The second octosyllable of each substanza draws a notional parallel. The narrator says in verses 170-71 that he has not seen the sorrows (*males*) or glories (*glorias*) of the Trojans. "Non los vjmos" is echoed in 173 by the more positive "oymos e leymos." The *glorias*, opposed to *males* in the first *quebrado*, is also metonymically related to the *estorias*. One is embodied in the other.

The second six-verse unit generalizes the contrast by extending the rejection of the ancient past to contemporary history. Again, the obvious parallels are in the *quebrados* (*d'ello/aquello*). But the play of words is an amplification of the octosyllables, where *saber* is notionally correlated with *olvidado* and *passado* with *ayer*. There are other parallels in stanza XV, but these examples suffice to show how the *copla* is divided. Two main units can be perceived: one dedicated to specific peoples (ABc ABc), the other to a more general denunciation of the impermanence of time (CDe CDe). Each of these units has two segments that replicate each other and that correspond to the rhyme scheme of the *copla manriqueña* (ABc ABc-CDe CDe). In each verse the word around which the parallel constructions are built carries the rhyme.

Though closure marks define each stanza of the poem, sometimes the parallel structure breaks the confines of a stanza and gives unity to a whole segment of the poem. It does so in the *ubi sunt* (XVI-XXIV), where the questions repeat themselves, with some variations, over eight stanzas. In the panegyric (XXV-XXVIII), the praise of don Rodrigo and the comparison of him to the Roman emperors also give evidence of an extraordinary degree of parallelism.

Groupings of stanzas or single stanzas that contain a high incidence of repetitious structures are easily detected. Less easy to perceive are the larger matrices in which they are imbedded. For example, the exploration of time's different aspects in the two examples cited resonates through other verse structures in other stanzas, making any one instance of parallelistic foregrounding concerning time dependent on a background of preceeding and succeeding symmetrical structures. These resonances flow sequentially into each other, along the entire length of the poem.

FOUR

Coplas por la muerte de su padre
A Reading

The *Coplas* can be divided into sections by theme, as illustrated in the preceeding chapter. Sections are determined by the closure marks of groups of stanzas that signal a shift in the thematic and argumentative structures of the poem. They are most conspicuous at the beginning and end of the *Coplas*, but also exist within its body.[1] These closure signals are the source of the perception that the poem is loosely based on the structures of classical oratory: I-III (Exhortation); IV (Invocation); V-VII, VIII-XIV (The World and Its Uses); XV, XVI-XXIV (The Bad Examples: The *Ubi sunt*); XXV-XXVI, XXVII-XXXII (The Good Example: Panegyric and Biography); XXXIII-XXXIX (Death and don Rodrigo); and XL (Epilog).[2] Although the reading of the poem given in this chapter follows these divisions as a practical way of handling the explication, the poem is a whole, coherent and consistent within itself. As this chapter will show, Manrique worked with care to create a lasting monument to the memory of his father.

EXHORTATION TO THE SOUL

I   Recuerde el alma dormida,   1
       abiue el seso e despierte
       contemplando
       cómo se passa la vida,
       cómo se viene la muerte   5
       tan callando,
           quán presto se va el plazer,
       cómo, después de acordado,
       da dolor;
       cómo, a nuestro parescer,   10
       qualquiere tiempo passado
       fué mejor.
       (*Cancionero* 89)

No other poem in Spanish literature realizes the objectives of the exordium so fully as the *Coplas*. The three parallel verbs of the first two octosyllables (*Recuerde, auive, despierte*) sound like a thrice-pealing bell calling the reader to attention. Several questions immediately arise about the poem. Who speaks? Who exhorts? Whose is the disembodied voice that addresses the sleeping soul? And who is that soul?

The *quebrado* raises a further question. Is contemplation the state that follows awakening (*despierte . . . contemplando*), or is it the cause of the awakening? Closer scrutiny reveals that the contemplative object of the soul is the fleetness of life and the approach of death. The thought is expressed in two verses whose symmetry tends to obviate their natural antithesis ("cómo se passa la vida, / cómo se viene la muerte" 4-5). Contemplation is therefore the agency (though not the cause) that makes the soul aware of the fact that life passes and death comes. The verbs *se passa* and *se viene* extend the personification of *alma, seso,* and *memoria,* which has been operative from the beginning, to encompass *vida* and *muerte.*

Contemplation of the movements of life and death is the silent exercise of three players: one who watches (the Soul, represented by two of its potencies, Reason and Memory), one who goes (Life), one who comes (Death). The stanza is also an allegory of an inner journey in search of understanding. The soul opens its mind to the truth and, instead of permanence, discovers movement and transcience. Verse 6 ("tan callando") is the key to the soul's realization that duration is a mirage. The silence that characterizes death's approach is due not so much to its stealth as to the inattention of the soul. Lost in its self-absorption, it does not notice the passage of time. The admonition is an expression of the power of the grace of God to illuminate the understanding through memory.

The movement that the soul suddenly notices is emphasized by the syntactic and metrical parallels of lines 4 ("cómo se passa la vida") and 5 ("cómo se viene la muerte"), and their echo in a more diffuse form in lines 8 ("cómo, después de acordado") and 10 ("cómo, a nuestro parescer"). Not death alone, the poem tells us, but both life and death, come and go—so quietly, that one fuses into the other before their movement can be noted. Sánchez de Talavera succinctly states the same thought in a verse in which all is process: "biuiendo se viene llegando / la muerte cruel, e esquiva."[3]

Manrique's metaphor presents life as a road travelled by the soul.[4] Along the way the soul meets other travellers. Pleasure (which metonymically recalls youth and power), for example, can be a travelling companion for awhile. But the alliteration that suddenly breaks the easy flow of the verse ("cómo, después de acordado, / da dolor", 8-9) reminds the reader that pleasure, by its very transcience, is an untrustworthy companion. The echo of the anaphoras of verses 4-5 in 8 and 10 ("cómo") reinforce the thought that the absence of pleasure is more keenly felt than the pleasure itself.

The first two tercets are marvelous in their economy of means. There are twenty-two words, of which eight are verbs or participles (*recordar, abivar, dormir, despertar, contemplar, passar*[*se*], *venir*[*se*], *callar*) and four are nouns (*alma, seso, vida, muerte*). There are no adjectives, no appeal to the senses. Nevertheless, powerful visual and aural associations expand the meaning of the verses. The sleeping soul at the moment of revelation recalls the medieval poetic dream tradition rooted in Augustine, with its garden, tree, open book, and admonition to read. As with the *Confessions* one is aware that the admonition invites one to begin an interior process.

Critics have proposed that the admonition to remember is based on a text of St. Paul (Epistle to the Ephesians 5: 14) or on a verse from a hymn attributed to St. Ambrose that was sung at the beginning of Advent in the Mozarabic rite.[5] Either text could have influenced Manrique, but the admonition to remember is commonly found in much of the religious literature of the time and in other biblical passages such as Hebrews 11: 13-16, where St. Paul again talks about those who died in faith before receiving the rewards promised them. These, he says, recognize themselves to be strangers in the world with a real home elsewhere: "Conforme a la fe murieron todos éstos sin haber recibido las promesas sino mirándolas de lejos, y creyéndolas, y saludándolas, y confesando que eran peregrinos y advenedizos sobre la tierra. Porque los que esto dicen, claramente dan a entender que buscan una patria. Que si se acordaran de aquella de donde salieron, cierto tenían tiempo para volverse."[6] St. Augustine joined St. Paul's text to his account of man's history and made it one of the foundations of his *City of God.* Later, Gregory the Great moved beyond St. Augustine's apologetic account of man's life in the world to explore the actual experience of life. Gregory defined the *populus peregrinus* of the Vulgate as a people who, while hastening toward the destiny of the elect, "know that they have a fatherland in the celestial; and the more this people hopes to find all that is its own, the more it considers all that passes away to be alien."[7] In Gregory, the image of the pilgrimage comes to symbolize the soul's essential "otherness" as it becomes aware of its condition.[8]

Manrique's soul, however, is anchored to a moment in time by the awareness brought about by contemplation. The *Coplas* looks at the journey of the soul from the perspective of the pilgrim, of the *homo viator*, but it is the world that flows by it, and not vice versa. The soul's journey becomes a metaphor for an intellectual experience initiated through memory. In

medieval philosophic discourse, understanding is considered
to be a form of remembrance. Words have significance only
when their meanings are known. But knowledge of the in-
telligible can only be reached through divine illumination in
memory, and with the compliance of reason and will.[9] In fact,
the tripartite division of the soul into memory, reason, and
will is an image of the Trinity. Memory represents the Father;
Reason, the Son; and Will, the Holy Ghost. Scholastics later
made Memory a part of Prudence, one of the four cardinal
virtues.[10] Reminiscence became a kind of moral habit to be
used to remember the past with a view to influencing present
and future conduct.

The soul's awareness of the passage of time naturally leads
it to an examination of its nature:[11]

II	Pues si vemos lo presente	13
	cómo en vn punto s'es ido	
	e acabado,	15
	si juzgamos sabiamente,	
	daremos lo non venido	
	por passado.	
	Non se engañe nadi, no,	
	pensado que a de durar	20
	lo que espera	
	más que duró lo que vió,	
	pues que todo a de passar	
	por tal manera.	
	(*Cancionero* 89-90)	

The *Coplas'* first stanza mentions the seeming superiority
of the past to the present (and, by extension, to the future).
The idea is quickly denied in the second stanza.[12] In the context of the poem, the present includes all things that exists in
the "now" (not *el presente*, but *lo presente*). These things are
evanescent, like all points in time ("en un punto s'es ido" 14).
From the present, time streches backward into the past and
forward into the future. Once the present takes its place in
time it becomes a dated experience belonging to the past. The

destiny of all future time is to pass through the present into the past. Movement and destruction are conjoined qualities (*ido e acabado*). Sight and judgment, as emphasized by the parallel structures, are also conjoined. To see without self-deception is to judge (13, 16). To judge is to accept the future (*lo non venido*) as the past, not because it has passed, but because it will pass. In this conceptual game, the verbs *venir*, *pasar*, and *ir* represent three time references: future, present, past. *Ir* and *venir*, like *pasado* and *futuro*, are antonyms that divide aspects of human experience into opposing realms. *Lo presente*, as the soul's experience of the tangible, and *passar*, as the process it experiences, function as synonyms. Thus, not only is the future (*lo non venido*), something that has yet to pass before our eyes (i.e., become the present). It is also something that can be judged as already having passed (*passado*), on the evidence of the past. Therefore, although they are opposing concepts, past and future can be equated. One can use the past to judge the future, because the future must follow the same road (*a de passar*) through the present (*presente*) and all the "presents" must end in the same place (*passado*).

The emphatic triple negative ("Non se engañe nadi, no / pensando que ha de durar / lo que espera / mas que duró lo que vió" 19-21) emphasizes the temporal equality of past and future. It reminds the reader that the object of the soul's contemplation is death. The soul sees death approaching. With death's arrival comes a last "present" before it is totally consigned to the past and to the memory of the living.

III	Nuestras vidas son los ríos	25
	que van a dar en la mar,	
	qu'es el morir;	
	allí van los señoríos	
	derechos a se acabar	
	e consumir;	30
	allí los ríos caudales,	
	allí los otros medianos	
	e más chicos,	
	allegados son yguales	

los que viuen por sus manos   35
e los ricos.
(*Cancionero* 90)

The opposition of movement and stasis in the first two
stanzas, so effectively synthesized in the duplication of the
participles in stanza II (*ido e acabado*) adumbrates the powerful
double metaphor of the third: "Nuestras vidas son los ríos /
que van a dar en la mar / qu'es el morir" (25-27). *Vidas* is
equated to *ríos* and *mar* to *morir.* Rivers run to the sea in a
process as relentless as life's journey toward death.[13] At the
end of life death awaits, not the feminine, gentler *la muerte,*
but the harsh, masculine *el morir,* our unpleasant fate. Its
inevitability is punctuated by the anaphoras of verses 28, 31,
32.[14]

The word *señoríos*—a phonological parallel of *ríos*—allows
the poet to demonstrate the extent of the power of death in
a sequence that moves from greater to lesser. The *señorío* is a
lordship below which the estates are ranged. Within the poem
it may encompass an even wider idea. Medieval chroniclers
divided the history of Spain into successive *señoríos* each with
its beginning, middle, and end, each identified with a people:
the Greeks, the Romans, the Goths, for example. The purpose
of the first verse may therefore be to expand the poem's in-
vestigation into the nature of time to include the whole history
of the human race and to demonstrate the power of death
over whole races, nations ("Allí van los señoríos"), and social
classes. The sequence is structured from greater to lesser: *señoríos, ríos caudales, medianos, chicos.* The three terms for rivers
denote the three estates of human society whose social dis-
tinctions are lost in death, just as the waters of the rivers lose
their singularity when they reach the sea.

The verse "allegados son yguales" (34) confirms the equalizing power of the sea. *Llegar* (from Latin *plicare*) and *allegar*
(from Latin *applicare*) can both mean to arrive, but only *allegar*
means "to bring together" and, by extension, "to make the
same." By using *allegar* the poem emphasizes the co-incidence
of arrival and equality. Furthermore, within the poem, to ar-

rive is to die. *Allegar* is therefore synonymous with *acabar*
("end") and *dar* (in the sense in which it is used in "que van
a dar en la mar" 26). All three verbs express the inevitability
of the flow of the waters to their end. To die, in human terms,
is to be interred. The sea, like the earth, is a mass grave in
which all remains are mixed without distinction, where one
lies (*allegado*) with one's fellow human beings.

The soul is the subject of the verbs of the first stanza (*recuerde, avive, despierte*). Because the act of contemplation is
directed by the narrator of the poem, however, it is a shared
event. The exhorter and the exhorted participate in a common
act of remembrance, making the soul both the subject of the
action and the recipient of the implied command. In stanza
four, however, the narrator assumes command of the discourse as he moves on to the invocation.

INVOCATION

The invocation consists of two parallel sections. The first
develops a common fifteenth-century topic of the invocation—the rejection of the pagan gods. The second begins the
invocation proper, which is addressed to Christ:

IV	Dexo las inuocaciones	37
	de los famosos poetas	
	y oradores;	
	non curo de sus fictiones	40
	que trahen yeruas secretas	
	sus sabores;	
	Aquél solo m'encomiendo,	
	Aquél solo inuoco yo	
	de verdad,	45
	que en este mundo viuiendo	
	el mundo non conoció	
	su deydad.[15]	

(*Cancionero* 90-91)

The rejection of the classical invocation to the gods or the Muses in favor of an invocation to Christ follows Gómez's similar refusal to call on the pagan gods in "El planto de las virtudes por el magnífico señor don Iñigo López de Mendoza."[16] But Manrique, unlike his uncle, sets up two antithetical terms for the comparison: the *fictiones* of the poets and orators, and Christ, or truth.[17] The stanza therefore develops between those two poles: fiction and truth. Each term alludes to a text with hidden meanings. The first tercet rejects the works of *poetas y oradores* by rejecting their invocations. In other words, by rejecting what they say. Because invocations are parts of a whole, of course, the books containing those invocations are rejected. The act of invoking, of calling for help, naturally brings another association to the fore. The invocation to the pagan gods is like *yerbas secretas*. *Yerbas* are consumed. They can be used to flavor food, or to cure. But they can also be used to poison. Their taste can hide an unpleasant consequence. The possible ambiguity of the verb *curar* (40), "to take notice of," "to appreciate," or "to cure," subliminally reminds the reader that the fictions of poets and orators cannot "cure" the soul like the truth of Christ.

That truth is also contained in a text that, though not mentioned, is implied: the Bible. The truth of scripture is therefore opposed to the fiction of poets. Fiction contains *yerbas secretas* that poison the soul, the biblical text heals the soul because it contains the life of Jesus, among whose attributes is that of being the soul's doctor and healer.[18]

THE WORLD AND ITS USES

V Este mundo es el camino
   para el otro, qu'es morada   50
   sin pesar;
   mas cumple tener buen tino
   para andar esta jornada
   sin errar;
    partimos quando nascemos,   55

andamos mientra viuimos,
y llegamos
al tiempo que feneçemos;
assí que quando morimos
descansamos.   60
(*Cancionero* 91)

Stanza five emphasizes the association of the narrator with
his auditor in the common act of remembrance by using the
first person plural (*partimos* [55], *viuimos* [56], *llegamos* [57],
feneçemos [58], *morimos* [59], *descansamos* [60], *vsásemos* [62],
deuemos [63], *nuestra fe* [64], *atendemos* [66], *sobirnos* [68], *entre nos* [70]). The narrator returns to his original metaphor
to explain how the world itself is the road that leads both
to death and to salvation. One enters into this life, says a
contemporary of Manrique, "para salir por la muerte, por
eso entramos llorando, a significar el amargura de la sali-
da. . . . Esta vida camino es; acabado el camino, conviene tornar a donde venimos, esto es, por la muerte."[19]
Manrique, however, is not a common versifier. The entire
stanza hides a conceptual game. The almost identical *quebrados*
(*sin pesar/sin errar*) hint at a notional parallel. What is *pesar*
(pain, sorrow), if not the result of *errar* (error)? But, what is
error, if not a straying (*errar*) from the true way? *Errar* therefore refers both to the act of straying and to its consequence:
error.[20] There follow two syntactically parallel octosyllables
and a *quebrado* ("partimos cuando nascemos, / andamos mientra viuimos, / y llegamos" 43-45), in which all of experience
is condensed into three verbs (*partir, andar, llegar*) in apposition to three other verbs corresponding to the stages of life
(*nacer, vivir, feneçer*):

        partimos quando *nascemos*,   55
        andamos mientra *viuimos*,
        y *llegamos*
        al tiempo que *feneçemos*;
        assí que quando *morimos*
        descansamos.   60

Manrique—while again stressing the brevity of life—equates
life with travel, and travel with travail (*pesar*). A *jornada* (journey) is a one-day march (though metaphorically it can be
extended to a part of a trip, or to the journey itself). It is also
one working day. The soul's journey through life is both brief
and difficult, so its end (*morir*) can be considered a rest (*descansar*). Verses 55 and 56 equate four verbs, *partir* and *nacer*,
andar and *vivir*, in rigorous parallel constructions (*partir* =
nacer, andar = *vivir*). The conceptual play continues in the
less obvious equations of *llegar* and *feneçer* (57-58), *morir* and
descansar (59-60). Furthermore, the two substanzas are tied
together by the relationship between *morada* (50), *llegar* (57),
and *descansar* (60). As the equivalent of *feneçer* and *morir*, the
verb *llegar* provides a transition from the first to the second
tercet of the substanza. The substanza, therefore, develops
along two planes within the same thematic context (the *pere-
grinatio hujus vitae*). One plane is metaphoric (*partir, andar,
llegar/descansar*), the other real (*nascer, viuir, feneçer/morir*). Both
seem to advance us linearly, from one point in time to another.
As before, however, the movement is both linear and circular.
Rivers begin at a source and flow away from it to end in a
sea where they are robbed of their singularity. Similarly, human life has a beginning and an end. It loses its uniqueness
when it ends. But the soul is not a river. It leaves its source,
but it can return to that source and find, not oblivion, but
rest. Movement therefore denotes life, while lack of motion
characterizes both death and heaven. The soul's objective is
to reach (*llegar*) the latter resting place—the "morada / sin
pesar" of verses 50-51—where its journey and its travails both
end. The *morada* is an image of enclosure like the *arraual de
senectud*, the *çelada*, and the *caua honda*. Behind it hides the
heavenly city, with its protective walls that intimate permanence and lack of toil.

The stanza contrasts those who travel and travail through
life in the hopes of finding rest at the end, and those who
blindly go forth without care or worry, completely engrossed
in the world. This opposition prepares for the transition to
the sixth stanza's focus on salvation. It suggests that rest—a

positive result of death in the eyes of the weary traveler—is
the reward of those who travel life's road *sin errar* and *sin
error*.

VI	Este mundo bueno fué	61
	si bien vsásemos dél	
	como deuemos,	
	porque, segund nuestra fe,	
	es para ganar aquél	65
	que atendemos.	
	Haun aquel fijo de Dios	
	para sobirnos al cielo	
	descendió	
	a nascer acá entre nos	70
	y a viuir en este suelo	
	do murió.	
	(*Cancionero* 91-92)	

The fifth and sixth stanzas are related by the repetition of
este.[21] Stanza V explained the nature of the world ("Este
mundo es el camino / para el otro" 49-50); stanza VI explains
that this world "es para ganar aquel / que atendemos" (65-
66). The process of winning salvation, however, is fraught
with dangers. It is only made possible by Christ's own journey
into the world:

> Haun aquel fijo de Dios
> para *sobirnos* al cielo
> *descendió*
> a *nascer* acá entre nos   70
> y a *viuir* en este suelo
> do *murió*.

The necessity of Christ's sacrifice is revealed in a sequence of
verbs that begins with two antonyms, *sobir* (68) and *descender*
(69, This last term is notionally equivalent to *partir* and *nascer*),
and by the apposition in the octosyllables of *Dios/nos* (67, 70)
and *cielo/suelo* (68, 71). Between them, *sobir* and *descender* en-

compass all of human experience (*nascer, viuir, morir* 70-72).
They are arranged in such a way as to allude to the circularity
of the movement (*descendió, nascer, viuir, murió = para sobirnos*).

Against that necessary sacrifice, man's obstinate pursuit of
the pleasures of the world (VII-XIV) acquires special significance.

VII	Ved de quánd poco valor	73
	son las cosas tras que andamos	
	y corremos,	75
	que, en este mundo traydor,	
	haun primero que muramos	
	las perdemos.	
	dellas deshaze la edad,	
	dellas casos desastrados	80
	que acaheçen,	
	dellas, por su calidad,	
	en los más altos estados	
	desfallescen.	
VIII	Dezidme: La hermosura,	85
	la gentil frescura y tez	
	de la cara,	
	la calor e la blancura,	
	quando viene la vejez,	
	¿cuál se pára?	90
	Las mañas e ligereza	
	e la fuerça corporal	
	de juuentud,	
	todo se torna graueza	
	cuando llega al arraual	95
	de senectud.	
	(*Cancionero* 92-93)	

The tone of the poem changes in stanzas VII-XIII. The narrator introduces his illustrations with a series of imperatives
and rhetorical questions (*Ved* 73, *decidme* 85, ¿*cuál*? 90, ¿*quién*?

111) that distance him from the soul once again. At the same time, the questions intimate the possibility of a dialogue between the soul and the narrator, but the dialogue never occurs.[22] Instead, these stanzas expose the lack value in man's earthly desires and pursuits.

Stanzas VII and VIII examine how the accidents of life—age and time—condemn goods, beauty, and physical prowess to disappear long before death approaches. Stanza VII is a transitional stanza that reminds us that one misuses the world when one runs after "las cosas del mundo." The principal parallels concern evaluation (*poco valor* 73, *mundo traydor* 76), desire (*andamos* and *corremos* 74-75), and consequences (*muramos* and *perdemos* 77-78). Stanza VIII is based on the widely held idea that man's life is divided into stages, each with its own characteristics and its own desires, each succeeding the other until the end.[23] Manrique, however, prefers to point to the fearsome qualities of old age, the *incommoda senectutis*, without dwelling on the specific stages of life. Again, the verb *venir* serves to mark the approach of death. Its arrival is intimated by the impermanence of *hermosura, frescura, calor, blancura*, and *tez*, which cannot resist the passage of time, and then by the transformation of *juventud* into *graveza*, as life arrives (*llegar*) "al arraual / de senectud." The "arraual de senectud" is the portal of death. Like "la mar qu'es el morir" it is an image of transition. The "arraual" is the outlying settlement without the strong protective walls of the city or castle. It therefore indicates the arrival of the soul at the border between life and death.[24] This movement continues in the next stanzas, as the poem casts an ever widening net over human society:

IX	Pues la sangre de los godos,	97
	i el linaje e la nobleza	
	tan crescida,	
	¡por quántas vías e modos	100
	se pierde su grand alteza	
	en esta vida!	
	Vnos, por poco valer,	

por quán baxos e abatidos
que los tienen;   105
otros que, por non tener,
con officios non deuidos
se mantienen.

X   Los estados e riqueza,
que nos dexen a deshora   110
¿quién lo duda?,
non les pidamos firmeza
pues que son d'una señora
que se muda:
    que bienes son de Fortuna   115
que rebueluen con su rueda
presurosa,
la qual non puede ser vna
ni estar estable ni queda
en vna cosa.   120

XI   Pero digo c'acompañen
e lleguen fasta la fuessa
con su dueño:
por esso non nos engañen,
pues se va la vida apriessa   125
como sueño;
    e los deleytes d'acá
son, en que nos deleytamos,
temporales,
e los tormentos d'allá,   130
que por ellos esperamos,
eternales.
(*Cancionero* 93-94)

The loss of youth is followed by a disquisition on the disappearance of nobility and power. The intratextual echo is
unavoidable. The rush of the nobility to extinction through
cowardice (97-98) and the assumption of forbidden trades
(103-108) recalls the dominant image of the second stanza
("nuestras vidas son los ríos" 25). The blood of Goths, the

clan, and the nobility are seen to run in sequence like swollen rivers (98-99) through their courses (100) and lose themselves in *menosvaler* and in *officios non deuidos*, the metaphoric equivalents of the *arraual de senectud*, which imply a moral or class turpitude. Similarly, estates and wealth (109-20) are subject to the whims of Fortune, who casts them off her wheel with their owners. These worldly goods cannot accompany one into the grave, but they lead one to it, and they can have dire consequences for their owners:

> e los deleytes d'acá　　　　　　127
> son, en que nos deleytamos,
> temporales,
> e los tormentos d'allá,　　　　　130
> que por ellos esperamos,
> eternales.

The conceptual play in the parallelisms of verses 127 and 130 (*deleytes d'acá* and *tormentos d'allf*) echoes the opposition in the first stanza betweem *plazer* and *dolor*, revealing another aspect of that *dolor*. With the loss of *deleytes* comes the fear of *tormentos*. Verses 128 and 131, though not as obviously parallel in their syntax, both expand on the meaning of the key noun in each tercet (*deleytes* and *tormentos*). Each verse ends with a verb (*deleytamos* and *esperamos*), before introducing the object and the main conceptual opposition in the *quebrado* (*temporales/ eternales*).

So far, death has been a traveller encountered on a road (5-6), and a sea in which all drown (25-27). It has even appeared briefly as the way to a dwelling where one can find peace and rest (60). Now, however, the more ominous characteristics of death appear. The poet examines the ways in which it lies in wait for the unwary.

> XII　　　　Los plazeres e dulçores　　　　133
> 　　　　　desta vida trabajada
> 　　　　　que tenemos,　　　　　　　135
> 　　　　　non son sino corredores,

e la muerte, la çelada
en que caemos.
   Non mirando a nuestro daño,
corremos a rienda suelta   140
syn parar;
desque vemos el engaño
e queremos dar la buelta
non ay lugar.

XIII   Si fuesse en nuestro poder   145
       hazer la cara hermosa
       corporal,
       como podemos hazer
       el alma tan gloriosa,
       angelical,   150
          ¿qué diligencia tan viua
       toujéramos toda hora,
       e tan presta,
       en componer la catiua,
       dexándonos la señora   155
       descompuesta!
       (*Cancionero* 94-95)

Plazeres e dulçores are another manifestation of the *deleytes d'acá*. They are now equated in the first substanza with the *corredores* of a hunter or a military leader (Death), who lies in wait for the soul in a *çelada*. *Plazeres e dulçores* are both the objects of the soul's pursuit and the instigators of its fall. They lead the foolish soul into a trap from which it cannot escape (142-44).

This foolishness of the soul is the subject of stanza XIII. Body and soul are differentiated by the possibility of change. The body, subject to aging, can be made to look young, but the aging process cannot be altered. The soul, on the other hand, can be perfected and made ready for its salvation. How foolish, therefore, for man to prefer body to soul, slave to master, death to salvation.[25]

XIV   Esos reyes poderosos   157
             que vemos por escripturas
             ya pasadas,
             con casos tristes, llorosos,   160
             fueron sus buenas venturas
             trastornadas;
                 assí que non ay cosa fuerte,
             que a papas y emperadores
             e perlados,   165
             assí los trata la Muerte
             como a los pobres pastores
             de ganados.
             (*Cancionero* 95-96)

The last images in the sequence link the Wheel of Fortune
to the Dance of Death (157-68), and reiterate the power of
death over all the orders of society, from *reyes* to *pastores*. The
first substanza opposes power and time. The power of kings
seen in *escripturas ya pasadas* goes the way of *plazeres e dulçores*,
when Fortune wills it. The second substanza extends the image to the other members of (noble) society and reaffirms the
equality of all before death.

THE BAD EXAMPLES

XV   Dexemos a los troyanos,
             que sus males non los vjmos,   170
             nj sus glorias;
             dexemos a los romanos,
             haunque oymos e leymos
             sus estorias,
             non curemos de saber   175
             lo d'aquel siglo passado
             qué fué d'ello;
             vengamos a lo d'ayer,
             que tan bien es oluidado

como aquello.   180
(*Cancionero* 96)

The assessment of power in stanza XIV is followed in XV by
the "rejection" of the stories of the Trojans and the Romans,
the greatest exemplars of earthly power and its fate among
the ancients. Normally, critics see a conflict between the sentiments expressed in this stanza and the comparison of don
Rodrigo with the Roman emperors in stanzas XXVII and
XXVIII. If the past must be rejected, why compare don Rodrigo to Roman emperors? They attribute this inconsistency
to discontinuities in the composition of the poem (the poet,
like Homer, nodding at times) or to an inherent distrust of
the written word by the poet.[26] Nothing could be further from
the truth.

Manrique does not reject the ancient past per se. In the
invocation and in stanza XV he reveals himself to be an avid
reader of what he forswears: "dexemos a los romanos / haunque oymos e leymos / sus estorias" (172-4).[27] Trojans and Romans, together with Castilian heroes, formed part of a familiar
triad on whose histories Castilian poets were nurtured and
from whom they normally drew their examples. The value of
that past for moral instruction was never questioned. Why
then does Manrique seem to reject it?

By stanza XV, the *Coplas* has already established the falsity
of the belief that "qualquiere tiempo passado / fue mejor" (11-
12). Manrique now proposes that it was also no worse. Other
periods of time may "seem" better or worse, but in reality
they are not. The value of the past and the present for moral
instruction is the same. There is therefore no inherent need
to resort to pagan history to prove that all human action is
subject to the same fate. That is Manrique's point. There is,
however, something that makes the present example pref-
erable to the ancient example. A clue may be found in Santillana's similar recommendation in the *Diálogo de la fortuna*:
"Dexa ya los generales, / antiguos e agenos dapños, / que
passaron ha mill años; / e llora tus propios males." Santillana
counsels that the examples drawn from general and ancient

afflictions be abandoned in favor of illustrations drawn from the pains that afflict one, because of the superiority of direct experience.

When rejecting the histories of the ancients, Manrique uses three verbs (*ver* 170, *oir* and *leer* 172) that allude to the way historians acquire knowledge of events. Scholars of the middle ages respected the authority of the text, but placed even greater value on visual testimony. The most respected histories were those written by witnesses. Dares and Dictys, for example, were considered the ultimate authorities about the destruction of Troy because they claimed to have been present. Second in order of value was to hear about an event from a witness. Least valuable was to read about an event. It follows that history can be seen, heard, or read (*visa, audita, lecta*).[28] Each verb takes a step further away from reality, moving from active participation in events to passive reenactment through reading. Manrique prefers to present a history for which he himself is an authority, a history which he has *seen*, and for which he can vouch, rather than ancient history that can only be heard or read. He proceeds immediately to evoke this history for his readers, for they too have shared in it.

XVI	¿Qué se hjzo el rey don Joan?	
	Los Infantes d'Aragón	
	¿qué se hizieron?	
	¿Qué fué de tanto galán,	
	¿qué de tanta jnujnción	185
	que truxeron?	
	¿Fueron sino devaneos,	
	qué fueron sino verduras	
	de las eras,	
	las iustas e los torneos,	190
	paramentos, bordaduras	
	e çimeras?	
XVII	¿Qué se hyzieron las damas,	
	sus tocados e vestidos,	
	sus olores?	195

¿Qué se hizieron las llamas
de los fuegos encendidos
d'amadores?
¿Qué se hizo aquel trobar,
las músicas acordadas   200
que tañjan?
¿Qué se hizo aquel dançar,
aquellas ropas chapadas
que trayan?

XVIII   Pues el otro, su heredero,   205
don Anrique, ¡qué poderes
alcançaua!
¡Quánd blando, quánd alag[u]ero,
el mundo con sus plazeres
se le daua!   210
       Mas verás quánd enemjgo,
quánd contrario, quánd cruel
se le mostró;
auiéndole seydo amigo,
¡quánd poco duró con él   215
lo que le dió!

XIX   Las dádiuas desmedidas,
los edificios reales
llenos d'oro,
las baxillas tan febridas,   220
los enriques e reales
del thesoro,
       las jaezes, los cauallos
de sus gentes e ataujos
tan sobrados,   225
¿dónde yremos a buscallos?
¿qué fueron sino rocíos
de los prados?

XX   Pues su hermano el jnnocente,
qu'en su vida sucessor   230
le fizieron,
¡qué corte tan excellente

tuuo e quánto grand señor
le siguieron!
Mas, como fuesse mortal,   235
metióle la Muerte luego
en su fragua.
¡O, juyzio diujnal,
quando más ardía el fuego,
echaste agua!   240

XXI   Pues aquel grand Condestable,
maestre que conoscimos
tan priuado,
non cumple que dél se hable,
mas sólo cómo lo vjmos   245
degollado.
Sus infinitos thesoros,
sus villas e sus lugares,
su mandar,
¿qué le fueron sino lloros?   250
¿qué fueron sino pesares
al dexar?

XXII   E los otros dos hermanos,
maestres tan prosperados
como reyes,   255
c'a los grandes e medianos
truxieron tan sojuzgados
a sus leyes;
aquella prosperidad
qu'en tan alto fué subida   260
i ensalzada,
¿qué fué sino claridad
que quando más encendida
fué amatada?

XXIII   Tantos duques excellentes,   265
tantos marqueses e condes
e varones
como vimos tan potentes,
dí, Muerte, ¿dó los escondes

e traspones?   270
E las sus claras hazañas
que hizieron en las guerras
i en las pazes,
quando tú, cruda, t'ensañas,
con tu fuerça las atierras   275
e desfazes.

XXIV   Las huestes ynumerables,
los pendones, estandartes
e vanderas,
los castillos impugnables,   280
los muros e valuartes
e barreras,
la caua honda, chapada,
o qualquier otro reparo,
¿qué aprouecha?   285
Quando tú vienes ayrada,
todo lo passas de claro
con tu flecha.
(*Cancionero* 96-101)

Stanzas XVI through XXIV are the second best known of the poem. It is a major achievement of Manrique's poetic genius that he takes a cliché of moral and elegiac poetry and turns it into a tantalizing evocation of a past that was as colorful and attractive as it was treacherous and deceitful.[29] Once again the underlying theme is duration, but it is now exemplified by historical figures known to Manrique and his audience.

It is here that the modern reader begins to lose contact with the specifics of the poem, even though he or she may understand the metaphoric value of the examples. Juan II; the Infantes of Aragón; Enrique IV; Prince Alfonso; Alvaro de Luna; Pedro Téllez Girón, master of Calatrava and his brother Juan Pacheco, master of Santiago are men of particular importance to don Rodrigo's biography.[30] Don Rodrigo often fought against Juan II and his favorite, Alvaro de Luna, and against Enrique IV. He briefly supported prince Alfonso in an abortive coup against Enrique IV—but saw the pretender's hopes dashed by an untimely death. Téllez and Pacheco were his constant rivals and occasional allies.

With these potent names, Manrique evokes the brilliance of early fifteenth-century court life. But this evocation exemplifies how the instability of the world dooms the mighty, revealing that court life is just one more aspect of the futile desire for wealth, power, and influence.

The repetition of *¿qué?* and *¿adónde?* gives these stanzas an antipophoretic structure that diminishes the individuality of the examples, while expanding the interpretation of the passage to include all human beings. The high incidence of parallel structures gives the section its coherence and reinforces the identification of the past ("lo d'ayer") with the present. Just as past heroes have vanished, so all will disappear.

The excellence of Manrique's *ubi sunt* lies in the way he avoids the repetition of one strict syntactical parallel structure in favor of variety:

> ¿Qué se hjzo el rey don Joan?
> Los Infantes d'Aragón
> ¿qué se hizieron?
> ¿qué de tanta jnujnción . . . ?   185

The syntactic parallel in lines 181-83 is tempered by the positional dislocation of "Los Infantes de Aragón" (182), by the ellipsis of the verb in 185, and by the interrogative in 187 ("¿Fueron sino devaneos . . . ?").[31]

The latter is itself the first of a group of syntactically parallel verses that will appear—as answers—in counterpoint to the *ubi sunt* ("¿qué fueron sino rocíos / de los prados?" 227-28, "¿qué le fueron sino lloros? / ¿qué fueron sino pesares?" 250-52, "¿qué fué sino claridad?" 262). Strict syntactic recurrence is also avoided by the alternation of singular and plural subjects and by the notional equation of wide categories of things. For example, the question—"¿Qué se hyzieron las damas?"—is followed by the grammatically coordinated "sus tocados e

vestidos, / sus olores," which describe aspects of daily life.
They can be equated among themselves as items within the
same semantic field and are stock phrases in fifteenth-century
poetry. The same is true of other noun doublets and triplets
scattered throughout the sequence (courtly events: "las iustas e los torneos" 190; knightly dress: "paramentos, bordaduras /e çimeras" 191-92; wealth: "los edificios reales / llenos
d'oro, / las baxillas tan febridas, / los enriques e reales / del
thesoro, / los jaezes, los cauallos / de sus gentes e ataujos"
217-24; etc.).

Sometimes a parallel series of nouns depends on another
element it amplifies, which is, in turn, part of a larger parallel
structure:

XVI	las iustas e los torneos, paramentos, bordaduras e çimeras?	190
XXIV	Las huestes ynumerables, los pendones, estandartes e vanderas, los castillos impugnables, los muros e valuartes e barreras, la caua honda, chapada, o qualquier otro reparo, ¿qué aprouecha?	280 285

Paramentos, bordaduras, and *cimeras* are part of the accoutre-
ments of knights in jousts and tourneys and refer to the mag-
nificence of those events. *Pendones, estandartes,* and *vanderas*
are the distinguishing insignia of *huestes ynumerables,* precisely
those things by which *huestes* can be ranked and counted.[32]
Muros, valuartes, and *barreras* are the defenses that make *castillos impugnables.* These noun triplets not only amplify other
nouns, but also often parallel similar triplets found in other
stanzas and modify structures that are themselves parallel.
The last example, however, has four rather than three am-

plifiers (281-83). The fourth, the "cava honda, / chapada" is immediately associated with death and prepares the reader for its appearance in the next sequence.

As in the initial stanzas of the poem, the serial nature of the parallel structures of the *ubi sunt*, amplified by their hierarchic and chronological order, leads to an ordered climax that echoes the structures of the Dance of Death. These stanzas lead the reader from greater to lesser individuals, and from older to more recent events: They begin with the courts of Juan II, Enrique IV, and the pretender, Prince Alfonso; continue with the great favorites: Luna, Girón, Pacheco; then list dukes, marquesses, counts, barons; and the multitudes in *huestes* and *castillos*. They describe life from the heights of the court to the depths of the "*cava honda / chapada*," with its unmistakable reminiscence of death.

While preterites dominate the sequence, and imperfects are occasionally used to indicate process (*alcançava, daua, ardía*), the whole section is strongly tied to the narrative present of the implied auditor, especially when the narrator addresses Death directly: *escondes / e traspones* 269-70, *ensañas* 274, *atierras / e desfazes* 275-76, *passas* 287. At the same time Manrique gives distance, yet prominence, to people and objects. He does so by means of the deictic use of the demonstrative (*aquel trobar, aquel dançar, aquellas ropas* 199-204; *aquel grand condestable* 241; *aquella prosperidad* 259), and by using the definite article as a demonstrative (*el rey don Juan; los Infantes d'Aragón; las justas; los torneos; las damas; las llamas; las músicas; las dádivas; los edificios; las baxillas; los enriques e reales; los jaezes; los cauallos; las sus claras hazañas; las huestes; los pendones, estandartes e vanderas; los castillos; los muros, e valuartes e barreras; la caua*).

The *ubi sunt* stanzas also evoke a sense of immaturity that is set in apposition to the section devoted to the panegyric. In part this section reflects a historical reality. Juan II and Enrique IV did not achieve advanced age; Alfonso died still a youth; Luna, a mature but still young man. This impression of youth that attaches to the *ubi sunt* is built on the description of those vain court occupations that engaged much of the courtier's time. It is based mostly on concrete nouns (*galanes, invenciones, iustas, torneos, paramentos, bordaduras, çimeras, da-mas, tocados, vestidos, olores, llamas de amadores, trobar, música acordada, dançar, ropas chapadas,* etc.), which are opposed by another series of nouns indicating their evanescence: *devaneos, verduras de las eras, rocíos de los prados.* As in the first part of the poem, the pursuit of the tangible results in *lloros, pesares,* and *claridad . . . amatada.* The tangible and its *placeres e dulçores* are the domain of Death.

It is noteworthy that the last image encountered in the *ubi sunt* is that of Death as an archer. The relentless nature of Death in its hunt for man is one of the dominant themes of the first part of the poem. It appears in stanzas XII (135-37) and XXIV (286-88). Its message is that those who seek the pleasures of this world do not realize that Death awaits, hidden in ambush. Those who do not take precautions die young. For those who are wise, however, Death is very different.

THE GOOD EXAMPLE

XXV   Aquél de buenos abrigo,
        amado por virtuoso   290
        de la gente,
        el maestre don Rodrigo
        Manrique, tanto famoso
        e tan valiente;
            sus hechos grandes e claros   295
        non cumple que los alabe,
        pues los vieron,
        nj los quiero hazer caros,
        pues qu'el mundo todo sabe
        quáles fueron.   300
        (*Cancionero* 101)

Unlike the introductory stanzas of the *Coplas,* which are dominated by verbs, the *ubi sunt* sequence is built on a series of concrete nouns, alluding to people or objects, with a few adjectives. The questions are not endowed with the calm

meditative repose of the first stanzas of the poem. They are
followed by answers in which nouns pile up on each other,
often without verbs, or with the verb delayed until the end
of the stanza (XIX, XXI, XXIII, XXIV). This lack of distinguishing characteristics reduces individuals to nonexistence.

The eight *ubi sunt* stanzas dedicated to the mutability of
fortune and the relentless enmity of Time are followed by
eight stanzas that sing the virtues of don Rodrigo. In contrast,
adjectives for the first time form a significant part of the lexicon. Their appearance signals the beginning of the panegyric.

Although a logical extension of what precedes it, the panegyric is in tension with the *ubi sunt* stanzas. Until the panegyric, the elegy belittles the value of the immediate past and
the present as part of its generally negative view of life. The
panegyric, on the other hand, must by its nature praise the
positive values represented by the illustrious dead. In so
doing it must prefer the immediate past to the present, as it
reveals the consequences of the death of a great man. In both
sections, the emphasis is on direct, visual knowledge of
events. This emphasis is revealed through the images evoked
by the *ubi sunt* questions, by the use of the verb "to see"
("más verás quánd enemigo" 211, "más sólo cómo lo vjmos"
245, "como vimos tan potentes" 268, "pues los vieron" 197),
and by the demonstrative pronoun *aquél*.

The transition from *ubi sunt* to panegyric is effected by the
demonstrative pronoun that introduces don Rodrigo ("Aquél
de buenos abrigo" 289). Although Manrique eschews the rhetorical repetitiveness of his uncle's "Defunzion del noble
cauallero Garcilasso dela Vega," the device is similar to one
used by Gómez to break the news of the death of Garcilasso
de la Vega to his mother:[33]

> XXII   Aquel que vos, noble señora, pariste
> aquel que criastes con tantos dolores,
> aquel sobrador de grandes temores
> aquien Garcilaso por nombre posiste,
> . . . aquel facedor de nobles fazañas

sabed que lo vi ayer sepultado.
(*Cancionero castellano* 30-1)

The conspicuous contrast between the life and deeds of Garcilasso and his end (*sepultado*), described in an anaphoric stac-
catto that extends over several verses, however, is very far
from Manrique's procedure. The single occurrence of *aquél* in
verse 289 circumvents the deictic nature of the demonstrative,
allowing a more personal sentiment to surface. In addition,
Manrique does not point at first to his father's accomplishments as a warrior, but to his role as protector of *buenos*, and
as someone loved for his virtue (290). The person is hidden
behind his deeds and not revealed until later (292). In fact,
though the demonstrative in "Aquél de buenos abrigo" (289)
echoes similar constructions in the *ubi sunt*, it represents a
very different use. The demonstrative pronoun functions
more like the demonstrative in the invocation ("Aquél solo
m'encomiendo yo / aquél solo invoco yo" 43-44). In the first
case, the pronoun is a metonymical reference to Jesus Christ,
in the second, the object is eventually stated, but its belated
appearance increases suspense. The textual echo draws a parallel between two exemplary individuals who did not stray
from their path.[34]
  The inability of the poet to recount the deeds of his father
is due to the fact that they are already so well known that it
is unnecessary to retell them. The refusal to speak, however,
is a ploy that Manrique uses to introduce the very encomium
of the father he seems to reject. The stanza once more shows
a preference for "hechos grandes e claros" known firsthand
by the poet and his audience, rather than distant events.

XXVI   Amjgo de sus amjgos,   301
            ¡qué señor para criados
            e parientes!
            ¡Qué enemigo d'enemigos!
            ¡Qué maestro d'esforçados   305
            e valientes!

¡Qué seso para discretos!
¡Qué gracia para donosos!
¡Qué razón!
¡Qué benjno a los sugetos!   310
¡A los brauos e dañosos,
qué león!
(*Cancionero* 102)

The reader expects an exposition of don Rodrigo's achievements to follow his introduction into the poem. The poem
does not provide this. Instead there is an assessment of the
man's greatness refracted through the experiences of those
who knew him. It is expressed in a hidden catalog of the
virtues of the knight: prudence, courage, temperance, and
justice. As in the *ubi sunt*, the frequent syntactic parallel structures in this section (302/307-8, 304-5/310-12) give emphasis
and clarity to the meaning of the passage. Every single line,
except 309, is built around an equation (*amigo/amigos; señor/
criados e parientes; enemigo/enemigos; maestro/esforçados e val-
ientes; seso/discretos; gracia/donosos; benigno/sugetos; bravos e daño-
sos/león*). These verses explore his relationships with friends
and vassals dependent on him and with his enemies. In turn,
these comparisons introduce those of the next stanzas.

Menéndez Pelayo thought stanzas XXVII-XXVIII the worst
stanzas in the *Coplas*. Quintana banished them from his edition. They are, however, an important nucleus in the section
dedicated to the glorification of don Rodrigo:

XXVII   En ventura Octavjano;
            Julio César en uencer
            e batallar;   315
            en la virtud, Affricano;
            Haníbal en el saber
            e trabajar;
            en la bondad, vn Trajano;
            Tyto en liberalidad   320
            con alegría;

en su braço, Abreliano;
Marco Atilio en la verdad
que prometía.

XXVIII Antoño Pío en clemencia;   325
Marco Aurelio en ygualdad
del semblante;
Adriano en la eloquencia;
Teodosio en humanidad
e buen talante.   330
Aurelio Alexandre fué
en deciplina e rigor
de la guerra;
vn Costantino en la fe,
Camilo en el grand amor   335
de su tierra.
(*Cancionero* 102-103)

The sequence continues the portrayal of the qualities of don Rodrigo begun in XXV and XXVI. The poet employs a modified form of a two-term comparison, attributing to don Rodrigo the characteristic virtues of certain Roman emperors and consuls.[35] Don Rodrigo is like Caesar in his enjoyment of battle and his luck in war. He is like Scipio in his knowledge, like Trajan in kindness, like Titus in liberality.

The form of Manrique's comparisons echos another of Gómez Manrique's compositions, the "Aguilando al conde de Paredes," an occasional poem that must have been well known within family circles:

Etor enla valentia,
Archiles en ardideza,
Alixandre enla franqueza,
Paris enla gentileza,
gauilan en fidalguia;   5
faga vos Dios tan gozozo
y placentero

enel año venidero
quanto vos fizo guerrero
e virtuoso.   10

Anibal en conquistar,
en defender Cipion,
enel seso Salamon,
en virtud otro Caton
Jullio Cesar en osar.   15
Tantos bienes temporales
os de Dios
quantos meresçedes vos,
pues fustes vno de dos
enlos mortales.   20

Para Castilla Camilo,
otro Cid contra Granada,
en la qual es vuestra espada
tanto temida e loada
e mas que la de Troylo;   25
devos Dios tanta riqueza
con salud,
quanta desde juuentud
vos dio bondad y virtud
y nobleza.   30

Estos dones por estrenas
tome vuestra señoria,
con esta poca valia
que vos da quien vos daria
otras si tuuiese buenas;   35
y no mireys no, señor,
la quantidad,
mas la buena voluntad
y pequeña facultad
del seruidor.   40

Fyn
Yo vos vea con mayor
dinidad

la viniente nauidad,
pues dello soys en verdad
merecedor.   45
(*Cancionero castellano* 2: 50)

Though only three comparisons are common to both
poems, the "Aguilando," a short celebratory lyric addressed
to don Rodrigo, is without doubt the source of these stanzas
in the *Coplas*. The objectives of the "Aguilando" and the *Coplas*, however, are very different. Gómez strings together
Greek, Roman, Biblical, and Castilian figures that recall a martial or an intellectual virtue: Hector (1), Achilles (2), Troylus
(3), Paris (4), Hannibal (11), Scipio (12), Solomon (13), Cato
(14), Caesar (15), Camillus (21), and the Cid (22).[36] Manrique
uses the comparisons to allude to the virtues that have disappeared from the surface of the earth with the death of don
Rodrigo. He uses fifteen Roman emperors and generals, many
of whom had something to do with the history of Spain, to
embody the qualities mentioned in stanzas XXV and XXVI
and to counterbalance the roster of the infamous dead in the
ubi sunt stanzas.[37]

One coincidence between the two poets, however, de-
serves note because of its significance. In both poems the
placement of Camillus, an early consul whose career spanned
the first half of the fourth century B.C., at the end of the
sequence contravenes chronology. It is not so surprising in
the "Aguilando"; although there is an obvious effort to retain
a chronological order (Greeks, Romans, Castilians), Gómez
Manrique breaks the Roman sequence by mentioning Sa-
lomon. In Jorge Manrique's poem, however, the order of
imperial succession is more or less preserved until the appearance of Camillus at the end. This alteration in a chrono-
logically ordered series is an intimation that Manrique had
his uncle's poem in mind when writing these stanzas. But it
does not explain why Gómez delays the appearance of Camillus until the end of the sequence, nor why Manrique accepts
the delay. The form of the comparisons provides a clue to
their origin. Curtius and María Rosa Lida de Malkiel consid-

ered the chronicles of Alfonso el Sabio to be the ultimate source of Manrique's stanzas.[38] A more likely candidate is Valerius Maximus' *Factorum ac dictorum memorabilium libri IX*, or an epitome of Valerius's work, or a work very much like it.[39] The *Factorum ac dictorum memorabilium*, known in Spain as the *Valerio Maximo*, plundered Roman history for examples of human virtue and frailty. The anecdotes, commonly used by students of rhetoric to embellish speeches with historical references, were gathered in ten books and divided into chapters such as: "De fortaleza," "De liberalidad," "De humanidad & clemencia," "De aquellos que hovieron piedad & amor a su patria," "De justicia," and "De fe publica." Each virtue or vice is associated with a Roman personage. Of Camillus, the *Valerio* says:

> E assi estando el en exilio: los gallos destruyero[n] la ciudad de roma / como arriba es contenido: mas camillo ayu[n]to los parie[n]tes suyos & amigos / & los fugitiuos q[ue] eran escapados de roma: & fizo vna grande hueste / et vino sobre los gallos: et ve[n]ciolos & cobro mucho delo q[ue] hauian robado enla ciudad: et dio lo todo por refazer la ciudad: por lo q[ua]l roma fue como refundada: y por esto fue llamado el segundo romulo: ca assi como romulo la fundo p[ri]merame[n]te: assi este otra vez la refizo. E assi este camillo antes que se co[m]batiesse co[n] los gallos / despues que houo tomada la ciudad de veyos: por el gra[n] amor q[ue] houo ala cosa publica: rogo q[ue] si algu[n] dios hauia embidia d[e] la prosperidad de roma / q[ue] el mal de aq[ue]lla viniesse a el. & luego q[ue] houo dicho aq[ue]sto cayo en tierra / en forma q[ue] el houo ome[n]es asaber significa[n]ça de su exilio / ca de[n]de a poco fue exiliado / y echado de la ciudad.[40]

Gómez, who probably knew the *Valerio*, was fond of calling his brother the "second Cid."[41] At the end of the "Aguilando" he mentions Camillus and the Cid in succession ("Para Castilla Camilo / otro Cid contra Granada"). Camillus, the savior and second founder of Rome after the Gallic invasion of 387/ 6 B.C., was often called the "second Romulus." Like the Cid, whose most famous victory was the capture of Valencia, and like don Rodrigo, who established his reputation by capturing Huesca, Camillus was renowned for the capture of Veii and Falerii.[42] Camillus was banished by his people but, because of his military ability, was recalled to fight the invading Gauls. For the love of his country, Camillus willingly forgot past ingratitudes and marched to its relief. He was justly rewarded and died in his eightieth year.

The association of Camillus (the second Romulus) with the Cid, and with don Rodrigo (the second Cid) was bolstered by the similarities of their heroic *vitas.* Like Camillus, don Rodrigo protected Castile from the Portuguese attack. Like the Cid, he warred with the infidel. Manrique does not mention the Cid but, like his uncle, ends his list with Camillus to bring out a paramount quality embodied in both the Roman consul and don Rodrigo: *amor patriae.*[43]

The similarity of these stanzas to the "Aguilando," however, does not imply slavish imitation.[44] Manrique had a superior concept of structure and a fine ear for rhythmic variations. The chiastic structure of stanza XXVII reverses the position of the members of the comparison from octosyllable to octosyllable, with the second octosyllable extending to the *quebrado*:

Octavian:	B = A	*En ventura* Octaviano
Caesar:	A = B	Julio Cesar *en uencer*
	C	*e batallar,*
Scipio:	B = A	*en la virtud,* Affricano;
Hannibal:	A = B	Haníbal *en el saber*
	C	*e trabajar;*
Trajan:	B = A	*en la bondad,* vn Trajano;
Titus:	A = B	Tyto *en liberalidad*
	C	*con alegría;*
Aurelius:	B = A	*en su braço* Abreliano;

Marcus
  Atilius: A = B Marco Atilio *en la verdad*
                      C   *que prometía.*

Stanza XXVIII shows a more rigorous parallel structure, in which almost invariably the subject of the comparison appears in the first half of the octosyllable. The resulting rhythms are finely modulated to balance the repetitive nature of the comparisons:

Anthony: A = B Antoño Pio *en clemencia;*
M. Aurelius: A = B Marco Aurelio *en ygualdad*
                      C   *del semblante;*
Hadrian: A = B Adriano *en la eloquencia;*
Theodosius: A = B Teodosio *en humanidad*
                      C   *e buen talante.*

Aurelius
  Alexander: A   Aurelio Alexandre fue
                 = B *en deciplina e rigor*
                      C   *de la guerra;*
Constantinus: A = B vn Costantino *en la fe,*
Camillus: A = B Camilo *en el grand amor*
                      C   *de su tierra.*

Salinas argues that in these stanzas Manrique magnifies the figure of don Rodrigo to bring him down later in his encounter with Death. Other critics accuse the poet of inconsistency when he rejects pagan inspiration and the stories of the ancients only to compare his father to the Romans.[45] Neither judgment appears to be correct. The Romans provided models for emulation, but in the *Coplas* they are simply symbols of qualities represented in don Rodrigo. Reference to their symbolic meaning is emphasized by the zeugma. In stanzas twenty-six through twenty-eight there is only one main verb, and its appearance is delayed until verse 331. Without a verb to guide, the nature of the relationship between the two parts of the comparison becomes a topic for debate. Are the elided verbs *fue como* ("En ventura [fue como] Octaviano")? Or is the comparison even bolder: "En ventura [fue]

Octaviano?" The ambiguity, also found in Gómez's "Aguilando," reinforces the perception that the great men mentioned in this catalog are personifications of intrinsic virtues
embodied in don Rodrigo, rather than reminders of a pagan
past.

The sheer number of the comparisons and the accumulation of similar verse structures show that don Rodrigo surpassed all of these men. Viewed from this vantage point,
stanzas XXVII and XXVIII do not contravene the rejection of
the classical world expressed in stanza XV, but rather reveal
agreement with Gómez Manrique, when he said that there
was no need to allude to "abtoridades nin enxemplos antiguos, pues los modernos bastan asaz."[46]

XXIX   Non dexó grandes thesoros,
        nj alcançó muchas riquezas
        ni baxillas;
        mas fizo guerra a los moros,   340
        ganando sus fortalezas
        en sus villas;
          i en las lides que venció,
        quántos moros e cauallos
        se perdieron;   345
        i en este officio ganó
        las rentas e los vasallos
        que le dieron.

XXX   Pues por su honra i estado,
        en otros tyenpos pasados   350
        ¿cómo s'uuo?
        Quedando desmanparado,
        con hermanos e criados
        se sostuuo.
        Después que fechos famosos   355
        fizo en esta mjsma guerra
        que hazía,
        fizo tratos tan honrosos
        que le dieron haun más tierra

que tenja.   360
(*Cancionero* 103-104)

The argumentative structure of the panegyric reveals Manrique's desire to concentrate on character before addressing
the question of his father's standing in the world. In the
"Aguilando" Gómez had wished his brother as many earthly
goods as he deserved ("Tantos bienes temporales / os de
Dios / quantos merescedes vos, / pues fustes uno de dos / en
los mortales" 16-20). Manrique points out that the uncle's
wish was not fulfilled. Don Rodrigo died without having ac-
cumulated great worldly possessions ("Non dexó grandes
thesoros, / nj alcançó muchas riquezas / nj baxillas" 337-39).

And yet, Manrique had to explain that even though his
father was far from rich, he had considerable power, influence, and estates scattered from the north of Spain to the
frontier. The three negatives of lines 337-39 are followed by
the explanatory *mas* of verse 340, which begins to declare why
the *fortalezas, villas, moros, cauallos, rentas,* and *vasallos* of don
Rodrigo, though as tangible as the worldly goods of the *ubi
sunt* sequence, are very different.

Lines 49-50 already established that material possessions
are good or bad, depending on the way they are obtained
and used. If they are part of the "dádivas desmedidas" of
kings to unworthy subjects, if they are dishonorably obtained
(106-8, 217-25, 247-49), or if they are frivolously squandered,
then they are evil. If, on the other hand, they are inherited
or are a reward for correct behavior, then they are honorable.[47] Historically, don Rodrigo's goods, except for Paredes—
and even there possession was confirmed by the king—were
all ultimately the result of royal favor. Manrique, however,
does not consider don Rodrigo's power and wealth to be due
to the king's irresponsible largesse, but to his father's own
effort, and to a grudging recognition of his worth.

XXXI   Estas sus viejas estorias   361
              que con su braço pintó
              en jouentud,

con otras nueuas victorias
agora las renouó   365
en senectud.
   Por su grand abilidad,
por méritos e ancianía
bien gastada,
alcançó la dignidad   370
de la grand Cauallería
dell Espada.

XXXII   E sus villas e sus tierras
ocupadas de tyranos
las halló;   375
mas por çercos e por guerras
e por fuerça de sus manos
las cobró.
   Pues nuestro Rey natural,
si de las obras que obró   380
fué seruido,
dígalo el de Portogal
i en Castilla quien siguió
su partido.
(*Cancionero* 104-105)

A short biography of don Rodrigo begins with stanza XXX. The poem tells how his inheritance was denied to him as a young man (349-51), yet shows that nevertheless he did not fail to support himself and his family (352-54), accomplish great deeds in battle (355-57), and enter into honorable arrangements that increased his holdings (358-60). In old age, when other men retire from the toils of life, don Rodrigo not only maintained his estate, but increased his activities (361-66). He obtained the mastership of Santiago by the election of the Castile chapter (367-72), although he had to free its holdings from the hands of don Juan Pacheco (373-78).

Pacheco, one of the "maestres tan prosperados" of the *ubi sunt* sequence, is the antithesis of don Rodrigo. Don Rodrigo earned his estates in war against the Moors; Pacheco obtained his from the king. The Pachecos allied themselves with the king of Portugal in the struggle between La Beltraneja and Isabel (379-84). Their great disservice to the crown is implied by the mention of their ally, the king of Portugal, who supported Juana against Fernando and Isabel (388-90).[49]

The biography is structured in two parts: the deeds of youth ("viejas estorias / que con su braço pintó / en jouentud" 361-63) and the deeds of old age ("nuevas victorias / agora las renovó / en senectud" 364-66). The *estoria* is the remembrance of an act or deed for the benefit of posterity. It can be a written, a painted, or an oral record. Don Rodrigo painted his *estoria* (362) in the sense that he established his reputation by his deeds. The effort is denoted in the choice of *braço* (not *mano*), revealing that he painted the memory of his deeds in blood with his sword. The "renovation" of those viejas *estorias* also signifies the refurbishing of don Rodrigo's reputation as a warrior. His fame spread by word of mouth and in writing. In the poem, *estorias* is invariably associated with hearing and reading ("haunque oymos e leymos / sus estorias" 173-74). Don Rodrigo's reputation survives imprinted in the memories of of those who witnessed his victories and experienced their own defeat (382-84). In written form, it survives in the work of his son. The term *estorias* therefore invests don Rodrigo with a mythic stature equal to or surpassing that of the ancient worthies with whom he is compared, for his fame was acquired as a young man, reaffirmed in old age, and witnessed by all those living in Castile at that time. The passage also reveals that don Rodrigo is an extraordinary individual who transcends the natural limitations of the *cursus aetatis*. The topos, for it is a rhetorical cliché, is the reverse of the *puer senex*, the *senex juvenis*. Geoffrey of Vinsauf's description of Pope Innocent in the *Poetria Nova* is an excellent example of the type: "Trans homines totus: ubi corporis ista juventus / Tam grandis senii, vel cordis tanta senectus / Insita tam juveni? Quam mira rebellio rerum: /Ecce senex juvenis!"[50] Geoffrey looks at his subject as both an old/ young and a young/old man, and the virtues he extolls are more spiritual than corporal. Manrique, on the other hand, shows us his father as a youth capable of mature acts and as an old man capable of youthful exploits. At both extremes of his life he evidences the virtues of the elect: prudence (*prudentia*), courage (*fortitudo*), measure (*temperantia*), and justice (*justitia*).

Unlike other parts of the poem, the panegyric retains an ascendant structure within each stanza and within each stanza grouping, generally ending with an assertion of the martial nature of the man. Stanza XXVI, which praises don Rodrigo's qualities, for example, ends by calling him a "lion" to those who seek mischief and evil. The comparisons with the Romans of stanzas XXVII and XXVIII end with Camillus, the protector of Rome against her enemies. The appraisal of don Rodrigo's material successes in stanza XXIX asserts that he won his possessions in martial encounters. Stanza XXX compares his destitute youth to the *tratos honrosos* of his maturity, and stanza XXXI covers the deeds of old age, culminating in the grandmastership of Santiago. Although don Rodrigo faced reversals in life, his career always reestablished itself in its true course. In this respect, the biography shares some characteristics with the *Entwiklungsroman*, where life is presented through the experience of a protagonist, and gives shape to his character and world view.[51] Unlike the *Entwiklungsroman*, however, Manrique follows his hero from the beginning of his chivalric life to the end. Manrique begins with the acquisition of those properties that guarantee his position as head of a lineage, continues with the martial accomplishments that protect and enhance those properties, and ends with those moral virtues that guarantee the respect of those who surround him. Don Rodrigo's life is therefore heroic at the beginning and at the end. The coming of death is not seen as the conclusion of a phase of decay but as one more heroic encounter of this *senex juvenis*.

DEATH AND DON RODRIGO

In the last third of the *Coplas* the sense of movement toward death initiated at the beginning of the poem and reiterated in each of its parts, vigorously reasserts itself. Death comes to issue don Rodrigo a final challenge.

XXXIII	Después de puesta la vida	385
	tantas vezes por su ley	
	al tablero;	
	después de tan bien seruida	
	la corona de su rey	
	verdadero;	390
	después de tanta hazaña	
	a que non puede bastar	
	cuenta cierta,	
	en la su villa d'Ocaña	
	vino la Muerte a llamar	395
	a su puerta,	
	(*Cancionero* 105)	

Death's challenge is a call to resume life's journey to its conclusion. But man is not capable of taking that last step without the mediation of Christ, who "para sobirnos al cielo / descendió" (68-69). The anaphoras that reiterate don Rodrigo's achievements (*Después de*, 385, 388, 391) introduce three subordinate clauses that delay the introduction of Death.[52] They run counter to the sense of duration established at the beginning of the poem, which emphasizes the quickness of Death's approach. In stanza XXXIII time stretches and Death waits, while the particularity of the man is emphasized. Death comes only after the poet points out once again that don Rodrigo has served "*su* rey" well (389). It comes to "*su* villa d'Ocaña" (394), calls on "*su* puerta" (396), and exhorts his heart to show "*su* esfuerço famoso" (401).

XXXIV	diziendo: Buen cauallero,	
	dexad el mundo engañoso	
	e su halago;	
	vuestro corazón d'azero	400
	muestre su esfuerço famoso	
	en este trago;	

e pues de vida e salud
feziste tan poca cuenta
por la fama,   405
esfuércese la virtud
para sofrir esta afuenta
que vos llama.

XXXV   Non se vos haga tan amarga
          la batalla temerosa   410
          qu'esperáys,
          pues otra vida más larga
          de la fama gloriosa
          acá dexáys,
             (haunqu'esta vida d'onor   415
          tampoco non es eternal
          nj verdadera);
          mas, con todo, es muy mejor
          que la otra temporal,
          peresçedera.   420

XXXVI   El biuir qu'es perdurable
          non se gana con estados
          mundanales,
          nj con vida delectable
          donde moran los pecados   425
          jnfernales;
             mas los buenos religiosos
          gánanlo con oraciones
          e con lloros;
          los caualleros famosos,   430
          con trabajos e afflictiones
          contra moros.

XXXVII   E pues vos, claro varón,
          tanta sangre derramastes
          de paganos,   435
          esperad el galardón
          que en este mundo ganastes
          por las manos;
             e con esta confiança

e con la fe tan entera   440
que tenéys,
partid con buena esperança,
qu'estotra vida tercera
ganaréys.

XXXVIII   Non tengamos tiempo ya   445
en esta vida mesqujna
por tal modo,
que mj voluntad está
conforme con la diujna
para todo;   450
    e consiento en mj morir
con voluntad plazentera,
clara e pura,
que querer hombre viuir
quando Dios quiere que muera,   455
es locura.

XXXIX   Tú que, por nuestra maldad,
tomaste forma seruil
e baxo nombre;
tú, que a tu diujnjdad   460
juntaste cosa tan vil
como es el hombre;
    tú, que tan grandes tormentos
sofriste sin resistencia
en tu persona,   465
non por mjs merescimjentos,
mas por tu sola clemencia
me perdona.
(*Cancionero* 106-109)

The last third of the poem moves from contemplation to
panegyric to active participation in the final moments of don
Rodrigo's life. It moves from the general to the specific, from
the death of all, to the death of many, to a particular death
that is unlike all the other deaths so far contemplated. The
present tense fixes a new point of view. Narrator and readers

now coincide with the temporal position of the characters in the poem.

Two voices speak: Death and don Rodrigo. But they do not converse. Normally, when Death comes calling on an unsuspecting soul an argument develops. The soul does not want to leave this world. In the *Coplas*, however, Death is a messenger from God who comes to reaffirm don Rodrigo's goodness and to announce the good news of his salvation.

In this respect, don Rodrigo's death is an extraordinary event. The reader is prepared for it, however, by the way in which the poem treats the old age of the hero. Medieval man was as ambivalent toward old age as he was toward death. He saw in old age a period of physical decay (as the poem shows in stanza VIII), and a period of danger, because of death's nearness. St. Isidore, for example, said of death: "Tria sunt autem genera mortis: acerba, inmatura, naturalis. Acerba infantum, inmatura juvenum, merita, id est naturalis, senum."[53] Natural death, which follows according to God's predestined plan and is no more than a process that leads to a natural end, is opposed to the two types of premature death, *acerba* and *immatura*, which break life's thread violently.[54] In all three cases death is inevitable, but one comes when expected, the other two do not. Fray Martín de Córdoba, a contemporary of Manrique, put it succinctly. Death, he said: "A los viejos está en la puerta, a los moços está en celada."[55] The source of the idea that death may be at one's door is found in two biblical parables: Mark 13: 33-37 and Luke 12: 36-38.[56] In Mark a porter awaits his master's return from a journey. In Luke, servants await their master's return from a wedding. Both parables were interpreted in their moral sense to signify the life of the individual at its end, when he is faced with death and judgment. St. Gregory, for example, in one of his homilies glosses Luke's text by identifying the *vigiliae* of the porter and the servants as the ages of man, and life as a dangerous sleep:

Qui ergo vigilare in prima vigilia noluit custodiat vel secundam, ut qui converti a pravitatibus suis in pueritia neglexit ad vias vitae saltem in tempore juventutis evigilet. Et qui evigilare in secunda vigilia noluit tertiae vigiliae remedia non amittat, ut qui in juventute ad vias vitae non evigilat saltem in senectute resipiscat.[57]

Gregory also identifies the coming of death with the Lord's knocking at the door: "Venit quippe Dominus cum ad judicium properat, pulsat vero, cum jam per aegritudinis molestias esse mortem vicinam designat."[58] Death, therefore, though personified as a man or a woman in the *Coplas*, is an allegory of the infirmities that afflicted don Rodrigo at the end of his life. But they are portrayed so that they become a reward for virtue. By presenting his father's death this way, Manrique is able to avoid being specific about the nature of those infirmities (according to one source, cancer of the face) and emphasize the idea that his father's natural death was a passage to a well-earned reward.

Fray Martín, in the work quoted previously, tells how one merits natural death:

. . . quieres bien morir, bive bien; quieres non themer a Dios después de la muerte thémelo en la vida. Este es el error común de los vanos que fazen grandes provisiones para la vida, ninguno non se provee para la muerte; alçan torres, fundan altos castillos, cércanse de gentes armadas, fázense provar las viandas, todo para aver segura vida; non curan de procurar segura muerte. E sería mejor proveer para despues de la muerte, que es tienpo perdurable, que para la vida que es como vapor transitorio.[59]

Those who care for life, build for life and find death. Those who fear God, build for death and consequently find life. Virtuous men, fray Martín adds, should not fear death. There is a natural will according to which all men, including Jesus, fear death. There is another will, which he calls "elective," by which man chooses that which reason dictates. The knight exposes himself to death for the public good or for his king;

the martyr, for his faith. Such a choice precludes the possibility of fearing death. The "elective" will, says fray Martín, "ha de echar el miedo de la natural voluntad o, si non lo puede echar, templarlo."[60] Don Rodrigo's final words are therefore another exposition of an ideal of Christian knighthood, which he affirmed throughout his life in his deeds and, in the poem, one last time in his hour of death. They also are further evidence of the virtues of old age that allow don Rodrigo to transcend the common *cursus aetatis: maturitas, gravitas,* and *sapientia.*

Death's reaffirmation of the value of Christian knighthood would be incongruous if the *Coplas* did not identify Death as an agent of God and as a guarantor of society. In the poem it is Death who sets forth the tripartite/trifunctional image of society that pervades medieval thought. Mankind, according to this image, is made up of three orders (*bellatores, oratores,* and *laboratores*) with three functions: fighting, praying, and working.[61] Of the three only the *oratores* and the *bellatores* produce cultural models of any significance. One is oriented toward the sacred (the cleric) and the other toward the profane (the knight).[62] The two vie with each other for the attention of men of letters and, depending on the author, one or the other predominates.

The aristocratic bias of the *Coplas* prefers the knightly model. Within the scope of the poem the *laboratores* are not mentioned at all, and the *oratores,* only in passing (427-28). Only the knight, the *bellator,* whose function is to undergo "trabajos e afflictiones / contra moros" (431-32) and to shed "sangre . . . / de paganos" (434-35), is thoroughly examined. The result is an imbalanced view of that tripartite vision that sees world order as resting on the labor of each of its components.[63] It is replaced by an overvaluation of knightly life that is structured around three conceptions of life enunciated in stanza XXXV: life in the world, life of fame, and eternal life. Life in the world, correctly led, has as its reward the life of fame and eternal life. Don Rodrigo is one of those knights who, in the words of stanza V, had the good sense to labor with care. He used the world according to its purpose ("para

ganar aquel / que atendemos") and won the *galardón* promised by God. Consequently, for him Death is a mediator,
whose appearance marks the end of a voyage and the attain-
ment of that "morada / sin pesar" mentioned in stanza V (50-
51).

EPILOGUE

XL   Assí, con tal entender,
          todos sentidos humanos   470
          conseruados,
          cercado de su mujer
          i de sus hijos e hermanos
          e criados,
               dió el alma a quien ge la dió   465
          (el qual la dió en el cielo
          en su gloria),
          que haunque la vida perdió,
          dexónos harto consuelo
          su memoria.   480
          (*Cancionero* 109)

The last stanza closes the circle. Don Rodrigo, in death,
returns to his home in heaven. The poem, which began with
an exhortation to the soul to remember the past, assess the
present, and contemplate the future, ends with a commemorative act that puts the reader in full command of a *memoria*.
It consoles one with the knowledge that there are individuals
whose life embodies the perfections of Christ, and who live
their lives "sin errar." Their reward, and that of those who
would emulate them, is to die surrounded by loved ones, in
full possession of their faculties, and worthy of returning to
God's grace.

Underlying the *Coplas* is a religious metaphor that portrays
man as an exile and this life as a pilgrimage. The metaphor
expresses itself at many points within the poem. Exile and
journey begin at birth and end in death (55-59). Life is a *camino*

(49) and a *jornada* (53). Things come and go along the way, (*vida/muerte* 4-5; *el presente* 13; *ríos* 25-36; *las cosas* 74; *la hermosura* 85-90; *juuentud* 93; *sangre, linaje,* and *nobleza* 97-98; *estados* and *riquezas* 109; *plazeres* and *dulçores* 133-34; *poder* 157), and they are fraught with care (*pesar* 51) and danger. The journey begins when the individual leaves the heavenly abode (*morada sin pesar* 50-51), and ends when he returns to it or is lost.

The metaphor implies the use of a large number of verbs of motion. The lexicon of the poem can be arranged along two axes, one representing physical movement (up/down/ [up]), and another representing displacement in time (past/ present/future). The first part of the poem (stanzas I-XXIV) is dominated by downward movement. Birth is a descent into life, or into the world, rivers flow downstream away from their source into the sea, men become prey and fall into death's trap, or fall from Fortune's wheel. Associated with this downward movement are a series of images of concealment or entrapment (*la mar / qu'es el morir, la celada, el arraual de senectud, la cava honda / chapada*) that are the opposite of the *morada sin pesar*. The only early exception to this negative view and to the generalized downward movement of the images occurs in the invocation and in the stanzas that follow it (IV, V, and VI). Those stanzas reveal the existence of a circular movement exemplified in Christ's descent into the world, his death, and his ascent back to heaven.

Semantically, the positive valuation of the world is marked by a verb that negates that valuation: *perder* (*perdemos,* 78; *se pierde,* 101; *perdieron,* 345).[64] Associated with *perder* are: *desfallecer* (*desfallecen,* 84); *parar* (141); *passar/passarse* (*passa* 4, *passado,* 11/18/176, *passar,* 23, *passas,* 287); *desfazer* (*desfazes,* 276); *aterrar* (*atierras,* 275); and *morir,* 27, 59. *Perder* and its allied verbs refer to people as a group, as categories (*el alma, la nobleza de los godos, emperadores, reyes*), and as specific individuals (don Juan, the infantes of Aragón, don Alvaro de Luna). All, however, are the same in that they are perceived as lacking transcendence.

Conversely, the negative valuation of the world incarnate

in don Rodrigo is expressed by the verb *ganar* (to win and to obtain: *ganar* 65, *ganando* 341, *ganó* 346, *gana* 422, *gánanlo* 428, *ganastes* 437, and *ganaréys* 444). Associated with *ganar* are *pintar* (*pintó* 362), *renovar* (*renovó* 365), *vencer* (*venció* 343), *batallar* (*batallar* 315 and the noun *batalla* 410); and *esperar* (*esperáys* 411, *esperad* 436). The implication is that those who seek the world lose it, and those who shun it, win it.

The opposition established by the poem between the two ways of looking at the world and its goods is also reflected in the uses of the verb *dar*. Along one axis of meaning, *ganar* and *dar* are opposites. *Ganar* means to acquire for oneself, *dar* means to give away. Like *ganar*, *dar* is related to material goods and is a synonym of *donar, regalar, proporcionar, entregar* (*las dádivas desmedidas*). In another context, however, *dar* and *ganar* function as synonyms. *Dar* denotes arrival, as in "que van a dar en la mar," and, at the end of the poem, the act of giving ("dió el alma a quien ge la dió 475) is synonymous with the conquest of heaven: to give is to receive, to lose is to win.

At the end of the poem, *morir* and *perder* are used in reference to don Rodrigo, but in a different context from the way they appear earlier. *Morir* is used as a noun in conjunction with the verb *consentir* ("e consiento en mj morir" 451—the only time that death waits for man's acquiescence), and again when it is introduced as an expression of God's own designs ("que querer hombre viuir / quando dios quiere que muera / es locura" 455). *Perder* appears associated with don Rodrigo only when it is obvious that the loss of his life is tempered by a greater gain ("que haunque la vida perdió, / dexónos harto consuelo / su memoria" 478). There are, therefore, two sets of verbs in antonymic relation (*perder* and *ganar, dar* and *ganar, morir* and *vivir*). They come together at the end, but with the meaning of one set modified by the other. Death explains the process that leads to that modification by enunciating the concept of the three lives: life of the body, life of fame, and everlasting life. The life of the body is of no value. Like all worldly things it is destined to become dust. The life of fame is of greater value because, although it partakes of death, it is more durable. The third life is eternal. Consequently, the arrival of Death is a departure from a lesser to a greater estate ("partid con buena esperança, / qu'estotra vida tercera / ganaréys" 442-44). It turns *morir* into a *nacer, partir* into a *llegar, perder* and *dar* into *ganar,* and *descender* into *subir.* Only at the end does *morir* again imply a return to our place of origin.

The ascending structure implicit in Death's final characterization of life further extends the poem's preocupation with motion. Up/down movement is implicit in the equivalences of two lexical triplets *nacer/vivir/morir,* and *partir/andar/llegar.*[65] *Nacer* and *morir, partir* and *llegar* are reversive antonyms. They denote change in opposite directions. One cannot be born and die or arrive and leave simultaneously. *Vivir* and *morir,* as noted in the discussion of the language of the love lyric, are complementary antonyms. They divide experience into two mutually exclusive realms. As in the lyric, however, the elegy undermines antonymy by means of paradox. Even though death is the end result of life, *vivir* and *morir* become synonymous as the poem progresses. Similarly, because the poem undermines the concept of duration by claiming that past, present, and future (another way of stating *nacer/vivir/ morir*) are nearly one, the opposition of *partir* and *llegar* is also undermined. Like *vivir* and *morir,* the semantic boundaries of *partir* and *llegar* lose their definition.

Don Rodrigo's willingness to abandon honor and wealth wins him salvation. This rejection of the very possessions that define his being as an aristocrat is emphasized by the verb *dexar,* the same verb used in stanza IX's evocation of the goods of the world. Goods are chains that bind man to the world, but they abandon him at death ("Los estados e riqueza, / que nos dexen a deshora" 109-10; "¿qué fueron sino pesares / al dexar?" 251-52). The poem advocates moderation in goods as an ideal, because they can readily be left for better things ("Non dexó grandes thesoros, / nj alcançó muchas riquezas / ni baxillas" 337-39) when death comes calling ("dexad el mundo engañoso / e su halago" 398-99).

One can reject the world, the poem's language explains, or be rejected because of it. By rejecting the world and by performing heroic deeds, don Rodrigo achieves salvation and fame, and leaves behind a memory ("pues otra vida más larga / de la fama gloriosa / acá dexáys" 412-14; "dexónos harto consuelo / su memoria" 479-80).[66]

The goods of the world are indicated by nouns clusters in the *ubi sunt* stanzas. *Justas, torneos, paramentos, çimeras, bordaduras, damas, llamas, trobar, músicas, dançr,* and *ropas* characterize the empty life at court. *Dádivas, edeficios, baxillas, enriques e reales, jaeces, caballos, gentes, atavíos, thesoros, villas, lugares,* are the outward manifestations of power and influence. The titles *duques, marqueses, condes,* and *varones* denote the honors of the world, represented also by the tangible manifestations of power: *huestes, pendones, estandartes, vanderas, castillos, muros, valuartes, barreras,* and *cavas.* The sequence of concrete nouns represents a view of the world and of life that is antithetical to the values sustained by the more spiritual qualities of don Rodrigo: *ventura, vencer e batallar, virtud, saber e trabajar, bondad, liberalidad, fortaleza, verdad, clemencia, ygualdad de semblante, eloquencia, humanidad e buen talante, deciplina e rigor, fe, amor a su tierra.*

Don Rodrigo's virtue is contrasted to examples that appear earlier in the poem. The blood of the Goths (their nobility) is lost in "officios no devidos" (107), don Rodrigo's is conserved and used for its purpose (430-32). Old age weighs man down with afflictions (95-96), don Rodrigo acts just as vigorously and forthrightly in old age as he did in youth (373-84). Furthermore, he is a man who "wins" in his old age (364-66), and who dies in possession of all of his faculties (469-71). Other contrasts can be drawn when the poem goes on to describe don Rodrigo's estate. The *altos estados* of the *ubi sunt* examples disappear, don Rodrigo's estate did not reach great heights, but it also was not lost.

Semantically, these stanzas revolve around an exposition of the values characterized by "honra i estado" (349). In stanza XXX these terms have a clear economic meaning. They are the estates used to sustain one's status, one's "hermanos e criados." But *honra* is associated with other lexical terms within the poem: *onor* (415); *famoso* (293, 401); *famosos* (355,

430); *fama* (405); and finally, *fama gloriosa* (413), and *gloria* (477).[67] It is significant that the term *honra* is never associated with Juan II, Enrique IV, and his courtiers. It could have formed part of that sequence of stanzas that refer to the estates of these great men, but it is excluded from that context. The reasons for the exclusion may be found in the views held by contemporary moralists about the nature of *honra*. When talking about moral virtues (the virtues summarized in stanzas XXXVII-XXXVIII of the poem), Alonso de Cartagena says that they are acquired by active participation in the life of the family, the city, and the state. The outward signs of these inner virtues are nobility, antiquity of lineage, and virtuous activity. Honor is the result of virtuous action and, therefore, not something that Manrique associates with the people he mentions in the *ubi sunt*.

The characterization of don Rodrigo also tempers the images of Death in stanzas XXIV-XL. In the first part of the poem Death is a boundless sea (26), a hunter who waits in ambush (137), a leader of an involuntary dance (163-68), a lady who throws men off her wheel (113-17), a blacksmith who throws souls into his forge (235-37), and an archer who shoots those who come before him (286-88). All of its appearances are associated with force, entrapment, or surprise. Death is a silent stalker; man, its victim.

In the second half of the poem, Death is a chessplayer (285-88) and a person who comes openly to don Rodrigo's house, knocks at his door, and addresses him with respect (395ff).[68] The first image implies a long, deliberate struggle, in which don Rodrigo faced Death many times, came away the victor, and gained the respect of his opponent. The second turns Death into an intercessor, who reaffirms the values for which don Rodrigo stood. When Death's checkmate comes, don Rodrigo is treated gently. All men must eventually lose out to Death. But, for a few, Death has great respect.

Critics have often sensed a conflict between an aristocratic and a clerical system of belief in the *Coplas*. This conflict, if it exists, is not the result of unsustained poetic inspiration. Rather, it is part of the society that produced the poem, and flows logically from it. The second half of the *Coplas* is as carefully contrived as the first.

In the *Coplas* significance is established in stanzas I-XV, and then the particular is interpreted by it. In this way, the poem's disquisition on the deceitfulness of the world serves as an introduction to the panegyric. The poem develops from the general to the specific. At the most general level, it moves from death to life; from the exordium that warns of the dangers of the world, to the drama of salvation.

The poem's preoccupation with death is the legacy of the textual tradition on which the first part of the *Coplas* is based. When the poem deals in generalities, its sentiments are orthodox, its point of view, otherworldly, its sources, ultimately rooted in the Bible, the Fathers, or their commentators. When the poem moves into history, the problems of life and the concerns of a specific community, the Manrique clan, express themselves openly. The general gives way to the particular. Classical examples are abandoned in favor of personal experience, of known people, and events. The poet prefers to work with the present or the recent past, which he criticizes and evaluates. But, though Manrique rejects the possibility that don Rodrigo's earthly life might be completely over with his death, he reaffirms his belief in the supreme value of eternal life.

Jorge Manrique also expresses his family's preocupations, and its need for solace, while he issues a challenge. The *Coplas* is as much a political statement as it is an elegy. All fifteenth-century poetry is deeply rooted in a sociopolitical context. Gómez Manrique's "El planto de las virtudes por el magnífico señor don Iñigo López de Mendoza," and the "Dezir a la muerte de Garcilasso de la Vega," for example, mourn the passing of a loved family member. They also make a statement on behalf of the family to king and court. In the "Planto" Gómez associates himself and his family with Santillana and makes an attempt to cast himself as an heir of the latter. The "Dezir" sounds a darker note, as Gómez subtly chides the king for his indifference to family rights and expectations.[69] In a similar fashion, the *Coplas* reflect the family's concerns following don Rodrigo's demise.

Don Rodrigo died shortly after reducing the Order of Santiago's Castilian headquarters—Uclés—to obedience, and just
when he seemed closest to realizing his lifelong ambition to
be fully recognized as *maestre* of Santiago. The next year,
Alonso de Cárdenas, don Rodrigo's bitter rival for the *maes-
trazgo*, was elected head of Santiago.

Alonso de Cárdena's election was a blow to the family,
which had to surrender Segura de la Sierra.[70] Adding insult
to injury, the Trece recognized Alonso de Cárdenas as successor, not of don Rodrigo, but of Juan Pacheco, the previous
legally constituted *maestre*.[71] The intervening years, during
which don Rodrigo had claimed to be *maestre*, were swept
aside by one man, who denied don Rodrigo in death the title
he had assumed in life. The *Coplas* restores that title to him.
Manrique could do nothing against a man to whom he owed
fealty and on whom the future expectations of many of the
Manriques depended. He could only create a monument to
the memory of his father that would outlast his enemies' spite
and remind others of the services don Rodrigo had rendered
to the crown.

The commemorative act represented in the elegy invokes
a prominent relative, recently deceased, in the name of a
group, in order to console and reaffirm clan bonds. The elegy
is written with the immediate family group as its audience.
It is both an expression of clan solidarity in an unfriendly
world and an instrument in the preservation of that community through the commemoration of its calamities and
triumphs.[72] But the poet also directs the elegy toward the
outside world, where he seeks to impress the collective
memory of society with the *pathos* of the history it com-
memorates.

He impresses this memory through the apotheosis of don
Rodrigo, which fixes in our mind the magnitude of his services. Don Rodrigo's life follows a christological model: birth,
death, transfiguration, resurrection, and ascent. It exemplifies
the effort of some men to reciprocate for God's condescension
toward man.

If one returns to the beginning of the poem and asks the
questions: What if the sleeping soul awakes? What if it re-

members that it is going to die? What should it do? Manrique's answer, given in the second half of the poem, is that if the soul belongs to a man like his father, then its duty lies in carrying its life to term, doing what it has been doing all along.

In a poem crafted by such a careful artificer, it is not accidental that the first verse begins with an exhortation to the soul to remember and the last ends by talking of the consolation of memory. What is this memory, if not the remembrance of a life dedicated to virtuous action by those who witnessed those actions? The acts of don Rodrigo Manrique were vividly etched in the memory of the family and of his son. The son took that memory and shaped it into a poetic *estoria*, a tangible, written account or memorial, which assured the continuation of his father's fame. In so doing, he provided witness for the reader, of the events of his father's life. The act of reading, in turn, permits the reader to consider the condition of the descendants, the injustices of the world, and remember the noble example of the father.

APPENDIX A

Pedro and Rodrigo Manrique

The brief biography of don Pedro Manrique below is part of a work known as *Generaciones y semblanzas*, written around 1450 by Fernán Pérez de Guzmán (ca. 1378-ca. 1468).[1] The *Generaciones* consists of a series of biographical sketches of principal personages of the first half of the fifteenth century. Don Rodrigo Manrique's biography is excerpted from *Claros varones de Castilla*, a work written toward the end of the fifteenth century by Fernando del Pulgar, a secretary to Fernando and Isabel who had served in high administrative office under Enrique IV.[2] It is part of a series of biographical sketches, which, like the *Generaciones y semblanzas*, is dependent on a literary tradition that conditions its rhetoric and structure, but evidences firsthand knowledge of the characters and events to which it alludes.

PEDRO MANRIQUE

Pero Manrrique, adelantado de León, fue un grande e virtuoso cavallero, e porque del linaje de los Manrriques es asaz dicho, resta de dizir como su madre doña Juana de Mendoça fue una notable dueña.

Era este adelantado muy pequeño de cuerpo, la nariz luenga, muy avisado e discreto e bien razonado e de buena conçiencia e temeroso de Dios. Amó mucho los buenos religiosos e todos ellos amavan a él. Ovo mucho buenos parientes de los quales se ayudó mucho en sus neçesidades. Fue onbre de grant coraçón e asaz esforçado. Algunos lo razonavan por bolliçioso e ambiçioso de mandar e rigir. Yo non lo sé çierto, pero si lo fue non lo avería a maravilla, porque todos los que se sienten dispuestos e sufiçientes a alguna obra e acto, su propia virtud los punje e estimula a la exerçitar e usar ca apenas verá onbre a alguno bien dispuesto a un ofiçio que non se deleite en lo usar e ansí este cavallero por su grand discriçión era bastante a rigir e governar. Veyendo un tienpo tan confuso e tan suelto que quien más tomava de las cosas, más avía dellas, non es mucho de maravillar si se entremetía dello. La verdad es ésta; que en el tienpo del rey don Johan el segundo en el qual ovo grandes e diversos mudamientos, non fue alguno en que él non fuese, non a fin de desservir al rey nin de procurar daño al reino, mas por valer e aver poder, de lo qual muchas vezes se siguen escándalos e males. E ansí en tales abtos pasó por diversas fortunas, prósperas e adversas. Ca algunas vezes ovo grant lugar en el rigimiento del reino e acreçentó su casa e estado, e otras vezes pasó por grandes trabajos, ca fue una vez desterrado e otra preso.

Algunos quisieron dizir que él allegava bien los parientes de los que avía menester e después los olvidava. Desto ovo algunos que se quexaron dél; otros lo escusavan diziendo que non avía tanto poder e facultad para que pudiese satisfazer a tantos e tan grandes onbres, o por ventura él faziendo su poder, ellos non se contentavan. Todavía él fue buen cavallero e devoto christiano e tan discreto e avisado que solía dél dizir don Sancho de Rojas, arçobispo de Toledo que <<quanto Dios le menguara del cuerpo, le acreçentara en el seso>>.

Murió en edad de çincuenta e nueve años.

RODRIGO MANRIQUE

Don Rodrigo Manrrique, conde de Paredes e maestre de Santiago, fijo segundo de Pedro Manrrique, adelantado mayor del reino de León, fue omme de mediana estatura, bien proporcionado en la conpostura de sus mienbros; los cabellos tenía roxos e la nariz un poco larga. Era de linaje noble castellano.

En los actos que fazía en su menor hedad paresció ser inclinado al oficio de la cauallería. Tomó hábito e orden de Santiago, e fué comendador de Segura, que es cercana a la tierra de los moros: e estando por frontero en aquella su encomienda, fizo muchas entradas en la tierra de los moros, donde ouo fama de tan buen cauallero, que el adelantado su padre, por la estimación grande en que este su fijo era tenido, apartó de su mayorasgo la villa de Paredes, e le fizo donación della, e el rey don Juan le dió título de conde de aquella villa. Este varón gozó de dos singulares virtudes: de la prudencia, conosciendo los tienpos, los logares, las personas, e las otras cosas que en la guerra conuiene que sepa el buen capitán. Fué asimismo dotado de la virtud de la fortaleza; no por aquellas vías en que se muestran fuertes los que fingida e no verdaderamente lo son; más así por su buena composición natural, como por los muchos actos que fizo en el exercicio de las armas, asentó tan perfectamente en su ánimo el ábito de la fortaleza, que se deleitaua cuando le ocurría logar en que la deuiese exercitar. Esperaua con buen esfuerço los peligros, acometía las fazañas con grande osadía, e ningún trabajo de guerra a él ni a los suyos era nueuo. Preciáuase mucho que sus criados fuesen dispuestos para las armas. Su plática con ellos era la manera del defender e del ofender el enemigo, e ni se dezía ni fazía en su casa acto ninguno de molleza, enemiga del oficio de las armas. Quería que todos los de su conpañía fuese escogidos para aquel exercicio, e no conuenía a ninguno durar en su casa si en él fuese conocido punto de couardía; e si alguno venía a ella que no fuese dispuesto para el uso de las armas, el grand exercicio que auía y veya en los otros, le fazía ábile e diestro en ellas. En las batallas, e muchos

recuentros que ouo con moros e con cristianos, este cauallero
fué el que mostrando grand esfuerço a los suyos, fería primero
en los contrarios: e las gentes de su conpañía, visto el esfuerço
de su capitán, todos le seguían e cobrauan osadía de pelear.
Tenía tan grand conoscimiento de las cosas del canpo, e
prouey[a]las en tal manera, que donde fué él principal capitán
nunca puso su gente en logar dó se ouiese de retraer, porque
boluer las espaldas al enemigo era tan ageno de su ánimo,
que elegía antes recebir la muerte peleando, que saluar la vida
huyendo.

Este cauallero osó acometer grandes fazañas: especial-
mente, escaló una noche la cibdad de Huesca, que es del reino
de Granada; e como quier que subiendo el escala los suyos
fueron sentidos de los moros, e fueron algunos derribados
del adarue, e feridos en la subida; pero el esfuerço deste capitán se inprimió a la ora tanto en los suyos, que pospuesta la
vida e propuesta la gloria, subieron el muro peleando, e no
fallescieron de sus fuerças defendiéndolo, aunque veyan los
unos derramar su sangre, los otros caer de la cerca. E en esta
manera matando de los moros, e muriendo de los suyos, este
capitán, ferido en el braço de una saeta, peleando entró en la
cibdad e retroxo los moros fasta que los cercó en la fortaleza:
es esperando el socorro que le farían los cristianos, no temió
el socorro que venía a los moros. En aquella ora los suyos,
vencidos de miedo, vista la multitud que sobre ellos venía
por todas partes a socorrer los moros, e tardar el socorro que
esperauan de los cristianos, le amonestaron que desanparase
la cibdad, e no encomendase a la fortuna de una ora la vida
suya, e de aquellas gentes, juntamente con la honrra ganada
en su hedad pasada; e requeríanle que, pues tenía tienpo para
se prouer, no esperase ora en que tomase el consejo nece-
sario, e no el que agora tenía voluntario. Visto por este cauallero el temor que los suyos mostrauan. No—dixo él—, suele
vencer la muchedunbre de los moros al esfuerço de los cristianos cuando son buenos, aunque no sean tantos: la buena
fortuna del cauallero crece cresciendo su esfuerço: e si a estos
moros que vienen cumple socorrer a su infortunio, a nosotros
conuiene permanecer en nuestra vitoria fasta la acabar o mo-

rir, porque si el miedo de los moros nos fiziese desanparar
esta cibdad, ganada ya con tanta sangre, iusta culpa nos por-
nían los cristianos por no auer esperado su socorro; es mejor
que sean ellos culpados por no venir, que nosotros por no
esperar. De una cosa—dixo él—, sed ciertos: que entre tanto
que Dios me diere vida, nunca el moro me porná miedo,
porque tengo tal confiança, en Dios e en vuestras fuerças, que
no fallecerán peleando, veyendo vuestro capitán pelear. Este
cauallero duró, e fizo durar a los suyos conbatiendo a los
moros que tenía cercados, e resistiendo a los moros que le
tenían cercado por espacio de dos días, fasta que vino el socorro que esperaua, e ouo el fruto que suelen auer aquellos
que permanescen en la virtud de la fortaleza.

Ganada aquella cibdad, e dexado en ella por capitán a un
su hermano llamado Gómes Manrrique, ganó otras fortalezas
en la comarca; socorrió muchas vezes algunas cibdades e villas
e capitanes cristianos en tienpo de estrema necesidad; e fizo
tanta guerra en aquellas tierras, que en el reino de Granada
el nonbre de Rodrigo Manrrique fué mucho tiempo a los moros grand terror.

Cercó asimismo este cauallero la fortaleza de Alcaráz, por
la reduzir a la corona real. Cercó la fortaleza de Uclés, por la
reduzir a la su orden de Santiago. Esperó en estos dos sitios
las gentes que contra él vinieron a socorrer estas fortalezas:
e como quier que la gente contraria vido ser en mucho mayor
número que la suya, mostró tal esfuerço, que los contrarios
no le osaron acometer, e él consiguió con grand honrra el fin
de aquellas empresas que tomó: dó se puede bien creer que
venció, más con el esfuerço de su ánimo, que con el número
de su gente.

Ouo asimismo este cauallero otras batallas e fechos de armas con cristianos y con moros, que requerían grand estoria
si de cada una por estenso se ouiese de azer minción: porque
toda la mayor parte de su vida trabajó en guerras e en fechos
de armas.

Fablaua muy bien, e deleitáuase en recontar los casos que
le acaescían en las guerras.

Usaua de tanta liberalidad, que no bastaua su renta a sus

gastos; ni le bastára si muy grandes rentas e tesoros touiera, segund la continuación que touo en las guerras.

Era varón de altos pensamientos, e inclinado a cometer grandes e peligrosas fazañas, e no podía sofrir cosa que le paresciese no sofridera, e desta condición se le siguieron grandes peligros e molestias. E ciertamente por esperiencia veemos pasar por grandes infortunios a muchos que presumen forçar la fuerça del tienpo, los cuales, por no sofrir una sola cosa, les acaesce sofrir muchas, e a muchos a quien de fuerça an de tener contentos para conseguir su poco sofrimiento.

Era amado por los caualleros de la orden de Santiago, los cuales, visto que concurrían en él todas las cosas dignas de aquella dignidad, le eligieron por maestre en la prouincia de Castilla por fin del maestre don Juan Pacheco.

Murió con grand honrra en hedad de setenta años.

APPENDIX B

Satiric Poetry

It is to be expected that in a time of social decay and political dissension poets would turn their attention to social criticism. Some of the most interesting poems of the fifteenth-century *cancioneros* are satires. Yet satire must have had little appeal for Jorge Manrique. Only three of his poems are satirical. Interestingly, all three are attacks on women, and all three subvert the courtly code to their ends. Though critics pass over them quickly, as if they were an aberration in an otherwise serious poet, they are also unexpectedly good.

The first, "A vna prima suya que le estoruaua vnos amores," views a love affair as the playing of an instrument which, if all parts are properly tuned, will produce a sweet melody:

> Quanto el bien tenprar concierta
> al buen tañer y conuiene,
> tanto daña y desconcierta
> la prima falsa que tiene;
> pues no aprouecha tenplalla,   5

ni por ello mejor suena,
por no estar en esta pena,
muy mejor sera quebralla
que pensar hazella buena.
(*Cancionero* 79)

The lover, however, is bothered by the discordant note of
a *prima* (the string highest in pitch, but also the word for
cousin). Since the *prima* will not be reduced to harmony by
being tuned (the verb used is *templar* which means both to
tune [or temper] and to make love), he concludes that it is
better to play without that string than to keep hearing its
odious note. The poem reveals an aspect of courtly service
suppressed in the courtly lyric itself. The favor sought by the
poet is undeniably sexual. To obtain it, he uses his instrument,
which, on the metaphoric level is a symbol of his song or
request, and on the real (if we accept the explanation of the
poem contained in the rubric) includes those around him who
take part in his courting. The betrayal of the string (*prima*),
destroys his song at the metaphoric level, and the betrayal of
his cousin (*prima*), destroys his suit at the real level. All of
this transpires in a rather cynical atmosphere. The *prima*'s
failure can be attributed to jealousy. The poet is willing to
silence her by making love to her in contravention of all
courtly rules, and failing that, he is not above murder!

The second poem, "Coplas a vna beuda que tenia empe-
ñado vn brial en la tauerna," is dedicated to a woman who
had dared to speak ill of the poet, and who is accused of
drunkenness. She has given up her velvet skirt as surety to
a tavern keeper for the wine that she consumes. The garment
that she gives up, which proclaims her gentility, now passes
into the hands of the tavern keeper's wife.[1]

The poem consists of five octosyllabic eight-line stanzas.
The first introduces the lady, the other four describe her mock
prayer to a series of saints (Valdeiglesias, Madrigal, Villareal,
Yepes, Coca, Luque, Baeza, Ubeda), which are really towns
famous for their wines.

The third is a longer composition more closely associated

with Manrique's private life. It is called the "Combite que hizo don Jorge Manrique a su madrastra," and describes a mock banquet given by the poet in honor of doña Elvira de Castañeda.[2]

As we have seen in chapter 1, relations between don Rodrigo's sons by his first marriage and the young countess of Paredes were probably not very good. After the *maestre*'s death, the countess of Paredes and the Manriques disputed the contents of the will. The case was not settled until 1485. The "Combite" was therefore probably written between 1476 and 1479.

The poem opens with an exhortation to the countess to prepare herself for a banquet:

> I Señora muy acabada:
> tened vuestra gente presta
> que la triste ora es llegada
> de la muy solemne fiesta.
> (*Cancionero* 81)

She is invited to enter the house by climbing a wall that leads to a dungheap. From there she proceeds to the poet's palace, a house without a roof, covered with cobwebs, and floored with nettles. She is taken to a reception room, furnished in the basest manner, where she waits to enter the banquet hall (stanzas 1-6). The banquet table is covered with a coarse cloth made of tow, the napkins are really undergarments, taken—we infer—from the naked attending servants. Only the poet retains his underclothes, albeit devoid of sleeves and collar, which were generally made of better quality cloth or lace, since they were the only parts to show. The rest of his apparel is old and worn (stanzas 7-8).

The banquet begins with soup, followed by a salad of wild onions, tow and frog heads dressed with gall, vinegar, and rose oil, and tossed in an old helmet. Then come the meats: a rooster in a pot, a hen with its chicks, two rabbits, birds cooked with their nests and fledglings—all accompanied by rice cooked in grease wrung from an old collar. Dessert consists of a tart made with lime and sand (stanzas 9-12).

At the end of the banquet a bizarrely dressed woman appears, perhaps to accompany the guests back to their houses:

XIII   La fiesta ya fenescida,
entrará luego vna dueña
con vna hacha encendida,
d'aquellas de partir leña,   100
con dos velas sin pauilos,
hechas de cera d'orejas;
las pestañas y las cejas
bien cosidas con dos hilos.

XIV   Y en ell un pie dos chapines   105
y en ell otro vna chinela;
en las manos escarpines
y tañendo vna vihuela:
un tocino por tocado;
por sartales vn raposo;   110
un braço desconyuntado
y el otro todo velloso.

XV   Y vna saya de sayal
forrada en peña tajada,
y vna pescada cicial   115
de la garganta colgada,
y vn balandrán rocegante
hecho de nueva manera:
las haldas todas delante
las nalgas todas de fuera.   120
(*Cancionero* 85-86)

The poem mocks doña Elvira by turning upside down the conventions of hospitality, and the duty owed to the lady as woman and mother. It does so by an inversion of the language and topics of courtly love. Doña Elvira is a "señora muy acabada," her ladies move "al trote," they go to a "triste fiesta," which they must enter not through the main gate, but over a wall. Once inside the house, they are placed in a "rincón" of the narrator's house and not in the place of honor. The poverty of the household perhaps alludes to the penury of Jorge Manrique, who had served don Rodrigo so long, but who was not generously remembered in his father's will.

NOTES

Preface

1. Juan Nícolás Böhl de Faber's anthology of early Castilian verse, for example, ends the *Coplas* with stanza XXIV. *Floresta de rimas antiguas castellanas*, 3 vols. (Hamburg, 1821) 1: 147-51. See below, chapter 3.

2. M. Menéndez Pelayo, *Historia de la poesía castellana en la edad media*, edited by Adolfo Bonilla y San Martín, 3 vols. (Madrid, 1914) 2: 393-96. "Las poesías menores de Jorge Manrique son muy poco numerosas, y no han sido coleccionadas nunca. Apreciables todas por la elegancia y limpieza de la versificación, no tienen nada que substancialmente las distinga de los infinitos versos eróticos que son el fondo principal de los Cancioneros, y que más que á la historia de la poesía, interesan á la historia de las costumbres y del trato cortesano. Sin la curiosidad que las presta el nombre de su autor, apenas habría quien reparase en ellas. Pero aunque no pasen de una discreta medianía, se dejan leer sin fastidio, y algo se deduce de ellas que para la biografía de su autor importa." Cejador basically concurred with Menéndez Pelayo. Jorge Manrique's poetic compositions, he said, "son como las comunes de sus coetáneos." Julio Cejador y Frauca, *Historia de la lengua y de la literatura castellana*, 13 vols. (Madrid, 1915) 1: 366. Romera Navarro calls him "uno de tantos poetas agudos y esmerados de los Cancioneros." M. Romera Navarro, *Historia de la literatura española* (Boston, 1928) 72.

3. Jaime Fitzmaurice-Kelly, *Historia de la literatura española*, tr. and enlarged by Adolfo Bonilla y San Martín, 7th ed. (Madrid, 1901?) 165.

4. R. Foulché-Delbosc, ed., *Cancionero castellano del siglo XV* 2 vols. (Madrid, 1915) 2: 632-33. Cited hereafter in the text as *Cancionero castellano*.

5. *Cancioneiro Geral de García de Resende*, edited by Andrée Crabbé Rocha, 5 vols. (Lisbon, 1973) 1: 52:

> Per boa confirmaçam
> que temos de Joam de mena,
> Joam rrodriguez del Padram,
> Manrrique, & quantos sam,
> ha[n] sospiros por moor pena.

6. "Fiestas de amor," *Cancionero de don Pedro Manuel de Urrea* (Logroño, 1513) fol. 18, quoted from Bartolomé José Gallardo, *Ensayo de una biblioteca española de libros raros y curiosos*, 4 vols. (Madrid, 1888-89) 4: 840-41.

7. Juan del Encina, *Obras completas*, edited by Ana María Rambaldo (Madrid, 1978) 47-48.

8. María Rosa Lida de Malkiel, "Una copla de Jorge Manrique y la tradición de Filón en la literatura española," *Revista de filología hispánica* 4 (1942): 167.

9. Pedro Salinas, *Jorge Manrique o tradición y originalidad*, 4th ed. (Buenos Aires, 1970) 189. All references to Manrique's poetry are to this edition and are noted in the text as *Cancionero* followed by the page number(s) in which the quoted material appears.

10. When this book was finished I received a copy of Serrano de Haro's new edition of the poetry: *Jorge Manrique: obras* (Madrid, 1986). Serrano's edition has a more complete critical apparatus for the *Coplas* than Cortina's, but he does not indicate which text, if any, he used as base.

1. The Historical Setting

1. The bibliography about the Trastámara period is extensive. For a more complete discussion see: Luis Suárez Fernández, *Juan I, rey de Castilla, 1379-1390* (Madrid, 1955); idem, *Los Trastámaras de Castilla y Aragón en el siglo XV, Historia de España*, Vol. 15 (Madrid, 1964) 1-318; idem, *Nobleza y monarquía: puntos de vista sobre la historia política castellana del siglo XV* (Valladolid, 1959; rev. ed. 1975); idem, "La crisis del siglo XIV en Castilla," in *La mutación de la segunda mitad del siglo XIV, Cuadernos de historia* 8 (Madrid, 1977) 33-45; Eloy Benito Ruano, *Los Infantes de Aragón* (Pamplona, 1952); Joaquín Gimeno Casalduero, *La imagen del monarca en la Castilla del siglo XIV: Pedro el Cruel, Enrique II, y Juan I* (Madrid, 1972); Inez Isabel Macdonald, *Don Fernando de Antequera* (Oxford, 1948); William D. Phillips, Jr., *Enrique IV and the Crisis of Fifteenth Century Castile, 1425-1480* (Cambridge, Mass., 1978); Julio Valdeón Baruque, *Enrique II de Castilla* (Valladolid, 1966); idem, *Los judíos de Castilla y la revolución Trastámara* (Valladolid, 1966); idem, *Los conflictos sociales en el reino de Castilla en los siglos XIV y XV* (Madrid, 1975); Jaime Vicens Vives, *Juan II de Aragón, 1398-1479: Monarquía y revolución en la España del siglo XV* (Barcelona, 1953); idem, *El segle XV, els Trastamares* (Barcelona, 1956). For an introduction to the life and reign of Isabel see Tarsicio de Azcona's *Isabel la Católica* (Madrid, 1964).

2. Salvador de Moxó, "De la nobleza vieja a la nobleza nueva: La trans-formación nobiliaria castellana en la baja Edad Media," in *Estudios sobre la sociedad castellana en la baja Edad Media, Cuadernos de historia* 3 (Madrid, 1969) 1-210. Moxó calls "old nobility" those families that existed in Castile before the fourteenth century and participated in the thirteenth-century reconquest of Andalusia. Documentation about these families begins to appear in the twelfth century. They were divided into two groups: the *magnates* or *ricos-hombres* and the *hidalgos* or *caballeros*. The first were the most important, because their actions had a national impact. These families generally held no title of nobility other than that of *ricahombría*. They were distinguished by their wealth, their lineage, and their employment in public office—the latter being a necessary supplement to their manorial incomes. These old clans became extinct in the fourteenth century (at least in their major branches) from natural causes (low fertility, endogamy, plagues), death in battles, and the persecutions of Alfonso XI, Pedro I, and Enrique of Trastámara. For further discussion see Stephen Haliczer, "The Castilian Aristocracy and the Mercedes Reform of 1478-1482," *Hispanic American Historical Review* 55 (1975): 449-67; Roger Highfield, "The Catholic Kings and the Titled Nobility of Cas-tile," in *Europe in the Late Middle Ages*, edited by J.R. Hale, J.R.L. Highfield, and B. Smalley (Evanston, Ill., 1965) 358-85; Salvador de Moxó, "El señorío, legado medieval," *Cuadernos de historia* 1 (1967): 105-18; idem, "Los señoríos. En torno a una problemática para el estudio del régimen señorial," *Hispania* 24 (1964): 185-236; Emilio Mitre Fernández, *Evolución de la nobleza en Castilla bajo Enrique III, 1396-1406* (Valladolid, 1968). The unusual munificence of the Trastámaras was amply recognized by their contemporaries. Pero Ferrús, in a poem written between 1379 and 1382, has the dead Enrique II say: "Nunca yo cese de guerras / treynta anos contynuados; / conquery gentes e tierras / e gane nobles rregnados; / fiz ducados e condados / e muy altos señorios, / e di a estraños e a mios / mas que todos los pasados" [*Cancionero de Baena*, 3 vols., edited by J.M. Azáceta (Madrid, 1966) 2: 657]. Ferrús could not foresee that other Trastámaras would outstrip Enrique II in generosity.

3. For a discussion of the nature of the Order of Santiago see below, note 11.

4. Doña Leonor was the posthumous daughter of a brother of Enrique II and Beatriz of Portugal.

5. He became king of Navarre in 1425 and king of Aragón at the death of his brother Alfonso V.

6. The youngest, don Pedro, did not receive much, nor did he achieve great prominence. There were also two daughters: María, who married Juan II of Castile, and Leonor, who married don Duarte of Portugal.

7. Moxó, "De la nobleza" 145-52. Serrano de Haro assembled most of what is known about the Manriques in *Personalidad y destino de Jorge Manrique* (Madrid, 1975). The fundamental work on the family, however, was done centuries ago, as part of Luis de Salazar y Castro's monumental *Historia genealógica de la Casa de Lara* (Madrid, 1697). It is to Salazar y Castro that these brief biographies of Jorge, Rodrigo, and Pedro Manrique are most indebted.

One must, however, be suspicious of the information given by Salazar about the origins of noble families. Genealogists and historians of the period courted the good will of patrons, who invariably wanted to trace their ancestry as far back as possible.

8. Medieval Spanish names followed no set rules. Normally a son would add to his own name that of his father, distinguishing the latter by the patronymic ending -ez (son of). Thus Manrique Pérez would be Manrique, son of Pero (Peter). Some families added to this a place name closely associated with them and distinguished by de: Manrique Pérez de Lara (Manrique, son of Pero of the city of Lara). In time, the village or *solar* of provenance became part of the family name. Very early on a few families, like the Manriques, began to use what can be properly called a last name, usually to indicate descent from a famous ancestor (Manric). The system can be complicated by the practice of naming some of the children of a marriage with the mother's name, or with the name of some ancestor who belonged to a related family. For example, doña Elvira de Castañeda and doña Guiomar de Meneses, both daughters of Pero López de Ayala, do not carry their father's name. Fortunately, the Manrique family usually did not follow this practice. They did, however, show a marked preference for certain given names that repeat themselves from generation to generation. Around the middle of the fifteenth century the family began to adopt some names of French, Italian, and Aragonese origin. Jorge Manrique seems to be the first to bear that name, perhaps because of his father's close allegiance to Aragón, whose patron saint is Saint George. His own children, Luis and Luisa, bear names that become popular in the late fifteenth century.

9. The courtship (or marriage?) is celebrated in a composition of Villasandino, *Cancionero de Baena* 1: 32.

10. Contemporary biographical sketches of Pedro and Rodrigo Manrique survive. See Appendix A.

11. The military Order of Santiago was subdivided into mayor commanderies ruled by *comendadores mayores*, five by the thirteenth century: Castile, León, Aragón, Portugal, and Gascony. Of these, Castile and León were the most important. From the beginning, many of the commanderies were carved out of Moorish territory. With Fernando III's conquest of Andalusia, the focus of the order shifted to its new and vast land holdings in the South, an area roughly delimited by Estepa, Medina Sidonia, and Segura de la Sierra. Segura was a sensitive point on the Moorish border. In 1245 the major commandery of Castile was transferred to it from Uclés. The basic study of the order is Derek W. Lomax's *La Orden de Santiago* (Madrid, 1965), to which one must go for complete bibliographic references. Also useful are: Francisco de Rades y Andrada, *Crónica de las tres órdenes y cavallerías de Sanctiago, Calatrava y Alcantara* (Toledo, 1572; facs. rep. Barcelona: El Albir, 1980); Eloy Benito Ruano, *Estudios santiaguistas* (León, 1978); and José Luis Martín, *Orígenes de la orden militar de Santiago, 1170-1195* (Barcelona, 1974).

12. Another of Santillana's sisters, Juana de Mendoza, was married to Diego Gómez Manrique, the great-grandfather of Manrique. Of doña Mencía,

Salazar y Castro says that she died before 1445 and was buried in the church of Nuestra Señora de la Peña, not far from Segura. From there her son Pedro, second count of Paredes, had the remains moved to Uclés, fearing that, because of the church's proximity to the frontier with Granada, they might some day be desecrated (Salazar y Castro, *Historia* X: 317-18).

13. Pacheco, for example, imposed his brother's ten-year-old son, Rodrigo Téllez Girón as master of Calatrava and obtained a papal dispensation to rule the order himself during his nephew's minority.

14. Doña Elvira brought Rodrigo Manrique a considerable dowry. As security for it, he gave his towns of Belmontejo and Parrilla. When he had to dispose of part of his holdings to cover the expenses incurred in the siege of Uclés, he arranged in his will that doña Elvira receive the money owed him by Fernando and Isabel.

15. The marriage took place in 1469. According to doña Elvira's testament, she had three sons by don Rodrigo: Enrique, commander of Carrizosa for Santiago; Rodrigo, commander of Manzanares and Villarrubia (not to be confused with Rodrigo Manrique, commander of Yeste and Taivilla, third son of don Rodrigo Manrique and doña Mencía); and Alonso, cardinal of Spain. They would have known the poet Jorge Manrique only as very small children. Of these youngest sons of don Rodrigo, Enrique, the oldest, inherited his mother's estates. Rodrigo held the commanderies mentioned. Alonso is by far the most interesting. Like his uncle Iñigo Manrique, who was bishop of Seville, Alonso joined the Church. He was made bishop of Badajoz by Isabel in 1499. His activities against Fernando after the death of the queen led to a brief period of imprisonment. After the improvement of relations between the Austrias and the king of Aragón, Alonso left for the Low Countries. He served Charles V as chaplain, and in time he was made bishop of Córdoba (1516), archbishop of Seville, grand inquisitor, and cardinal (1531). He died in 1538. See Salazar y Castro, *Historia* I: 14; also, *Diccionario de historia eclesiástica de España,* edited by Quintín Aldea Vaquero, et al. (Madrid, 1972) 2: 1408; and, l'abbé C.B., *Dictionnaire des cardinaux* (Paris, 1857) 1183. After the death of Jorge Manrique's son, Luis Manrique, Alonso tried to obtain, without avail, the commandery of Montizón for his brother Rodrigo (Simancas, Memoriales, Cámara de Castilla).

16. The Trece elected the master of Santiago and helped to rule the order. They met for important decisions at either San Marcos de León or Uclés.

17. The Aragonese were encamped behind the city walls of Olmedo. The chronicles relate how Prince Enrique approached the city from the nearby royal camp to see the disposition of the enemy troops. The Aragonese saw a good opportunity to capture the crown prince and quickly sallied forth, forcing Enrique to flee. Juan II, offended by the boldness of the invaders, ordered his troops to attack, and in the fighting that ensued, several men died. The battle was decisively won by Juan II. Rodrigo Manrique took a prominent part in the encounter on the side of the insurgents, a fact not flatteringly recalled in the *Coplas de la panadera,* an anonymous satiric poem written shortly after the battle:

Con lengua brava parlera
y corazon de alfenique
el comendador Manrique
escogio bestia ligera
e dio tan gran corredera
fuyendo muy a desora
que seis leguas en un ora
dexo tras si la barrera.

18. Salazar y Castro, *Historia* X: 294, and "Pruebas del Libro X" 385-87. Salazar maintains that Rodrigo Manrique had a clear right to be master of Santiago, and that the Pope confirmed his claim, thanks to the intercession of Alfonso V of Aragón. See also Diego de Valera, *Memorial de varias hazañas*, edited by Juan de Mata Carriazo (Madrid, 1941) 279.

19. Salazar y Castro (*Historia* X: 299) summarizes the accord whereby Enrique IV accepted the succession of Alfonso and released him into the custody of the marquess of Villena. The incident reveals how far Enrique IV was willing, or was forced, to go in order to avoid a confrontation with his opponents.

20. Alonso de Palencia, *Crónica de Enrique IV*, ed. and trans. by A. Paz y Melia, 5 vols. (Madrid, 1905) 1: 457-59.

21. The nobles who wished to succeed the marquess of Villena were his son, Diego López Pacheco, the duke of Medina Sidonia, the count of Benavente, and the marquess of Santillana. None were members of the order, so technically they were not qualified. Among the members, the postulants were the duke of Alburquerque, the count of Osorno, don Alonso de Cárdenas, Diego Alvarado, and Rodrigo Manrique. In a move that presaged the solution to the problem posed by the military orders, Queen Isabel requested that the Pope vest her with the administration of Santiago.

22. He died, according to Palencia, from a cancerous sore that consumed his face.

23. Serrano de Haro, *Personalidad y destino* 60.

24. Salazar y Castro, "Pruebas," 414. See also note 12.

25. Recently, Enrique Toral Peñaranda has maintained that Siles, a dependance of Segura, was the probable site of the birth in his book *Ubeda 1442-1550* (Jaén, 1975) 44. He offers no documentation to support his statement.

26. José Martín Jiménez, "Filiación de los linajes de Jorge Manrique (consideraciones sobre el lugar de su nacimiento, su fisonomía moral y su personalidad literaria," *Boletín de la Real Academia de Córdoba de Ciencia, Bellas Letras y Nobles Artes* 38 (1969 [1972]): 183-207.

27. *Crónica del halconero de Juan II, Pedro Carrillo de Huete*, edited by Juan de Mata Carriazo (Madrid, 1946) 347-8.

28. Tierra de Campos and Palencia, so closely identified with the Manriques, are also occasionally mentioned as possible birthplaces. Another city closely identified with Jorge Manrique, though not as a birthplace, is Toledo.

In that city he married and was captain of the Hermandades. Toledo has a portrait of him that Francisco Caravaca attributes to Pedro Berruguete or a disciple in "¿Quién fue el autor del retrato de Jorge Manrique?" *Papeles de son Armadans* 65 (1972): 89-99. Pedro Berruguete and his son Alonso were born in Paredes de Nava, and it is known that Pedro dwelt for some time in Toledo toward the end of Jorge Manrique's life: Diego Angulo, *Pedro Berruguete en Paredes de Nava* (Barcelona, 1946). If the attribution is correct the likeness of Jorge Manrique may be accurate. Serrano de Haro, however, believes the painting to be of the eighteenth century, *Personalidad y destino* 145.

29. Serrano de Haro's biography, *Personalidad y destino*, does a plausible job of reconstructing what Manrique's childhood may have been like.

30. Eloy Benito Ruano, "Algunas rentas de Jorge Manrique," *Hispania* 25 (1965): 114.

31. See pp. 69-70, 112-13.

32. Palencia, *Crónica de Enrique IV* 1: 284 and 2: 362. Gómez Manrique remembers the death of Garcilasso in some very moving lines. "Defunzion del noble cauallero Garcilasso dela Vega," in Foulché-Delbosc, *Cancionero castellano* 2: 28-33.

33. On Diego's death see A. Pretel Marín, *Una ciudad castellana en los siglos XIV y XV. Alcáraz, 1300-1475* (Albacete, 1978) 156-60.

34. *Hechos del condestable don Miguel Lucas de Iranzo*, edited by Juan de Mata Carriazo (Madrid, 1940) 405.

35. Lucas de Iranzo also tried to exchange Montizón for the archbishop of Toledo's nephew, Fernando de Acuña, who had fallen into his hands, but don Rodrigo was not about to release the castle and its strategic lands as ransom for anyone. *Hechos del condestable* 480.

36. E. Benito Ruano, "Autógrafos de Jorge Manrique," *Archivum* 18 (1968): 107-16. The documents are interesting because they reflect a moment in the poet's life during which he was caught between the desires of his father to become master and the wishes of the pretender, don Alfonso, that Pacheco (the marquess of Villena) hold that office. The first document is dated August 28, 1467, before the capitulation of the fortress. It explains that Manrique had received a letter from the prior of Uclés and the Trece informing him of the election of Pacheco, and another letter from the master, demanding that Manrique pay hommage to him for Montizón. In his reply, contained in the same document, Jorge Manrique explains that the fortress was not yet in his hands, but that he would render hommage to Pacheco within sixty days of its capitulation. The second document names a vassal of don Rodrigo to stand in Jorge Manrique's stead and swear fealty to Pacheco. It is dated November 15, 1467.

37. Benito Ruano, "Autógrafos" 111-12.

38. Serrano de Haro, *Personalidad y destino* 196-200.

39. "Relacion que hizo Francisco de Leon, comendador de Bastimentos de Leon, de su mandado, al mui magnífico y virtuoso señor don Alonso de Cardenas, maestre de la orden, de las villas, fortalezas y encomiendas que le pertenecían con arreglo a la visita que hizo el señor maestre don Juan

Pacheco. Año de 1468," Archivo Histórico Nacional, Ordenes militares, 1233C. The same document reveals that in addition to Montizón and Chiclana, Jorge Manrique also received part of the rents of Belmonte de la Sierra and Torre de Juan Abad.

40. The couple had two children. Luis succeeded his father as commander of Montizón and was also a Trece. Luisa married Manuel de Benavides, lord of Javalquinto and Espeluy (Salazar y Castro, "Pruebas" 443). It is not known if Luis had any children, though it is unlikely that he had male issue because, as mentioned, after his death his uncle Alonso (the cardinal) attempted to have Montizón vested on Luis's brother Rodrigo (Simancas, Memoriales, Cámara de Castilla). Luis was eventually a *veinticuatro* of Granada and one of the witnesses of the last will and testament of Gonzalo Fernández de Córdoba. Luisa had at least one daughter, Mencía Manrique de Benavides, who married don García de Toledo. In her will of 1506, Elvira de Castañeda stipulates that in the case of the death of her son Enrique and descendants, or of her nephew Pedro López de Ayala and descendants, her estate was to go to Luisa Manrique, daughter of Jorge and Guiomar.

41. Benito Ruano, "Algunas rentas" 116-17.

42. *Relaciones de los pueblos de España ordenadas por Felipe II*, edited by Carmelo Viñas and Ramón Paz (Madrid, 1963) 2, pt. 3: 524. Rodrigo Manrique's residence was in the parish of San Román, where Jorge Manrique probably also resided when in the city. His palace may have been part of the properties that by the mid-sixteenth century belonged to doña Luisa de la Cerda and were frequently visited by Santa Teresa de Jesús. See Linda Martz and Julio Porres Martín Cleto, *Toledo en 1561* (Toledo, 1974) 126; Luis Salazar de Mendoza, *Crónica del cardenal don Juan Tavera* (Toledo, 1603) 387; Efren de la Madre de Dios, OCD, and O. Stegginck, O. Carm., *Tiempo y vida de Santa Teresa* (Madrid, 1968) 352ff; and E. Benito Ruano, *Toledo en el siglo XV* (Madrid, 1960).

43. Salazar y Castro, "Pruebas" 400-407. The estate was not settled during the life of the second count of Paredes. It was finally settled by doña Leonor de Acuña, his widow in 1485.

Throughout this period it was Gómez Manrique who seems to have taken most to heart the dying request of his brother Rodrigo to protect the countess and their young sons. Gómez stipulated in his testament that if his granddaughters died without issue, his estate was to go to Enrique Manrique; if he died, then it was to go to Alonso, and then to don Rodrigo. Because Alonso was a priest and Rodrigo a knight of Calatrava, the failure of Enrique to have issue would have eventually brought Gómez's estate to the counts of Paredes. Gómez Manrique's pain at the death of his brother in 1476 and of Jorge in 1479 is expressed in an answer to the *Carta consolatoria* that the protonotario Juan de Lucena sent to him on the occasion of the death of Gómez's daughter Catalina. Lucena mentions the passing of so many of Gómez's relatives, among them don Rodrigo and Jorge. Gómez responds: "me amenguays diziendo en el comienço con quanto viril coraçón sofrí los infortunios passados de las muertes de tales y tantos ermanos y sobrinos, en especial del señor don Rodrigo Manrique, mi señor y ermano, tan digna de ser sentida, y la de aquel hijo con tanta razón de ser querido, tanto que yo era ensemplo de consolación a todos atribuyéndome muy grandes y muy bien dichos lohores, haziéndolos más crecidos por acrecentar mi fortaleza, conformándovos con aquel dicho que dize que la virtud alabada cresce." Biblioteca Nacional ms 22021, fols. 3r-8v, printed in "Gómez Manrique y el protonotario Lucena," *Revista de archivos, bibliotecas y museos* 81 (1978): 564-82.

44. See Appendix B.

45. Palencia, *Crónica de Enrique IV* 2: 362-63.

46. Palencia, *Crónica de Enrique IV* 2: 361; Galíndez de Carvajal, *Crónica de Enrique IV*, edited by Juan Torres Fontes (Murcia, 1946) 395-96; Valera, *Memorial* 181.

47. Salazar y Castro, *Historia* 2: 310 and 408.

48. This event provides a rare glimpse into Jorge Manrique's marital life. After the poet's death, doña Guiomar asked for the return of the dowry, or the observance of the marriage settlement whereby she was to receive an undetermined income from certain towns that had belonged to don Rodrigo. The towns had been used to pay for the military campaigns in the marquisate of Villena. In her deposition doña Guiomar wrote that she was pressured by her husband into accepting the sale against her will: "el dicho maestre de Santiago (don Rodrigo Manrique) queriendo disponer de los dichos vasallos la fizo contra toda su voluntad e que por temor suyo que ella oviese de consentir en la de venta e que ella viendo su gran poder e mando e asimismo del dicho D. Jorge su marido a quien no le convenía en cosa contradecir sin que ella recibiera gran peligro de su persona e causa a le dar mala vida continuo dix que quixo mas secretamente dando reclamo de la dicha fuerza et miedo que así se le facía e dix que ovo de prestar consentimiento a la tal venta contra toda su voluntad." Serrano de Haro, *Personalidad y destino* 142.

49. Palencia, *Crónica de Enrique IV* 4: 375; also, Serrano de Haro, *Personalidad y destino* 180-92.

50. Fernando and Isabel revived the Santa Hermandad, an institution that was in decay, to counterbalance the power of the great nobles. The Santa Hermandad began in 1476 in the city of Burgos and was rapidly adopted by other cities in the realm. See Antonio Alvarez Morales, *Las hermandades, expresión del movimiento comunitario en España* (Valladolid, 1974). Jorge Manrique's presence in the Hermandad of Toledo, though not documented before 1478, coincides with Gómez's appointment as *corregidor* (mayor) of the city. Serrano de Haro, *Personalidad y destino* 273.

51. Pedro de Baeza in *Memorial histórico español: colección de documentos, opúsculos y antigüedades* (Madrid, 1853) 5: 503-504. The event is also amply described in Alonso de Palencia's *Fourth Decade*. See Richard P. Kinkade, "The Historical Date of the *Coplas* and the Death of Jorge Manrique," *Speculum* 45 (1970): 216-24; and, J. Labrador, A. Zorita, and R.A. Difranco, "Cuarenta y dos, y no cuarenta coplas en la famosa elegía manriqueña," *Boletín de la Biblioteca Menéndez Pelayo* 61 (1985): 37-95. Labrador, et al., agree with Kin-

kade's interpretation of Palencia's evidence about the composition of the *Coplas*. According to them, the *Coplas* were composed, though not necessarily in a final version that satisfied the poet, shortly before the siege of Garci-muñoz. Hernando del Pulgar's *Crónica de los reyes católicos don Fernando y doña Isabel* (Madrid, 1953) 339, reveals that reprisals on both sides followed the death of Jorge Manrique. Though the chronicle does not directly relate the reprisals to Manrique's death, they are so presented in a *romance* printed in 1550. See Alonso de Fuentes, *Libro de los cuarenta cantos de diuersas e peregrinas historias* (Sevilla: Domenico de Robertis, 1550); also, A. Durán. *Romancero general* (Madrid, 1921) 2: 67.

52. The day was not generally known until Derek Lomax, in a review of Serrano de Haro's book on Manrique, *Bulletin of Hispanic Studies* 44 (1967): 287-88, revealed that the exact date was given in the Calendar of Uclés. The Calendar is a list of all the religious feasts and saints' days of the year. The friars wrote between the lines the names of the benefactors of the order for whom they had to pray. Among them is Jorge Manrique, with the notation that he died on the twenty-fourth of April, 1479.

53. Their recollections are incorporated into the *Relaciones de los pueblos de España*, but they are suspect. See J. Labrador et al., 47-48.

54. See Dimas Pérez Ramírez, *Uclés, último destino de Jorge Manrique* (Cuenca, 1979).

2. The Minor Lyrics

1. For a list of the extant manuscripts see J. Steunou and L. Knapp, *Bibliografía de los cancioneros castellanos del siglo XV y repertorio de sus géneros*, 2 vols. (Paris, 1975-78); J. González, "Cancioneros manuscritos del prerenacimiento," *Revista de literatura* 40 (1978): 177-215; Brian Dutton, "Spanish Fifteenth-Century *Cancioneros*: A General Survey to 1465," *Kentucky Romance Quarterly* 26 (1979): 445-60; and the fundamental *Catálogo índice de la poesía cancioneril del siglo XV* (Madison, Wisc., 1982).

2. The most important authors of the thirteenth and the fourteenth centuries, Alfonso X, don Juan Manuel, and Juan Ruiz wrote lyrics in Castilian. Their Castilian lyric production, however, cannot compare in quantity with that of fifteenth-century lyric poets.

3. For Antony van Beysterveldt the tardy appearance of courtly love in Castile seems to be a result of socio-religious circumstances: *La poesía amatoria del siglo XV y el teatro de Juan del Encina* (Madrid, 1972) 102. There are, however, economic reasons as well. The appearance of great estates in private hands provided resources not previously available to nobles who were not members of the royal family.

4. See Roger Boase, *The Troubadour Revival: A Study of Social Change and Traditionalism in Late Medieval Spain* (London, 1978).

5. John G. Cummins, "Pero Guillén de Segovia y el MS 4.114." *Hispanic Review* 41 (1973) 6ff.

6. All citations of Manrique's poetry are taken from A. Cortina's *Jorge*

Manrique: cancionero, 4th edition (Madrid, 1960). They are noted as *Cancionero* in the body of the text. Numbers refer to pages in Cortina's edition.

7. Because few of Manrique's lyric poems survive in manuscript form, editors have relied on the *Cancionero general* of Hernando del Castillo (Seville, 1511; edited by A. Rodríguez Moñino, Madrid, 1958) for the texts of Manrique's minor lyrics. The 1511 edition of Hernando del Castillo's anthology attributes forty-two poems to Manrique. The second edition (1514) drops "Alla veras mis sentidos," "Guay d'aquel que nunca tiende," "Ni miento ni m'arrepiento," and "Quanto mas pienso serviros," but adds three: "Cada vez que mi memoria," "No tardes muerte, que muero," and "Por vuestro gran merescer." The 1535 edition (Sevilla: Juan Cromberger) adds the *Coplas* and "Oh mundo pues que nos matas." Only one poem, "Con tantos males guerreo," is of doubtful origin. It follows another poem ascribed to Manrique, but is preceded by an imprecise rubric: "Otra canción." Two poems not included in the editions of the *Cancionero general,* "Mi saber no es para solo" and "O muy alto Dios de Amor," are found in Gómez Manrique's *cancionero* and in an eighteenth century copy of the *Cancionero de Pero Guillén de Segovia.* Both were published by Cortina.

8. P. Le Gentil, *La Poésie lyrique espagnole et portugaise à la fin du moyen âge,* 2 vols. (Rennes, 1949) 1: 461-519. The fictitious debate has its roots in medieval Latin literature and, more specifically, in goliardic poetry. Examples in Castilian poetry are the "Disputa del agua y del vino," and the "Elena y María." The narrative debate is a dialogue that takes place within a larger narrative poem, such as the "Comedieta de Ponça" of the Marqués de Santillana. The *pregunta* evolves through the century from a form often used for discussion of serious themes into a type of occasional poetry. See Rafael Benítez Claros, "El diálogo en la poesía medieval," *Cuadernos de literatura* 5 (1949): 171-87; John Cummins, "Methods and Conventions of the Fifteenth Century Poetic Debate," *Hispanic Review* 31 (1963): 307-231; idem, "The Survival in the Spanish *Cancioneros* of the Form and Themes of Provençal and Old French Poetic Debates," *Bulletin of Hispanic Studies* 42 (1965): 9-17; and especially, José J. Labrador, *Poesía dialogada medieval: La pregunta en el Cancionero de Baena, estudio y antología* (Madrid, 1974).

9. Without a definite hint on the part of the poet, the language of the *preguntas* could be as ambiguous to those to whom it was addressed as it is to us. A *pregunta* of Mossén Crespí de Valdaura, possibly inspired by Manrique's poem, illustrates the point:

> Entre dos fuegos me quemo,   1
> el vno el cuerpo atiza
> y el otro haze ceniza
> ell alma con tal extremo,
> que razon va descompuesta   5
> sin ser la causa d'amores:
> ¿que pena puede ser esta,
> dezid, grandes trobadores?
> (*Cancionero general* 159r)

Mossén Crespí uses the language of the love poetry to create and then defraud certain expectations in his audience. Two fires consume the poet. The first burns and provokes the body (*hacer tiza*, and *atizar*), the second reduces the soul to ashes (*hacer ceniza*); both result in the *descomposición* of *razón* (the unraveling, or unsettling, or overthrow of reason). Just when one expects to be asked about the two types of love, one finds out that the origin of the combustion is not love. What, then, is this pain? The answer given by Mossén Aguilar and Luis Crespí (the son of Mossén Crespí) is that the fire that afflicts the body originates in Mossén Crespí's preference for the *vida activa* (*Cancionero general* 159r). The active life burns the body with worldly cares, and the soul is forlorn because it is separated from God, who is only reached by the *via contemplativa*. One cannot be sure that this interpretation coincides with what Crespí had in mind, though one suspects that it does. But at least Crespí gave clear indication of what he did not want considered. The manner in which he did it, however, shows that he expected his audience to anticipate a question about love.

10. Serrano de Haro, *Personalidad y destino* 231-32 and 280. Serrano also raises the possibility that the poem is about Jorge's difficulties with Fernando and Isabel over the attempted assault on Baena. Guevara's answer would refer to the poet's command of the troops of the Holy Brotherhood of Toledo. Both explanations seem farfetched.

11. *Cancionero general* 1: 630.

12. See, for example, the poems that begin on pages 3, 18, 28, 35, 47, 59, and 60 in Manrique's *Cancionero*.

13. Le Gentil, *La Poésie lyrique* 1: 218ff; Tomás Navarro Tomás, *Métrica española* (Madrid, 1974) 146.

14. There are seven *esparsas* among Manrique's poems. The *canciones*, one of the most popular short lyric forms of the fifteenth-century are represented by eight works.

15. Le Gentil, *La Poésie lyrique* 2: 261ff; Rudolf Baehr, *Manual de versificación española*, tr. K. Wagner and F. López Estrada (Madrid, 1973) 326ff.

16. On the length of the *canción* see Le Gentil, *La Poésie lyrique* 2: 275ff.

17. See, for example, the first two verses of the *vuelta* in "Quien tanto veros dessea."

18. See, for example, "Por vuestro gran merescer" (*Cancionero* 61-62) and "Justa fue mi perdiçión" (*Cancionero* 63-64).

19. Baehr, *Manual* 330ff. See also: Hans Janner, "La glosa española: Estudio histórico de su métrica y de sus temas," *Revista de filología española* 27 (1943) 181-232.

20. J. Huizinga, *Le Déclin du moyen âge* (Paris, 1967) 243.

21. Jorge Manrique's motto is appropriate for an accomplished love poet but not for the other Manriques, who prefer to allude to pride of family. Salazar y Castro cites other *motes* used by the Manriques, among them: "Es de los Manrique, que vienen de los Godos" and "Non descendemos de reyes, sino los reyes de nos." This is an allusion to the descent of the House of Lara from count Fernán González, Salazar y Castro, *Historia* I: 30. A further elaboration of these mottoes can be read on a stone balustrade that leads to

the presbytery of the monastery of the Holy Trinity in Burgos (founded by the first counts of Castañeda): "Manriques, Sangre de Godos, Defensa de los christianos, y espanto de los paganos. Y pues tales sois Manriques, no ay a do poder bolar, sino al cielo a descansar."

22. The *Cancionero general* and the *Cancioneiro Geral de García de Resende* contain sections devoted to *motes*. The rubric of poem 533 of the *Cancionero general*, for example, explains the symbolic meaning of Juan de Lezcano's headgear at a tournament: "Sacó Juan de Lezcano por cimera una luna, seyendo servidor de doña María de Luna y dijo: 'A todos da claridad / sino a mi que la deseo / que sin veros no la veo.' "

The practice of donning symbolic headgear and explaining its significance in a motto or in some lines of verse was very common in fifteenth-century peninsular tournaments. See Le Gentil, *La Poésie lyrique* 1: 214-17. Paolo Giovio in his *Dialogo dell'imprese militare et amorose* (Lyons, 1574), gives several examples of symbolic headgear carried in tournaments by late fifteenth and early sixteenth-century Castilian gentlemen, and even mentions the use of a waterwheel as an *impresa* of the Castilian knight Diego de Guzmán (33-35).

23. Eugene Vance, *Mervelous Signals: Poetics and Sign Theory in the Middle Ages* (Lincoln and London, 1986) 93.

24. Juan Alfonso de Baena, *Cancionero de Baena,* edited by José María Azáceta, 3 vols. (Madrid, 1966) 1: 15.

25. See R. Dragonnetti, *La Technique poétique des trouvères dans la chanson courtoise* (Bruges, 1941); Glynnis M. Cropp, *Le Vocabulaire courtois des troubadours de l'époque classique* (Geneva, 1965); Georges Lavis, *L'Expression de l'affectivité dans la poésie lyrique française du moyen âge (XIIe-XIIIe s.) Etude sémantique et stylistique du réseau lexical 'joie-dolor'* (Paris, 1972); Paul Zumthor, *Essai de poétique médiévale* (Paris, 1972).

26. In "Con el gran mal que me sobra" (30), he says:

> Y como tardé en me dar
> esperando toda afruenta
> después no pude sacar
> partido para quedar
> con alguna fuerą esenta.

27. Diego de Valera, in his *Tratado de providencia contra fortuna*, Biblioteca de autores españoles: *Prosistas castellanos de siglo XV*, 2 vols (Madrid, 1959) 1: 143, advises that the proper maintenance of fortresses is one of the means to allay the attacks of Fortune. He goes on to say that "el mayor e mas principal bastimento, e que mas a tarde se falla, es virtuoso coraçón para las guardar."

28. Rodrigo de Arévalo, when talking about the preparations of a city for war, cites Plato and Aristotle, saying "toda cibdad o reino es como un cuerpo mixto, quiere dezir que es fecho a semejança del cuerpo y persona humana de guisa que, para ser la tal cibdad o reino bien fundado, deve ser semejante a prudente varon." Prudence consists of following good, fleeing evil, and

defending oneself against those who would give offense. He goes on to say that the object of all war is to live virtuously in peace and quiet (*Suma de la política*, Biblioteca de autores españoles: *Prosistas castellanos de siglo XV*, 2 vols. [Madrid, 1959] 1: 267-68).

29. Francisco de Osuna's *Tercer abecedario espiritual* ([Madrid, 1972] 198) uses a similar image to represent the perils of the soul. In the *Abecedario*, the heart, the castle of the soul, is besieged by Carne, Mundo, and Demonio. Castidad, Liberalidad, and Caridad confront them.

30. Reason and Will are the most common personifications found in the lyric and in the doctrinal poetry of the fifteenth century. See, for example, Juan de Mena's "Coplas Contra los Pecados Mortales o Debate de la Razón y la Voluntad" and Gómez Manrique's continuation (*Cancionero castellano* 1: 120-33, 133-52). Mena was among those who believed in the independence of the Will. The opposing viewpoint is found in Fray Iñigo de Mendoza's "Historia de la questión y diferencia que ay entre la Razón y la Sensualidad." Mendoza's poem presents the struggles between Reason and Sensuality in the guise of a joust. Reason captains those who seek *bienaventurança* (salvation); Sensuality leads those addicted to *brutas deletaciones* (brutish pleasures). They both contend for the Will, a force that can be bent either way, and which, in most men, takes the side of the senses, helping them overcome reason. Beysterveldt, *La poesía amatoria* 137-50.

31. The theme of the Order of Love is also developed by Juan de Mena (*Cancionero castellano* 2: 204) and Gómez Manrique: "En lugar de castidad / prometo de ser constante: / prometo de voluntad / de guardar toda verdad / que a de guardar ell amante: / prometo de ser suiecto / all amor y a su seruicio; / prometo de ser discreto, / y esto todo que prometo / guardallo será mi oficio" (*Cancionero castellano* 2: 238).

32. Rainer Warning, "Moi lyrique et société chez les troubadours," in *Archéologie du signe*, edited by Lucie Brind'Amour and Eugene Vance (Montréal, 1981) 81.

33. See, for example, the poem "De don Jorge Manrique quexándose del Dios de Amor, y cómo razona el uno con el otro" (*Cancionero* 3ff).

34. See also *Cancionero* 27.

35. María de los Dolores Mateu Ibars, *Iconografía de San Vicente Martir*. Tomo I: *Pintura* (Madrid, 1980).

36. The poem is a judicial appeal against an unjust sentence. As such it takes the judicial process as its guiding metaphor and is related to a type of poetry with antecedents in French, Provençal, and medieval Latin literature. See for example, *'Le Court d'Amours' of Mahieu le Poirier*, edited by T. Scully (Waterloo, Ontario, 1976), or the *Arretz d'Amour* of Martial of Auvergne, edited by J. Rychner (Paris, 1951). Its immediate roots, however, are in Castilian literature. The *Cancionero de Baena* contains many debates between poets that end up before a third party for judgment. See nos. 231-36, 373/375, 412/413, 431/435/439, 488-89. Sometimes, as the poets debate the question, the tone of the poems becomes more acrimonious, and there is a need to resort to a "cooler" head to adjudicate a settlement. In the most extreme cases—

and these are almost always fictitious debates—the work has a courtroom setting from the start. It then becomes a *pleito* (lawsuit) rather than a *debate*— a term used by the poets themselves to distinguish this type of composition. In poem 488 of the *Cancionero de Baena* (3: 968-69), Nicolás de Valencia brings a suit before Fray Diego de Valencia against a lady who has stolen his heart. The lady refuses to return it, and he appeals to the Fray Diego to give a just sentence as a *buen letrado*. Fray Diego, impartial judge that he is, sentences Nicolás to continue to serve the lady (3, no. 489: 970-71). Nicolás challenges the sentence, saying that the judge was "vandero en ansi judgar," and appeals to Don Amor (3, no. 490: 971-72). Two poems from Fray Diego follow. In them he responds to Nicolás' accusations, orders him to pay the cost of the trial, voids his appeal, and banishes the ill-mannered lover (3, nos. 491 and 492: 973-75). A similar lawsuit is the object of the composition called "Pleito del manto" in the *Cancionero de obras de burlas provocantes a risa* (Valencia, 1519).

37. María del Rosario Fernández Alonso, *Una visión de la muerte en la lírica española: La muerte como amada* (Madrid, 1971).

38. Jorge Manrique's father also seemed to engage in this peculiar romance with death. Don Rodrigo's *cancionero* consists of only about a dozen poems, but twice he glossed the stanza: "mis sentidos no's quejeis / de veros en tal afrenta /que el morir es buena cuenta," and in another song he argued:

> Lo seguro de la vida
> tiene el muerto que reposa
> qu'el mundo es tan fiera cosa
> que no hay cosa conocida;
> lo mas cierto es desear
> lo que ha de permanecer
> gloria para descansar
> muerte para fenecer.

His portrayal in the *Coplas* echoes the robust defiance of these lines. Don Rodrigo is possibly a source of Jorge Manrique's sensibility to the theme of death, which frees the *Coplas* from the allegorical artificiality of the elegies of his time.

39. Keith Whinnom summarizes traditional critical opinion about *cancionero* love poetry, and offers an alternative view. *La poesía amatoria cancioneril en la época de los Reyes Católicos*. Durham Modern Language Series, HM 2 (Durham, 1981) 9-20).

40. Its language is in some respects an unforegrounded language. I use the term in the sense defined by Bohuslav Hrávanek to mean "the use of the devices of language in such a way that this use itself attracts attention and is perceived as uncommon, as deprived of automatization." "The Functional Differentiation of the Standard Language," in *A Prague School Reader on Esthetics, Literary Structure, and Style*, edited by Paul L. Garvin (Washington, 1964) 10. Jan Mukarovsky applies the concept to poetry. "Standard Language and Poetic Language," in *A Prague School Reader* 17-30. The language

of Mena's didactic poetry is a good contrast to that of the lyric. Its most important foregrounding elements are his use of neologisms and latinate syntactic structures. One is still hampered, however, in an assessment of the poetic tradition that underlies fifteenth-century poetry because of a lack of sufficient basic studies on individual poets. It is impossible, therefore, to judge whether the poetic sensibilities of the first half of the century differ in a significant way from those of the second half of the century. To a great extent, the *cancionero* lyric remains a mass of undifferentiated poetry.

41. Paul Zumthor, "Mémoire et tradition poétique," in *Jeux de mémoire: Aspects de la mnémotechnie médiévale*, edited by Bruno Roy and Paul Zumthor (Montréal, 1985) 16.

42. Keith Whinnom, "Hacia una interpretación y apreciación de las canciones del *Cancionero general* de 1511," *Filología* 13 (1968-69): 361-81. My count of the verbs and nouns that appear more than once in the ten *canciones* of Jorge Manrique generally agrees with Whinnom's tally and reveals the following frequency: *ser* (18), *querer* (13, *querido*, 3), *satisfacer* (11), *perder* (8, *perdida* 3, *perdimiento* 1, *perdición* 1), *vida* (12), *amor* (4, *amores* 4, *amado* 1, *amador* 2), *esperar* (7, *esperanza* 1), *morir* (6, *muerte* 2), *poder* (5), *ver* (5), *conoscer* (4), *venir* (4), *vencer* (4), *fe* (4), *ausencia* (3, *ausente* 1), *desear* (3), *estar* (3), *olvidar* (3), *quedar* (3), *servir* (3), *tener* (3), *contento* (3), *cuidado* (3), *enemigo* (3), *confianza* (3), *presencia* (3), *alcanzar* (2), *causar* (2), *cegar* (2), *condiciones* (2), *consentir* (2), *desamparar* (2), *dolor* (2), *galardón* (2), *gastar* (2), *grado* (2), *guerra* (2), *herida* (2), *merescimiento* (2), *mudanza* (2), *partir* (2), *pasión* (2), *peligro*(2), *remedio* (2), *sospiros* (2), *victoria* (2).

43. The longer love lyrics and the satires allow for a larger, though still restricted, proportion of concrete nouns and of adjectives. In satiric poetry the language of the courtly love lyric and everyday language coexist, one parodied by the other.

44. As the following verses by Gómez Manrique show, this use of a series of verbs to achieve a climax is a common feature of the shorter lyrics:

> Con la beldad *me prendistes,*
> con la graçia *me robastes,*
> con la bondad *me feristes*
> al punto que *me mirastes.*
> (*Cancionero castellano* 2: 13)

45. "The paradox of simultaneous difference and similarity is partly resolved by the fact that opposites typically differ along only one dimension of meaning: in all other respects they are identical, hence their semantic closeness; along the dimension of difference they occupy opposing poles, hence the feeling of difference." D.A. Cruse, *Lexical Semantics* (Cambridge, 1986): 197. The analysis of recurrence and patterning in Manrique's poetry makes use of this study of complementaries and antonyms. Although, because of the introductory nature of this book this is not the place to go into its details, lexical semantics can provide a means of describing what takes place in the language of the lyric. Briefly stated, complementaries di-

vide a conceptual domain into two mutually exclusive areas (198), for example: true : false, dead : alive. If one is denied, then the other is true. Generally, complementaries are either verbs or adjectives (201). They can be of four types: reversive, interactive, satisfactive, and counteractive. All of these come into play in the lyric. In the *Coplas* reversives are very important. In the set, to be born : live : die, the outer members are reversives. They denote change in opposite directions (entering life, leaving life). This is one of the oppositions that is central to the poem's paradoxes.

46. Lavis studied the frequency and context of the vocabulary that expresses joy and suffering in the *chanson* of the *trouvères*. He found that the meaning of *joie* and *dolor* depend on a lexical micro-system organized according to the principles of opposition and substitution (*L'Expression* 583). The syntactic-semantic possibilities of *joie* and *dolor* can be organized according to three dicotomous oppositions, which he calls *comportement/non comportement*, *englobant/englobé*, *continuité/discontinuité* (585f). Lavis concludes that the affective vocabulary of the chanson of the *troubadours* and of the *trouvères* is fairly similar.

47. Jakobson suggested that the study of the selection, distribution and interrelation of morphological classes and syntactic constructions in a poem would reveal symmetries and antisymmetries, balanced structures, accumulation of equivalent forms and salient contrasts, and rigid restrictions in the repertory of morphological and syntactic constituents. "Poetry of Grammar and Grammar of Poetry," in Roman Jakobson, *Selected Writings* Vol. III: *Poetry of Grammar and Grammar of Poetry*, edited by Stephen Rudy (The Hague: 1981) 92f. In a letter to Haroldo de Campos, Jakobson applied his methodology to a poem by Martin Codax, but his suggestions have in general not been taken up by students of the Castilian lyric. "Martin Codax's Poetic Texture," *Poetry of Grammar and Grammar of Poetry* 169-75.

48. H. Sopher, "Parallelism in Modern English Prose; Its Formal Patterns, Rhetorical Functions and Notional Relations," *English Studies* 63 (1982): 45f.

49. Nowhere in the love lyric, however, are these positional parallels as obvious as in the *Coplas*.

50. Other examples of chiasmus: "*Callé por mucho temor; / temo por mucho callar*" (67), "*Es plazer en c'ay dolores, / dolor en c'ay alegría . . . vn esfuerço en c'ay temores / temor en c'ay osadía*" (17), "*mi beuir que presto muera / muera porque biua yo*" (39).

51. See stanzas XXVII-XXVIII for another example of the use of diaphora.

52. E.R. Curtius, *European Literature and the Latin Middle Ages* (New York, 1953) 162.

53. Dragonnetti, *La Technique poétique* 541; P. Zumthor, "Recherches sur les topiques dans la poésie lyrique des XIIᵉ et XIIIᵉ siècles," *Cahiers de civilization médiévale* 2 (1959): 409-27.

54. Pedro Salinas, *Jorge Manrique* 43. Salinas echoes Menéndez Pidal's assessment of fifteenth-century poets as being "faltos de positiva inspiración." "La primitiva poesía lírica española," *Estudios literarios* (Madrid, 1920) 273.

55. Baena clearly states this when he says that the poet must feint at being in love. *Cancionero de Baena* 1: 15.

56. "Le sujet de l'oeuvre ne saurait être confondu avec sa donnée. Le thème n'est qu'un prétexte. C'est l'oeuvre formelle elle-même qui est le sujet." R. Guiette, "D'une poésie formelle en France au Moyen âge," *Revue des sciences humaines* (1949): 65. Dragonnetti calls this utilization of traditional materials the "dynamic cliché" because, though known and expected to appear in the poetry, it still had the power to move the auditors. *La Technique poétique* 451.

57. Whinnom, *La poesía amatoria* 17. See also J.M. Aguirre's excellent article: "Reflexiones para la construcción de un modelo de la poesía castellana del amor cortés," *Romanische Forschungen* 93 (1981): 55-81.

3. *Coplas por la muerte de su padre:* The Background

1. The Selected Bibliography at the end of this book contains a partial list of editions.

2. See F. Caravaca, "Foulché-Delbosc y su edición 'crítica' de las *Coplas* de Jorge Manrique," *Boletín de la Biblioteca Menéndez Pelayo* 49 (1973): 229-79. All references are to A. Cortina's 4th edition, *Jorge Manrique: cancionero* (Madrid, 1960); line numbers are my own.

3. Antonio Pérez Gómez, "La primera versión impresa de las *Coplas* de Jorge Manrique, Zaragoza s. a. (1482-83)," *Gutenberg-Jahrbuch* 40 (1965): 93-95; and "Notas para la bibliografía de Fray Iñigo de Mendoza y de Jorge Manrique," *Hispanic Review* 27 (1959): 30-41; also Caravaca, "Foulché-Delbosc" 252.

4. Ricardo Senabre, "La primera edición de las *Coplas* de Jorge Manrique," in *Serta philologica F. Lázaro Carreter* (Madrid, 1983) 2: 509-17.

5. For a discussion of the authenticity of these stanzas see: F. Caravaca, "Notas sobre las llamadas 'coplas postumas' de Jorge Manrique," *Boletín de la Biblioteca Menéndez Pelayo* 50 (1974): 89-135.

6. The exceptions are Juan Hurtado de la Serna and A. González Palencia, eds., *Jorge Manrique: coplas y glosas* (Madrid, n. d.); and A. Bonilla y San Martín, ed., *Antología de poetas de los siglos XII al XV* (Madrid, 1917).

7. J. Labrador, A. Zorita, and R.A. Difranco, "Cuarenta y dos, y no cuarenta coplas en la famosa elegía manriqueña," *Boletín de la Biblioteca Menéndez Pelayo* 61 (1985): 37-95. The article points out that sixteenth- and seventeenth-century readers were as likely as not to read a version of the *Coplas* with the two un-canonical stanzas. The two stanzas appear in Longfellow's translation, intercalated between stanzas XXIV and XXVI. In modern editions they are normally printed as an appendage to the poem.

8. José Manuel Quintana, *Poesías selectas castellanas* (Madrid, 1829) xx; R. Burkart, "Leben, Tod, und Jenseits bei Jorge Manrique und Francois Villon," *Romanische Stil- und Literaturstudien Leo Spitzer* (1931) 1: 271-301; Anna Krause, *Jorge Manrique and the Cult of Death in the Cuatrocientos*, Publications of the

University of California 1 (Berkeley, 1937) 54; A. Cortina, *Jorge Manrique* xlii; H. Petriconi, "El argumento de las *Coplas* de Jorge Manrique," *Investigación y progreso* (Madrid, October, 1932) 151-53; Pedro Salinas, *Jorge Manrique* 218f; Adolfo Prieto, "El sentimiento de la muerte a través de la literatura española," *Revista de literatura moderna* 2 (1960): 141-61; Stephen Gilman, "Tres retratos de la muerte en las *Coplas* de Jorge Manrique," *Nueva revista de filología hispánica* 13 (1959): 308.

9. For a discussion of the characteristics of the classical elegy see: Georg Luck, *The Latin Love Elegy* (Edinburgh, 1969); L. Alfonsi and W. Schmid, "Elegie" in *Reallexikon für Antike und Christentum* 4 (1959): 1026ff. The Italian and French elegists of the Renaissance used the form (in *terza rima*) for love poetry, while the neo-latin elegy admits all subjects. See P. van Tieghem, *La Littérature latine de la renaissance* (Paris, 1944) 86.

10. Francisco Caravaca, "Estudios manriqueños. Notas sobre el título: *'Coplas' de Jorge Manrique 'a la' muerte de su padre,"* *La torre* 73/74 (1971): 185-221. Caravaca points out that the first edition of the *Coplas* (Zaragoza, 1482?) gives the poem the title: "Dezir de don jorge manriq / por la muerte de su padre." The title *Coplas* appears for the first time in the *Cancionero de Iñigo de Mendoza* (1483) and is commonly used thereafter. Both titles seem to be the creation of the printers. The composition was in all likelihood untitled until after the death of Manrique. The term *dezir* was used in the *cancioneros* of the fifteenth century to denote a strophic poem, longer than usual, of varied subject matter, destined to be read rather than sung (though there are indications that some were sung). The *dezires* tended to be composed of octosyllabic eight-line stanzas, but with the passage of time the term was applied less precisely, until it meant just a long poem, generally of a sententious nature. The *cancioneros* begin to replace the term *dezir* with *coplas* toward the end of the century. See P. Le Gentil, *La Poésie lyrique* 2: 180-86; and R. Baehr, *Manual* 114.

11. See Donald R. Howard, *The Three Temptations: Medieval Man in Search of the World* (Princeton, 1966); Robert Bultot, *Christianisme et valeurs humaines. La doctrine du mépris du monde*, 6 vols. (Paris and Louvain, 1964).

12. The following studies provide a good introduction to the study of death in the Middle Ages: Philippe Ariès, *Essais sur l'histoire de la mort en Occident du moyen âge à nos jours* (Paris, 1975); idem, *L'Homme devant la mort* (Paris, 1977); T.S.R. Boase, *Death in the Middle Ages. Mortality, Judgment, and Remembrance* (London, 1972); E. Camacho Guisado, *La elegía funeral en la poesía española* (Madrid, 1969); C. Cohen, "Les éléments constitutifs des quelques planctus du Xe et XIe siècles," *Cahiers de civilization médiévale* 1 (1958): 83-86; E. Dubruck, *The Theme of Death in French Poetry of the Middle Ages and the Renaissance* (London, The Hague and Paris, 1964); J. Filgueira Valverde, "El planto en la historia y en la literatura gallega," *Cuaderno de estudios gallegos* 4 (1945): 511-606; Fr. Joukovsky, *La Gloire dans la poèsie française et neolatine du XVIe siècle* (Geneva, 1969); Alberto Tenenti, *La Vie et la mort à travers l'art du XVe siècle* (Paris, 1952); idem, *Il senso della morte e l'amore de la vita nel rinas-*

cimento (Turin, 1957); Claude Thiry, *La Plainte funèbre. Typologie des sources du moyen âge occidental*, Fasc. 30 (Louvain, 1978).

13. Also known as *De Miseria Humane Conditionis* and *De Contemptu Mundi.* See Lotario dei Segni (Innocent III), *De Miseria Condicionis Humane*, edited by R.E. Lewis (Athens, Georgia, 1978). There are 672 extant manuscripts of the work.

14. The *Vado mori* was published by Guyot Marchant in 1485 at the foot of one of the engravings of his *Danse macabre*. For the 1486 edition of the *Danse*, Marchant added the *Dit des trois morts et des trois vifs*, thus bringing together the best known poems about death of the thirteenth, fourteenth, and fifteenth centuries. See Stefan Glixelli, *Les cinqs poèmes des trois Morts et des trois Vifs* (Paris, 1914).

15. "Where is my son, the happiness of my life, the solace of my old age, my only heir?" Amador de los Ríos, *Historia crítica de la literatura española* (Madrid, 1961-65) 2: 334ff. Amador published several Iberian Latin elegies written before the fourteenth century in his *Historia*. In addition to this literary tradition and to the vernacular laments mentioned by Prieto and Camacho Guisado, there is a folkloric tradition that has not left many tangible signs of its existence. M. Alvar assembled some of its last vestiges, still sung in the 1950s among North African Sephardic Jews whose ancestors were expelled from Spain in 1492. At that time they continued to maintain their Hispanic traditions and language. These songs, most commonly called *endechas*, celebrate the passing of an individual in simple verse. They begin with a lament, which is followed by a praise of the individual, and they utilize some of the themes and motifs of literary funeral poetry. Most notably absent is any note of consolation for the survivors. Learned poetry occasionally describes funeral customs and gives an idea of the social context in which the *endechas* came into being. M. Alvar, *Endechas judeo-españolas* (Madrid, 1969).

16. Prov. *planh*, Fr. *plainte*, It. *pianto*, Sp. *planto/llanto*, Eng. *plaint*.

17. Prieto, "El sentimiento" 120-126; Camacho Guisado, *La elegía* 99-111.

18. Le Gentil characterizes Castilian attitudes in the following manner: "La Mort ne hante pas en Espagne les imaginations, elle ne les remplit pas de visions d'horreurs et d'épouvante. Elle s'impose à la réflexion presque uniquement au décès des grands personnages. On la maudit, mais on sait aussi l'accepter; on ne la décrit pas; elle reste une puissance mystérieuse, qu'on ne songe pas à se représenter sous la forme d'un cadavre hideux et repousant. . . . Certes, sous l'influence de la *Danza de la Muerte*, l'esprit macabre apparaît, çà et là, dans quelques oeuvres du *Canc. de Baena*: le mort sort de sa tombe, ou nous mande un suprême message pour nous sermonner et nous inspirer un effroi salutaire; mais ce n'est pas ce corps en décomposition, dont parle la légende des trois Morts et trois Vifs. Une pudeur instinctive arrête ici les poètes castillans et portugais." Le Gentil, *La Poésie lyrique* 1: 392.

19. Joël Saugnieux, *Les dances macabres de France et de l'Espagne et leur prolonguements littéraires* (Paris, 1972) 17.

20. For background on the Dance of Death see Saugnieux, also J.M. Clark, *The Dance of Death in the Middle Ages and the Renaissance* (Glasgow, 1950); L.P. Kurtz, *The Dance of Death and the Macabre Spirit in European Literature* (New York, 1934); E. Mâle, *L'Art religieux à la fin du moyen âge en France* (Paris, 1949) Part II, Chapter 2: *La Mort*; L. Reau, *L'Iconographie de l'art chrétien*, 6 vols. (Paris, 1955-59) II, 2: 637-62.

21. Camacho Guisado, *La elegía* 67ff.

22. Foulché-Delbosc, *Cancionero castellano* 2: 28-32.

23. In a characteristic mixture of emotion and erudition, Gómez Manrique ends the poem by saying: "El qual escriui con tanto tormento / como tenian las dueñas troyanas / en ver a su rey mesando sus canas / aquel negro dia de su perdimiento." *Cancionero castellano* 2: 32.

24. The *Crónica de Enrique IV* describes how the king callously approached the dying knight to see the effects of the poison. Galíndez de Carvajal, *Crónica de Enrique IV* 133.

25. Dialogue is part of the Dance of Death. It also appears in medieval debates, such as those of the body and the soul, and occasionally in the lyric, either as a monologue in which death acts as a passive listener (for example, Fray Diego de Valencia's "Dezir a manera de discor"), or as an active interlocutor (for example, Juan de Mena's "Razonamiento que faze Juan de Mena con la muerte").

26. Serrano de Haro, *Personalidad y destino* 366. Serrano goes on to divide the work into four parts. He considers *coplas* I-XIV to be a moral sermon; XV-XXIV, an historic discourse; XXV-XXXIII, a presentation and panegyric of don Rodrigo; and finally, XXXIV-XL, a dramatic exchange between don Rodrigo and Death.

27. The whole problem of the division of the *Coplas* in light of the lack of a definitive text has been amply discussed by F. Caravaca in "Foulché-Delbosc." Caravaca points out that Foulché-Delbosc did not give an accurate description of the text that he designates as A, the *Cancionero de Iñigo de Mendoza*, Escorial ii-X-17, and which is another copy of the Palermo incunabulum described by Pérez Gómez in 1965, Biblioteca Comunale di Palermo sign. Esp. XI-F.56, no. 3. Foulché-Delbosc seems to have followed as his base text Escorial iii-K-7 in his edition of 1902. Other critics and editors have accepted his description of the texts. Cortina, for example, does not mention the unusual stanza order of Escorial ii-X-17. Most critics have based their explications on either the stanza order of the Foulché-Delbosc or Cortina editions. Caravaca goes on to point out that the favorite tripartite division of the *Coplas* does not fit with the text represented by Escorial ii-X-17 or Palermo Esp. XI-F.56, no. 3. It seems to him that the source of this stanza order was an unknown manuscript, perhaps even belonging to Jorge Manrique, which was given to the printer by a friend or a member of the family. Caravaca doubts that a printer would have altered the order of the stanzas of his own accord, thinking it more likely that whoever gave the work to the printer made the changes, because he was bothered by the late appearance of don Rodrigo. Moving this one section forward entailed, as a consequence,

the moving of the twelve stanzas that deal with contemporary figures and events, and their placement between stanzas XXIV and XXVI.

28. Quintana, *Poesías selectas* 37, n. 3. In addition to taking Jorge Manrique to task for failing in sentiment toward his father, Quintana calls the elegy a funeral sermon about the nothingness of the things of the world, the disdain for life, and the power of death. Quintana ends his edition with stanza XXVI, deeming that the reader would have tired of Manrique's meter by that point.

29. G. Ticknor, *History of Spanish Literature* (Boston, 1845) 407.

30. J. Blanco White, *Variedades o mensagero de Londres* (London, 1923/24) 150.

31. Menéndez Pelayo, *Historia de la poesía* 2: 401.

32. Caravaca, "Foulché-Delbosc" 272ff.

33. Senabre, "La primera edición" 511.

34. Burkart, "Leben, Tod, und Jenseits."

35. Krause, *Jorge Manrique*; Cortina, *Jorge Manrique*.

36. Salinas, *Jorge Manrique*.

37. This is not to say that other structural divisions have not been suggested. Serrano de Haro at one point departed from the traditional tripartite division. In 1967, German Orduna compared the *Coplas* to the five parts of a medieval discourse and came up with the following structure: I-III (*Exordium*), IV-VI (*Narratio*), VII-XIV (*Argumentatio*), XV-XXXIX (*Peroratio*), and XL (*Epilog*). "Las *Coplas* de Jorge Manrique y el triunfo sobre la muerte," *Romanische Forschungen* 89 (1967): 139-51. Aubrun divides the poem into I-III (Instrospection), IV-V (Invocation), VI-IX (Distanciation), X-XIII (Oraison), XIV-XXIV (Evocation du passé), XXV-XXXIII (Dithyrambe), XXXIV-XXXVIII (Débat tragico-lyrique), and XXXIX-XL (Prière et finale). There is also the problem posed by the posthumous *coplas*, which, in Labrador's view, are a fitting end to the first large movement of the poem (Labrador, "Poesía dialogada 70ff).

38. Only two of the eleven known glosses treat stanzas XXVII-XXXV. On the glosses see Nellie E. Sánchez Arce, *Las glosas a las Coplas de Jorge Manrique* (Madrid, 1956).

39. See Navarro Tomás, *Métrica española* 91-92 and 133-38. Navarro Tomás considers the stanza to be an evolution of the six-line stanza found in the "Gozos de Santa María" of the archpriest of Hita, adding that it is the only fifteenth-century stanza that has survived to modern times (168). P. Le Gentil and R. Baehr see the characteristic verse of the *lai* in fifteenth-century French poetry as a more likely source. The *lai* used a twelve verse stanza that repeated a three verse rhyme (aab). Most elegiac French verse of the time used the same form. In any case, Manrique is most directly indebted to Juan de Mena, whose poem, "El fuego más engañoso" (*Cancionero castellano* 1: 204), seems to be the first to use the stanza.

40. Quintana, *Poesías selectas* xxi.

41. Dorothy Clotelle Clarke, *Morphology of Fifteenth Century Castilian Verse* (Pittsburgh, 1964) 219-22. The alternation of long and short lines does not imply a difference in the duration of these lines, because the pronunciation of the *pie quebrado* is slower, making it as long in duration as the octosyllable.

It does accelerate and slow down the reading of the verses. One can say that the octosyllables embody the sorrow felt by the poet, while the *pie quebrado* sustains the contemplation and introspection that results from it. Gustavo Correa, "Lenguaje y ritmo en las *Coplas* de Jorge Manrique a la muerte de su padre," *Hispania* 63 (1980): 185.

42. "The charm of the elegiac couplet . . . may be explained in a number of ways. There is an element of surprise in the pentameter: it seems to begin like the hexameter which has preceded it . . . but instead of rolling along majestically, it suddenly stops and reverses, becoming its own echo. Moreover there is an intensely 'personal' element in the pentameter: instead of reaching out to embrace the world, it hesitates, it reconsiders and ends on an abrupt final note—whose abruptness is softened immediately by the renewal of the rolling beat of the following hexameter." Luck, *The Latin* 28.

43. *Philosophia antigua poetica,* edited by A. Carballo Picazo, 3 vols. (Madrid, 1953) 2: 292f.

44. Tomás Navarro Tomás, "Métrica de las Coplas de Jorge Manrique," *Nueva revista de filología hispánica* 15 (1961): 170f. The comments on the rhythms of the *Coplas* are indebted to this article. The 320 octosyllables of the poem are regular. Of the 160 four-syllable lines 28 are longer or shorter than four syllables by the count of one, but they can be considered regular when one considers that synalepha is common in Spanish poetry, and that fifteenth-century poets compensated for the shortness of a line by adding a syllable to the next. See Aurelio Espinosa, "La sinalefa y la compensación entre versos en la versificación española. Algunas observaciones adicionales," *Romanic Review* 19 (1928): 289-301.

45. Navarro Tomás, "Métrica" 175f.

46. Such as *impugnables, trasponer, innumerables, edificios, delectable, sujetos,* and *senectud.* The work also captures the reader's attention in the first part by inviting him or her to join in the meditative process. The invitation is at first vaguely formulated in the exhortation (*Recuerde, avive*), then more clearly in the associative verse that begins: "Nuestras vidas son los rios;" and finally, in the argumentative structure of the first part, with its constant repetitions of *pues, mas, porque, si, aun, pero, digo, por esso, que son sino,* and *desque.* The poem also shows certain alternations between the forms of words that reflect the instability of fifteenth-century vocabulary and pronunciation, for example: *dudança/duda* (doubt), *olvidança/olvido* (forgetfulness), *tristura/tristeza* (sadness), *ferir/herir* (to wound), *facer/hacer* (to make or do), and *fazaña/hazaña* (deed). Without an autograph manuscript, however, one hesitates to attribute some of these alternations to the author.

47. *Cancionero* 47ff. Among the poems of Jorge Manrique's uncle, Gómez Manrique, there is one where *contemplando* is also used in a *quebrado* as a rest for the previous line and as a pivot between octosyllables:

> Nunca esta noche dormi
> *contemplando*
> En el dolor muy extremo

Que sufro triste de mi
bien amando.
(*Cancionero castellano* 10)

48. "Cada vez que mi *memoria* / vuestra beldad representa / mi penar se torna gloria, / mis seruicios en victoria, / mi morir vida contenta" (*Cancionero* 64); also poems XXVI, XXXIV, and XLII.

49. Jakobson, "Poetry of Grammar" 87-97.

50. Sopher, "Parallelism" 37-48.

51. Notional relations establish equivalences in a text. The relationships can be contrasts, equivalences, or equations. The test for contrast is the possibility of interpolating a contrastive linking word between the parallels, the test for equivalence is the possibility of interpolating *is*, or an equivalent, between the parallels. The test for equation is the possibility of coordinating the parallels with *and*. Sopher, "Parallelism" 45f.

4. *Coplas por la muerte de su padre*: A Reading

1. For the purposes of this analysis, we accept as standard the sequence of stanzas found in Cortina's edition.

2. For a discussion of the rhetorical structure of the *Coplas* see Rodolfo Borello, "Las *Coplas* de Jorge Manrique: estructura y fuentes," *Cuadernos de filología* 1 (1967): 49-72.

3. "Dezir a la muerte del almirante Roy Diaz de Mendoza," *Cancionero de Baena* 3: 1074. On the possible Latin sources of Manrique's verses 4-6 see María Rosa Lida de Malkiel, "Para la primera de las *Coplas de don Jorge Manrique por la muerte de su padre*," *Romance Philology* 16 (1962): 170-73. The movement of life into death gave rise to many mottoes. The *Spiegel van den Ouden* 3rd ed. (Dordrecht, 1635) 150, contains one as lapidary as Sánchez de Talavera's verse: "Il tempo va, la morte viene."

4. See F.C. Gardiner, *The Pilgrimage of Desire* (Leiden, 1971).

5. St. Paul is proposed by Cortina, *Jorge Manrique* xlvii, Krause, *Jorge Manrique* 170, and Cangiotti, *Les Coplas* 19, among others. The hymn of St. Ambrose, "Mens iam resurgat torpida," is proposed by Lida de Malkiel, "Una copla" 170. The Mozarabic rite was still in use in Ocaña when don Rodrigo died, so it is not implausible that Manrique might have heard it sung there, shortly after his father's death.

6. I quote from Cipriano de Valera's translation of the Bible in an edition done in Madrid, 1916. *The Oxford Annotated Bible* (New York, 1962): "These all died in faith, not having received what was promised, but having seen it and greeted it from afar, and having acknowledged that they were strangers and exiles on the earth. For people who speak thus make it clear that they are seeking a homeland. If they had been thinking of that land from which they had gone out, they would have had opportunity to return."

7. J.P. Migne, *Patrologia Latina* 76, 63; trans. quoted from Gardiner, *The*

Pilgrimage 14. Gardiner shows how, from St. Paul's days to our own, this fruitful metaphor for man's sojourn in the world has been used to express an inner reality. In the Middle Ages, the image was so familiar, that by using only a few words writers could bring it to mind.

8. Jean Leclercq, *The Love of Learning and the Desire for God*, tr. Catharine Misrahi (New York, 1977), 31ff. Leclercq traces the evolution of this vocabulary of desire, noting that the first result of experiencing man's condition leads to detachment from the world. For Gregory detachment results from the compunction of fear and the compunction of desire, a spiritual pain that results from an awareness of the existence of sin and a desire for God.

9. The idea goes back to St. Augustine's *De magistro*, X, xiv. See G. Weigel, ed. *De magistro* (Vienna, 1961).

10. Fortitude, Temperance, Justice, and Prudence.

11. See Frances Yates, *The Art of Memory* (Chicago, 1966) 62; also Richard Sorabji, *Aristotle on Memory* (London, 1972). The love lyric also draws upon the same ideas concerning memory.

12. The idea of the superiority of the past was one of the clichés of the lyric that expressed how the lover, once rejected by the lady, pined for past favors. In a composition in the *Cancioneiro Geral de García de Resende*, for example, the Portuguese poet, Jorge de Aguiar, develops as a *mote* "Qualquyera tiempo pasado / fue mejor:"

> Jorge d'Aguyar a este mote
> Qualquyera tiempo passado
> fue mejor.
> Ho bevir mal empleado,
> ho dia, mucho peor
> que qual quyer tiempo passado
> fue mejor.
> Ho vida la que bevy
> muerte la que ora byvo,
> ho plazer, que fue de ty;
> no te veo, ja te vy
> en servir a quien yo syrvo;
> que dire yo desdichado
> pues callar me es peor;
> vivo tan mal a my grado
> que qual quyer tiempo passado
> fue mejor.
> (*Cancionero de Resende* 2: 160)

Jorge de Aguiar, a knight of Santiago, wrote during the reigns of Afonso V and João II. His poetry was collected in the *Cancionero de Resende*, where he appears as a participant in the well-known debate on *cuidar e sospirar*. The *mote* cited above is one of two poems he wrote in Spanish. His oldest datable poems are from 1481. He died in 1508. See Diego Barbosa Machado, *Biblioteca lusitana*, 4 vols. (Lisbon, 1931) 2: 726; also the *Grande dicionario da literatura portuguesa e de teoria literaria* (Lisbon, 1969) 1: 90.

13. The association memory and rivers also appears in the "Castillo de amor" (*Cancionero* 22): "y cerca a las otras partes, /vn río mucho crescido, / qu'es membrar."

14. Ecclesiastes 1:7 "All streams run to the sea, / but the sea is not full; / to the place where the streams flow, / there they flow again."

15. John 1:10 "He was in the world, and the world was made through him, yet the world knew him not."

16. Gómez Manrique's composition was dedicated to the memory of Jorge Manrique's great uncle, the marquess of Santillana, one of the two great poets of the preceding generation. Note that Gómez does not directly name those whose invocation he refuses—*las planetas, las cirras, las hermanas discretas, la madre de cupido, la Tesaliana.* He makes of the refusal an artifice that does exactly what he proposes not to do: call specific deities to the reader's attention:

> Non invoco las planetas
> que me fagan elocuente
> non las cirras muncho netas
> nin las hermanas discretas
> que moran cabe la fuente
> ni quiero ser socorrido
> de la madre de cupido
> ni de la Tesaliana
> mas del nieto de sant ana
> con su saber ynfinido.
>
> Dexo las invocaciones
> a los non sabio ynotas
> que grandes exclamaciones
> a las bajas discreciones
> son e deben ser remotas.
> (*Cancionero castellano* 2: 68, 72)

Gómez's invocation is very much in accord with fifteenth-century poetic practice in poems of a moralizing nature. For example, Padilla's "Retablo de la vida de Cristo:" "Dexa por ende, las falsas ficciones / de los antiguos gentiles salvages, /las quales son unos mortales potages / cubiertos con altos y dulces sermones." (*Cancionero castellano* 1: 494). On this topic see Joaquín Gimeno Casalduero, "San Jerónimo y el rechazo y la aceptación de la poesía en la Castilla de finales del siglo XV," in *La creación literaria de la edad media y del renacimiento* (Madrid, 1977) 45-65.

17. Another important echo of Gómez Manrique may derive from the latter's best known work: the "Coplas a Diego Arias." Stanzas 23 and 24 of Gómez's work may have served as models for the posthumous *coplas* of Manrique. The closest parallels can be found in stanza 24:

¡O mundo pues que nos matas
fuera la vida que diste
toda vida
mas según acá nos tratas
lo mejor y menos triste
es la partida
de tu vida tan cubierta
de males y [de] dolores
tan poblada
de los bienes tan desierta
de placeres y dulzores
despoblada!

18. "Jhesus, salus et medecine / De toute creature humaine." *Ovide moralisé,* edited by C. de Boer (Amersterdam, 1915-38) Book 7: 732-33. The name of Jesus was etymologically related by the moralist to the root *eis,* which means to cure or animate.

19. Fray Martín de Córdoba, *Compendio de la fortuna,* in *Prosistas castellanos del siglo XV,* edited by P. Fernando Rubio, O.S.A. 2 vols. (Madrid, 1964) 2: 61.

20. Compare in the love poetry:

VII   Ese Dios alto sin cuento   61
        bien sé yo qu'es mayor;
        mas, con mi gran desatiento,
        le tengo muy descontento
        por servir a ti, traidor,   65
            que con tu ley halaguera
        m'engañaste, y has traído
        a dexar la verdadera,
        y seguirte en la manera
        que sabes que t'e seguido.   70

VIII   En ti solo tuve fee
        después que te conoscí,
        pues ¿cómo paresceré
        ante'l Dios a quien erré
        quexando del que serví?   75
        (*Cancionero* 6-7)

21. The textual references seem to point to John 3: 16.

22. Of course, the dialogue never gets established. The rhetorical questions set the stage for it, but only the narrator assumes the stage, and carries forth the argument: "Pero digo c'acompañen" (121).

23. St. Isidore's *Etymologiae,* for example, divided the ages of man into six: "Gradus aetatis sex sunt: infantia, pueritia, adolescentia, iuventus, gravitas atque senectus." *Etymologiarum libri XX,* edited by W.M. Lindsay (Oxford, 1911), Bk. 11, Chapter 2.

24. Joseph Silverman, "Concerning the *arrabal de senectud* in Manrique's

Coplas por la muerte de su padre," in *Studies in Honor of Everett W. Hesse* (Lincoln, Nebraska, 1981) 135-41.

25. María Rosa Lida de Malkiel traced the origin of this concept from Philo of Alexandria's *On the Origin of the World,* to what she believed to be Manrique's probable source in the *Epistola paraenetica ad Valerianum cognatum de contemptu mundi et saecularis philosophiae* of St. Eucherius, bishop of Lyons. In that work, the opposition body/slave to soul/mistress appears in a context that is similar to the entire sequence of stanzas in which it is embedded in the poem. Not only does St. Eucherius complain about those who would care for the body (slave) instead of for the soul (mistress), but he also deplores the reckless pursuit of riches. He also describes ancient and modern kingdoms, which are now forgotten. In both Philo and St. Eucherius, however, body and soul are antithetical pairs, not *cara* and *alma.* Mrs. Malkiel herself points to the occurrence of the topic, in the form Manrique gives it, in the *cancionero* of Alvarez Gato ("Por her la cara hermosa / tornar ell ánima fea," *Cancionero castellano* 1, no. 102). The most immediate sources may therefore be found in the Castilian poetry of Manrique's time. The opposition of *cara* and *alma* better fits the youthful recklessness that the first part of the *Coplas* evokes. Lida de Malkiel, "Una copla" 168.

26. Serrano de Haro, *Jorge Manrique* 260.

27. Also "Esos reyes poderosos / que vemos por escripturas / ya pasadas." *Cancionero* 157-9.

28. M. Schulz, *Die Lehre von der Historischen Methode bei den Geschichtsschreibern des Mittelalters VI.-XIII. Jh.* (Berlin, 1909) 25-26.

29. See Rodolfo A. Borello, "Para la historia del *ubi sunt,*" in *Lengua, Literatura, Folklore. Estudios dedicados a Rodolfo Oroz* (Santiago de Chile, 1967) 81-92; idem, "Las *Coplas*" 49-72; idem, "El *ubi sunt* en la poesía española antes del siglo XV," *Cuadernos de filología* 6 (1972): 87-117; J.F. Gatti, "El *ubi sunt* en la prosa medieval española," *Filología* 8 (1962): 105-21; M. Liborio, "Contributi alla storia dell'*ubi sunt,*" *Cultura neolatina* 20 (1960): 114-209; Margherita Morreale, "Apuntes para el estudio de la trayectoria que desde el *¿ubi sunt?* lleva hasta el '¿Qué le fueron sino . . . ?' de Jorge Manrique," *Thesaurus* 30 (1975): 471-519; Ricardo G. Villoslada, S.I. "El tema del *ubi sunt*: Nuevas aportaciones," *Miscelánea Comillas* 45 (1966): 5-114.

30. For a discussion of the events in which these people participated, and their relation to the Manrique family see chapter 1. Though Manrique may have considered the age of the Infantes as long gone, he wrote his poem as the last of the players in that drama disappeared: Don Rodrigo (1476) and Juan II of Aragón (1479).

31. The interrogative reappears in 188: "¿qué fueron sino verduras?"

32. The *banderas* are the insignia of kings, dukes, marquesses, counts, viscounts, admirals, and barons; the *pendones* designate the forces of the military orders; and the *estandartes* knights who have men at arms under their command. Diego de Valera, *Tratado de las armas,* Biblioteca de autores españoles 116: *Prosistas castellanos del siglo XV* (Madrid, 1959) 132.

33. In both passages the subject is delayed, inviting the reader to continue.

34. David H. Darst, "Poetry and Politics in Jorge Manrique's *Coplas por la muerte de su padre*," *Medievalia et Humanistica* 13 (1985) 197.

35. Mentioned are: Augustus Octavianus Caesar, the adopted son and inheritor of Julius Caesar; Scipio Publius Cornelius, surnamed Africanus, a Roman general, and the vanquisher of Hannibal; Hannibal, a Carthaginian general, renowned for his virtue and learning; Trajan, born in Itálica, Spain; Titus Vespasianus; Aurelianus; and Regulus Marcus Atilius, a Roman consul and a successful campaigner against the Carthaginians. Atilius was eventually captured, but allowed to return to Rome to negotiate a cessation to the hostilities and arrange an exchange of prisoners. Instead, he dissuaded the Senate from acceding to the Carthaginian demands. He was bound by oath to return to Africa, and was put to death under gruesome circumstances. Antoninus Titus, surnamed Pius, the adopted son of Adrian; Antoninus Marcus Aurelius, the adopted son of Antoninus Titus; Hadrian; Theodosius Flavius; Marcus Aurelius Antoninus, surnamed Caracalla; Flavius Valerius Constantinus; and Marcius Furius Camillus.

36. The use of such figures to illustrate moral qualities pervades fifteenth-century poetry and prose. Diego de Burgos, for example, in the "Triunfo del Marques" (*Cancionero castellano* 2: 535ff) has a whole gallery of ancient and modern figures render homage to the marquess of Santillana in no discernible order. Among them are: Africano, "veras la virtud del buen Africano"; Marco Antonio, "que en alta tribuna / estouo gran tiempo, mas no bien seguro"; Cesar; Regulo Atilio, "que quiso morir / en Africa antes que en Roma venir, / diziendo palabra que no fuese recta"; Trajan, "si fue de Castilla el justo Trajano;" Adriano, "principe docto"; Tito, "enemigo de todos auaros, / famoso en las guerras, sin armas benigno"; Constantino, "que fue con la Iglesia assi liberal, / por do tiene agora por mas principal / su dote terreno que el culto divino." Among the Castilian worthies only four deserve mention: Fernán González, the Cid, Pero Gonçálvez, and Garcilasso de la Vega. Similarly, in his *Generaciones y semblanzas*, Fernán Pérez de Guzmán describes the ancient emperors from the point of view of the qualities they embody, rather than their place in history. The chapter on Antoninus Pius, for example, has the rubric "De como este noble enperador fue de maravillosa clemençia e piedat e muy humano, e que en su tienpo fizo mucho por non matar ninguno e si ser podía, antes los perdonava." *Generaciones y semblanzas*, edited by R.B. Tate (London, 1965) 65. What Manrique owes Gómez Manrique, though again it is common property, is the form the comparison takes in the "Aguilando." The comparison also appears in a letter Gómez wrote to Pero Gonçalez de Mendoza on the death of the latter's father: "se puede dezir que perdio en este otro Fabio para sus consejos; otro Cesar para sus conquistas; otro Camilo para sus defensas; otro Livio para sus memorias . . . en las guerras mostrandose vn Marco Marcello en el hordenar, e vn Castino enel acometer" (*Cancionero castellano* 2: 67). The outdoing comparison is also common in dedications. Diego de Valera's *Tratado de las armas*, for example, eulogizes

Alfonso V of Aragón saying: "por otro Salomón sois avido, e donde execución, esfuerço o veril osadía no fazen mengua Cipión ni Aníbal; e donde liberalidad se requiere, a Trajano e Alixandre sobráis." 117.

37. I disagree with Salinas, who thinks that Manrique does not believe that his father's fame could outlast that of the more prominent figures in the *ubi sunt* stanzas. *Jorge Manrique* 189. While no fame is everlasting, Manrique's point is precisely that his father's fame will outlive that of his enemies.

38. Ernst R. Curtius, "Jorge Manrique und der Kaisergedanke," *Zeitschrift für Romanische Philologie* 52 (1932): 129-52.

39. Ed.C. Kempf (Berlin, 1888).

40. Hugo de Urries, *Valerio Maximo* (Zaragoza: Paulo Hurus, 1495), fols. 18-24. See also 57-58, 109, 132, 210. Urries's work is a translation of the Simon de Hedin's French translation of the *Valerius*. Hugo de Urries was "copero mayor" of Juan II of Aragon, and a member of the royal council. His version of the *Valerio* was actually translated in Bruges in 1467 at the request of duke Charles of Burgundy, when Hugo was ambassador to the ducal court. Interest in the *Valerius,* however, antedates the publication of Urries's version. The Latin version was known especially among the clergy due to the utility of the work in the preparation of sermons and orations. Not long before Urries translated Simon de Hedin's *Valerius,* Diego Rodríguez de Almella wrote an imitation of the *Valerius* for Jorge Manrique's uncle Juan. *Valerio de las estorias escolasticas et de españa dirigido al noble & reverendo señor don ioha[n] ma[n]rrique, prothonotario de la santa fee ap[ostol]ica Arcidiano de valpuesta del consejo del Rey nuestro señor* (1462). Rodríguez de Almella's book follows the structure of the *Valerius,* but draws its *exempla* from the Bible and from the history of Spain.

41. "En aqueste mesmo lugar donde esta / le armo cauallero en vna gran lyd / Rodrigo Manrrique, el segundo Cid, /a quien de su muerte mucho pesara" (*Cancionero castellano* 2: 29). "Deuos el Señor del mundo, / tantos bienes temporales /quantos a dado de males / e trabajos desiguales / a vos, el buen Cid segundo" ("Estrenas al señor conde de Paredes," *Cancionero castellano* 2: 43).

42. Veii and Falerii where Etruscan cities close to Rome. Veii was captured in 396 B.C. Livy, 5. 1-22; Plut. *Vitae Parallelae,* "Camillus" 2-6.

43. According to Gómez, patriotic fervor is a characteristic of the lineage and can be counted among those goods inherent in the blood. (*Cancionero castellano* 2: 112).

44. Gómez Manrique's comparisons are generally built on the pattern A = B (verses 1-5, 11, 15), B = A (verses 12-14 where A is the man and B the quality); and he runs them in series (verses 1-5, A = B; verses 12-14, B = C). Only one of his comparisons extends to a *quebrado.*

45. Pedro Salinas, *Jorge Manrique* 189.

46. *Cancionero castellano* 2: 113. Fernando del Pulgar, for example, compares each of the subjects of his biographies to a famous Roman, only to indicate that the Castilian surpassed the Roman in the particular virtue he embodied. See *Claros varones de Castilla,* edited by J. Domínguez Bordona (Madrid, 1923).

47. Jorge Manrique's attitude is consistent with his class ethos. Gómez Manrique, for example, says of goods: "Procurar deuen los nobles e virtuosos onores, riquezas e tenporales estados que, como Seneca dize, nunca fue la nobleza e virtud a perpetua pobreza condenada; pero tal deue ser procuraçion sin manzellar la fama e menos la conçiencia; e con esto los ya dichos inquerir pueden los tales bienes e reçebir quantos assi onesta mente les vinieren, e retenerlos en sus casas, mas non deuen fincarlos en los coraçones, e seran sus arcas ligeras de abrir, mas non foradadas, por via que dellas salgan muchas cosas, mas no ninguna se cayga; e avn lo que mas de fazer es graue, que si estas riquezas e mouibles estados se fueren, que no corran tras ellos, mas que sin ninguna queden turbaçion, como aquellos a quien estas riquezas no lieuan, saluo assi mesmas." *Cancionero castellano* 2: 65.

48. The stanzas allude to don Rodrigo's early victories against the Moors that secured Segura from Moorish incursions, and led him to the conquest of Huesca; to the misfortunes of the young commander following the battle of Olmedo, when the king confiscated his lands; and finally, to the peace negotiations that confirmed his hold on Paredes and obtained for him the title of count (see chapter 1).

49. The passage may contain an implied criticism of the king's actions. Don Rodrigo did not receive a reward for his service. He died too soon. But in the period that followed his death the king favored don Rodrigo's enemies rather than his family.

50. "You transcend all men: where will a youthful body be found in such an aged man, or where such a mature heart in one so young? What strange rebellion in nature: a young old man!" E. Faral, ed., *Les Arts poétiques du XIIe et du XIIIe siècles* (Paris, 1924), 11. 20-3.

51. See M.M. Bachtin, "Du discours romanesque," in *Esthétique et théorie du roman* (Paris, 1978).

52. See stanza XXXIX for another example of this delaying structure.

53. *Etymologiarum libri XX* 2: 76: "Three are the types of death: premature, immature, and natural. Premature death is that of infants, immature death is that of youths, and merited death, that is to say, natural death, that of the old."

54. The idea is very old, and had its clearest expression, perhaps, in Manilius's saying: "Nascentes morimur, finisque ab origine pendet" (We die when we are born, and the end depends on the beginning). In other words, life is no more than the process of death, which leads slowly to the decay and eventual decomposition of the body. This type of death, however, as Isidore explains, is merited. It is positive because there is a sense of fulfillment or plenitude at the end.

55. M. de Córdoba, *Compendio de la fortuna* 61. Another elaboration of the idea can be found in Juan del Encina's *Coplas de la muerte cómo llama a un poderoso cavallero* (*Obras completas,* 2: 136), but the idea that man's life is a sleep from which he awakens by the knocking of death at his door is a common topic. In *The Parlement of the Thre Ages,* for example, man dreads the moment when death comes knocking: "And now es dethe at my dore

that I drede moste; / I ne wot which daye ne when ne whate tyme he comes"
11. 292-93, quoted from T. Turville Petre, "The Ages of Man in *The Parlement of the Thre Ages*," *Medium Aevum* 46 (1977): 66-76.

56. "Beatus quem cum venerit dominus et pulsaverit," Luke 12: 36-37.

57. "So let him who has not been wakeful in his first watch look to it in his second, so that if he has failed to turn from his wickedness in boyhood, he may at least wake up to the ways of eternal life in the period of his maturity. And let him who has not woken up in his second watch make sure to remedy that in his third, so that if he has not woken up to the ways of eternal life in maturity, he may at least come to his sense in old age." Gregory, *XL Homiliarum in Evangelia*, Bk. I, Hom. 13 (*PL* 76.1125), tr. quoted from J.A. Burrow, *The Ages of Man* (Oxford, 1986) 68.

58. "The Lord comes when he hastens to judgment, and he knocks when he represents to us by afflictions of sickness that death is near" *PL* 76.1124; tr. quoted from Burrow 70.

59. M. de Córdoba, *Compendio de la fortuna* 61-62.

60. "Segund ésta, el fuerte cavallero se pone a la muerte por la causa pública o por defension de su rey; segund ésta, los martires menospreciaron la muerte; segund ésta, el Apóstol deseava morir e ser con Christo. Esta voluntad electiva ha de echar el miedo de la natural voluntad o, si non lo puede echar, templarlo. Dévesle dezir: ¿Para qué themes lo que non puedes escusar? ¿Para qué themes lo ques es tu provecho, que es ser librado de la angustia de este mundo? El cuerpo cárcel es del ánima, pues morir non es sino soltar el preso." M. de Córdoba, *Compendio de la fortuna* 62.

61. See Georges Duby, *Les Trois ordres ou l'imaginaire du féodalisme* (Paris, 1978). Translated by Arthur Goldhammer as *The Three Orders: Feudal Society Imagined* (Chicago, 1980).

62. Georges Duby, "The Diffusion of Cultural Patterns in Feudal Society," in *The Chivalrous Society*, trans. by Cynthia Postan (Berkeley, 1977) 175.

63. The imbalance is common to all works that deal with the medieval conceptions of social structures. Depending on the bias of the author, works that discuss the tripartite nature of society concentrate on the *oratores* or on the *defensores*. The *laboratores* are seldom mentioned.

64. The paradox of victory in defeat, of life in death, is also common to the love lyric. There is a strange echo of don Rodrigo's submission to his destiny in *canción* XX:

> Justa fue mi perdición,
> de mis males soy contento.
> Non espero galardón,
> pues vuestro merescimiento
> satisfizo mi passión.
> Es victoria conocida
> quien de vos queda vencido,
> qu'en perder por vos la vida
> es ganado lo perdido.

> Pues lo consiente razón,
> consiento mi perdimiento
> sin esperar galardón,
> pues vuestro merescimiento
> satisfizo mi passión.
> (*Cancionero* 63)

65. Aristotle divided life into three stages, which could be compared to an arch that mounts and descends. This pattern corresponds to the lexical triads of the poem: *partir, caminar, llegar; nacer, vivir, morir.*

66. Note that the verb *dexar,* like *venir,* functions to advance the narrative of the poem from past to present. Within specific stanzas, *dexar* and *venir* embody the essential characteristics of life and death. Across stanzas, they advance the movement of the poem from the past to the present, and from the general to the specific (for example, stanza sixteen).

67. See Pio Colonnello, "Honra e honrar nelle *Coplas por la muerte de su padre* di Jorge Manrique: Loro ambito semantico," *Annali dell'Istituto Orientale.* (Naples) *Sezione Romanza* 19 (1977): 417-34.

68. Catherine Swietlicki, "Life as a Game: The *Tablero* Image in Jorge Manrique's *Coplas por la muerte de su padre,"* *Kentucky Romance Quarterly* 26 (1979): 433-44.

69. "Este, muriendo, al rey fizo pago, / pues que delante sus ojos fue muerto, / su orden muy bien guardando por çierto / de nuestro patron señor Santiago, / faziendo enlos moros non menos estragos / que los desçendientes de sy de Cadino, / mostrandose bien sin duda sobrino / del noble marques de Buytrago." *Cancionero castellano* 2: 29.

70. Queen Isabel, warned that Alonso de Cárdenas was moving toward Uclés with his men, moved her court from Valladolid to the convent to block the election. She reminded the electors that it was traditional for the post to be held by a member of the royal family and, to avoid dissension, requested that the assembled members ask the Pope to place the administration of the order in Fernando's hands. The king and queen clearly foresaw that a hasty election would lead to internal dissent and to an eventual armed confrontation. They must have had considerable support from within the order, possibly from the Manrique family, who might have seen it as a way of blocking Alonso de Cárdenas's candidacy. The Pope entrusted the king with the administration of the order for six years, but by November of 1477 Fernando must have considered tempers sufficiently cooled to allow the election of a *maestre.* With the obvious approval of the king, Alonso de Cárdenas became the head of the order and was thus rewarded for his support of the royal cause during the war with Portugal. Cárdenas held the post until 1493. The days of the independent *maestres,* however, were numbered. The end of the war in Granada sounded the death knell for the independence of the military orders. By the beginning of the next century, the crown had taken over the direction of all the orders, and in 1523 the papal bull *Dum intra nostrae* allowed the king of Spain to assume the title of *maestre* in perpetuity.

71. Palencia, *Crónica de Enrique IV* 4: 478.

72. Eugene Vance defines the act of commemoration in the epic as "any gesture, ritualized or not, whose end is to invoke, in the name of a social group, some remembered essence or event that is either anterior in time or ontologically prior to what is present, in order to animate, fecundate, mark, or celebrate some moment in the present." Eugene Vance, *Mervelous Signals* 51.

Appendix A

1. Fernán Pérez de Guzmán, *Generaciones y semblanzas*, edited by R.B. Tate (London, 1965) 27.

2. Edited by J. Domínguez Bordona (Madrid, 1923) 97-103.

Appendix B

1. The situation has a proverbial flavor. Celestina when talking about her tavern-hopping with Pármeno's mother says: "entrauamos en la primera tauerna y luego mandaua echar medio açumbre para mojar la boca. Mas a mi cargo que *no le quitaron la toca* por ello, sino cuanto la rayauan en su taja, y andar adelante." *Tragicomedia de Calisto y Melibea*, edited by M. Criado de Val and G.D. Trotter (Madrid, 1970) 74.

2. The "Combite" was first printed in the *Cancionero general* of 1511 and included in all subsequent editions. It also circulated as a chapbook. For this poem, as for other poems of the period, we depend on the rubric it carries in the *Cancionero general* for the identification of the target. The poem does not name doña Elvira.

SELECTED BIBLIOGRAPHY

The following list of manuscripts and early editions of Jorge Manrique's works is substantially derived from Brian Dutton's *Catálogo índice de la poesía cancioneril del siglo XV* (Madison, Wisc., 1982), and Jacqueline Steunou and Lothar Knapp's *Bibliografía de los cancioneros castellanos del siglo XV y repertorio de sus géneros poéticos* 2 vols. (Paris, 1975). We do not list Manrique's poems in editions of the *Cancionero general* subsequent to the princeps or in other sixteenth-century *cancioneros*. We do, however, indicate the new poems added to the 1514 and the 1535 editions of the *Cancionero general*. Dutton or Steunou's manuscript descriptors follow the place and shelflist numbers of manuscripts, or the titles of imprints. When a citation appears in both Dutton and Steunou only Dutton is listed to avoid redundancy or confusion over foliation disagreement between both bibliographies. The place of a poem in the sequence of works in a manuscript or imprint, and the folio(s) or page number(s) where it appears, are given after the first line of the poem. The "General Bibliography" contains works on Jorge and Gómez Manrique. Works of a more general nature used in this study are cited in the notes. Additional bibliographical information about Manrique can be found in Manuel Carrión Gútiez's *Bibliografía de Jorge Manrique 1479-1979* (Palencia, 1979), and Sister Mary Appolonia Matjasic's *The History of the Criticism of Las Coplas de Jorge Manrique* (Madrid, 1979). For editions of later glosses of the poem see works by Nellie Sánchez de Arce and Antonio Pérez Gómez.

MANUSCRIPTS

Coplas por la muerte de su padre

Escorial, monastery K-III-7, Fray Iñigo de Mendoza and others, ca. 1485. [Dutton EM6]. "Recuerde el alma dormida" 15 (215v-255r).
Harvard, Houghton fMS Sp 97, Cancionero de Oñate-Castañeda, ca. 1485. [Dutton HH1]. "Recuerde el alma dormida" 79 (421v-424v) [34 stanzas].
London, British Library Eg. 939-Plut. 541b, ca. 1475. [Dutton LB3]. "Recuerde el alma dormida" 4 (15r-18v) [39 stanzas].
Madrid, Nacional 4114, Cancionero de Pero Guillén de Segovia. Eighteenth-century copy. [Dutton MN19]. "Recuerde el alma dormida" 67 (407r-418r) [31 stanzas].
Madrid, Palacio 617, compiled between 1560-70. [Dutton MP2] "Recuerde el alma dormida" 199 (211r-215r)
Paris, Nationale Esp. 37, Baena, "O," ca. 1445-50. [Dutton PN1c]. "Recuerde el alma dormida" 576c

Minor Lyrics

Barcelona, Universitat Central 151, 1484. [Dutton BU1]. "Quien tanto veros dessea" 36 (82r).
Escorial, monastery K-III-7. [Steunou I: 143]. "Es amor fuerça tan fuerte" 14 (214r-215r).
Evora, Biblioteca Pública cXIV.I.17. [Steunou I: 147]. "Yo soy quien liure me vy" 89 (43r).
London, British Library Add. 10431, ca. 1500. [Dutton LB1] "No se porque me fatigo" 3 (2r); "Pues el tiempo es ya pasado" 170 (50r) [Attrib. to Mena]; "Estos y mis enojos" 250 (81v); "Quien tanto veros dessea" 408 (110r-v).
Madrid, Biblioteca particular de Rodríguez Moñino. [Steunou I: 216]. "Sin Dios sin vos y sin mi" 87 (32r); "Yo soy quien libre me vi" 88 (32r).
Madrid, Nacional 3777, Obras de Garci Sánchez de Badajoz. Dated copy [1843] of a sixteenth-century manuscript. [Dutton MN14]. "Quien no estuviera en presencia" 52 (122); "No se porque me fatigo" 10 (29-30).
Madrid, Nacional 4114. Cancionero de Pero Guillén de Segovia. Eigh-

teenth-century copy. [Dutton MN19]. "Mi saber no es para solo" 45 (351r-v); "Oh muy alto Dios de amor" 65 (399r-404r); "Entre bien y mal doblado" 68 (419r); "Despues que el fuego s'esfuerça" 70 (419v-420r).

Madrid, Nacional 7817, Obras de Gómez Manrique, ca. 1475. [Dutton MN24]. "Mi saber no es para solo" 87 (137r).

Madrid, Palacio 617, compiled between 1560-70. [Dutton MP2] "Justa fue mi perdicion" 113 (163v) [Attrib. to Costana]; "Quien no estuviera en presencia" 134 (166r-v) [Anon.].

Madrid, Palacio 1250, Obras de Gómez Manrique, ca. 1475. [Dutton MP3]. "Mi saber no es para solo" 112 (420-21).

Madrid, Palacio 1335, ca. 1500 with additions until 1520. Cancionero musical de Palacio. [Dutton MP4a]. "Justa fue mi perdicion" 27 (31v-32r).

Modena, Estense Alpha.R.8.9. [Dutton ME1]. "Quien no estuviera en presencia" 8a (22v) [Anon.].

Oxford, All Souls College 189. [Steunou I: 280-1]. "Quien no estuuiere en presencia" 52 (31v); "No se porque me fatigo" 74 (52v); "Es amor fuerça tan fuerte" 104 (72v-73v).

Salamanca, Universitaria 2763. A fifteenth and a sixteenth-century manuscript bound in one volume. [Dutton SA106] "Entre bien y mal doblado" 144 (85r), "No se porque me fatigo" 96-17 (27v).

Segovia, Cathedral [no shelf list number]. musical MS, ca. 1500. [Dutton SG1]. "Justa fue mi perdicion" 164 (207r)

EARLY EDITIONS

Coplas por la muerte de su padre

Fray Iñigo de Mendoza. *Vita Christi*. Zamora(?), 1482(?) [Dutton 82*IM]. "Recuerde el alma dormida" 3 (X1r-X4v).

Fray Iñigo de Mendoza. *Vita Christi*. Zamora(?), Antonio Centenera(?), 1483(?) [Dutton 83*IM]. "Recuerde el alma dormida" 12 (67r-70r).

Fray Iñigo de Mendoza. *Vita Christi*. Zaragoza, Paulo Hurus, 1495. [Dutton 95VC]. "Recuerde el alma dormida" 15 (109r-112r).

Coplas a la muerte de su padre. Salamanca(?), 1483(?). [Dutton 83*JM]. "Recuerde el alma dormida" 1 (1r-4v).

Coplas a la muerte de su padre. Sevilla, Ungut y Polono, 1494. [Dutton 94JM]. "Recuerde el alma dormida."

Cancionero de Ramón de Llavía. Zaragoza, Juan Hurus, 1490-1495(?) [Dutton 94*RL]. "Recuerde el alma dormida" 9 (73r-76r).

Cancionero general (Sevilla, 1535). "Recuerde el alma dormida" (201v).

Coplas (con la glosa de Alonso de Cervantes). Lisbon, Valentim Fernándes, 1501. [Dutton O1JM]. "Recuerde el alma dormida" 1 (3r-20r).

Coplas (con la glosa de Alonso de Cervantes). Toledo, Hagenbach suc., 1505-1510(?). [Dutton 08JM]. "Recuerde el alma dormida" 1 (3r-20r).

Coplas (con la glosa de Alonso de Cervantes). Sevilla, Jacobo Cromberger, 1508-1510(?). [Dutton 09JM]. "Recuerde el alma dormida" 1 (a3r-c4r) [39 stanzas].

Coplas (con la glosa de Alonso de Cervantes). Sevilla, Cromberger, 1511-1512(?). [Dutton 11JM]. "Recuerde el alma dormida" 1 (3r-20r).

Coplas a la muerte de su padre. Sevilla, Cromberger, 1515(?). [Dutton 15JM]. "Recuerde el alma dormida" 1 (1r-4v).

Minor Lyrics

Cancionero general de Hernando del Castillo. Valencia, Cristóbal Kofman, 1511. [Dutton 11CG]. "Con el gran mal que me sobra" 186 (96v-97r); "Ve discreto mensagero" 187 (97r-v); "Yo calle males sufriendo" 188 (97v); "Hallo que ningun poder" 189 (97v); "Calle por mucho temor" 190 (97v-98r); "Pensando señora en vos" 191 (98r); "Es amor fuerça tan fuerte" (98r); "Porqu'el tiempo es ya passado" 193 (98r-v); "Guay d'aquel que nunca atiende" 194 (98v); "Estando triste seguro" 195 (98v-99r); "Ni miento ni m'arrepiento" 196 (99r); "Alla veras mis sentidos" 197 (99r); "Hame tan bien defendido" 198 (99r-v); "En una llaga mortal" 199 (99v-100r); "Vos cometistes traicion" 200 (100r); "Quanto el bien temprar concierta" 201 (100r); "Segun el mal me siguio" 202 (100r); "Los fuegos qu'en mi encendieron" 203 (100r-v); "Que amador tan desdichado" 204 (100v); "Fortuna no m'amenazes" 205 (100v-101r); "Mi temor ha sido tal" 206 (101r); "Ni beuir quiere que biua" 207 (101r-v); "Acordaos por Dios señora" 208 (101v); "Ved que congoxa la mía" 209 (101v-102r); "Con tantos males guerreo" 282 (122r); "No se porque me fatigo" 328 (125r); 94 (203r); "Justa fue mi perdicion" 329 (125r) [Anon.]; "Quien tanto veros dessea" 330 (125r); "Es una muerte escondida" 419 (130r); "Cuanto mas pienso serviros" 420 (130r); "Estos y mis enojos" 516 (141r); "Yo soy quien libre me vi" 597 (143v); "Siempre amar y amor seguir" (143v);

"Quiero pues quiere razón" 598 (143v-144r); "Quien biuiere con su grado" (153r); "Entre dos fuegos lançado" 712 (153r); "Entre bien y mal doblado" 714 (153r); "Despues que el seso s'esfuerça" 719 (153v-154r); "Porque me hiere un dolor" 723 (154r); "Los males que son menores" 726 (154r-v); "Con dolorido cuydado" 876 (185r); "Señora muy acabada" 966 (221r-v); "Hanme dicho que se atreue" 1027 (233v-234r).

Cancionero general de Hernando del Castillo. Valencia, Jorge Costilla, 1514. [Dutton 14CG]. "Cada vez que en mi memoria" 64 (108v); "No tardes muerte que muero" 64 (108v); "Por vuestro gran merescer" 66 (108v); "Justa fue mi perdicion" 123 (139v) [Anon.].

Juan Agraz. *Coplas a Juan Marmolejo, etc.* Burgos, Basilea, 1512-1515(?) [Dutton 14*JA]. "Hanme dicho que se atreve" 3 (4r-v).

Cancionero de Ramón de Llavía "Es amor fuerça tan fuerte" 11 (78r-78v)

Cancioneiro Geral de García de Resende "No se porque me fatigo" 515 (109r)

Pater noster de las mugeres, etc. Toledo, Villaquirán, 1515-1520(?) [Dutton 18*PN]. "Señora muy acabada" 2 (2r-3r).

SOME MODERN EDITIONS

Alda Tesán, Jesús Manuel, ed. *Poesía*. Salamanca, 1965.

Azáceta, José Mª, ed. *Poesía cancioneril*. Barcelona, 1984.

Beltrán, Vicente, ed. *Jorge Manrique: cancionero y Coplas a la muerte de su padre*. Barcelona, 1981.

Caravaggi, Giovanni, ed. *Poesía: Jorge Manrique*. Madrid, 1984.

Cortina, Augusto, ed. *Jorge Manrique: cancionero*. 4th edition. Madrid, 1960.

Foulché-Delbosc, R., ed. *Coplas que fizo Jorge Manrique por la muerte de su padre*. Barcelona, 1902.

———, ed. *Cancionero castellano del siglo XV*. 2 vols. Madrid, 1915. See "Jorge Manrrique" 2: 228-56.

Santiago, Miguel, ed. *Jorge Manrique: obra completa*. Madrid, 1975.

Serrano de Haro, Antonio, ed. *Jorge Manrique: obras*. Madrid, 1986.

Smerdou Altolaguirre, Margarita, ed. *Poesía*. Madrid, 1975.

Suñén, Luis, ed. *Jorge Manrique*. Madrid, 1980.

GENERAL BIBLIOGRAPHY

Aaron, M. Audrey. "Manrique and Cardenal: No elegía sino alegría." *Proceedings of the Pacific Northwest Conference on Foreign Languages* 26 (1975): 184-91.

Acosta Polo, Benigno. "Jorge Manrique o la novedad de lo eterno." *Bolívar* (Colombia) 12 (1952): 325-40.

Alamo Salazar, A. "¿Cuándo escribió Jorge Manrique las *Coplas a la muerte de su padre?*" *El diario Palentino*, Nov. 13, 1976.

Allue y Morer, Fernando. *De Jorge Manrique a Jorge Guillén*. Malaga, 1971.

———. "Leyendo a Jorge Manrique." *Poesía hispánica* 285 (1976): 10-13.

Alonso, Martín. *Segundo estilo de Bécquer*. Madrid, 1972. See "Jorge Manrique y Bécquer, poetas intemporales" 216-23.

———. *Evolución sintáctica del español*, 3rd ed. Madrid, 1972. See "La sintaxis intemporal desde Jorge Manrique a Góngora" 234-95.

Alonso Cortés, Narciso. *Sumandos biográficos*. Valladolid, 1939. See "Gómez Manrique" 9-20.

Alvarez Martínez, María Angeles. *Formas de contenido literario de un tema manriqueño*. La Laguna, 1984.

Antolín, G. "Sobre el traductor latino de las 'Coplas de Jorge Manrique'." *Revue hispanique* 14 (1906): 22-34. Also in *La ciudad de Dios* 138 (1924): 241-65.

Antonio, Nicolás. *Bibliotheca Hispana Vetus*. 2 vols. Madrid, 1778. See "Georgius Manriquius" 2: 342, no. 856; and "Gomezius Manriquius" 2: 342-44.

Astrana Marín, Luis. *El cortejo de Minerva*. Madrid, n.d. See "Jorge Manrique: sus *Coplas* y sus glosas" 58-64.

Aubrun, Charles V. "La mort du père (*Coplas de Jorge Manrique*). Structure et signification." In *Culture et marginalités au XVIe siècle. Mélanges offerts à Pierre Le Gentil. Documents et travaux de l'équipe de recherche culture et société au XVIe siècle*. Edited by José Luis Alonso Hernández, et al. Paris, 1973. 1: 75-84.

Baquero, Gastón. "Jorge Manrique en América." *Poesía hispánica* 288 (1976): 8-12.

Basave, Agustín. "Fondo y forma en las *Coplas* de Manrique." *La nueva democracia* 36 (1956): 41-47.

Bayo, Marcial José. "Nota sobre *La Celestina*." *Clavileño* 1, no. 5 (1950): 48-53.

192   *Bibliography*

Bell, Alan S. "Tradition and Pedro Salinas' Original Approach to Jorge Manrique." *South Atlantic Bulletin* 39 (1974): 38-42.

Benigno Flórez, Manuel. "Vísperas de las *Coplas.*" In *Tertulia 76.* Palencia, 1976. 9-12.

Benítez Claros, Rafael. "El diálogo en la poesía medieval." *Cuadernos de literatura* 5 (1949): 171-87. See 185f on the *Coplas.*

Benito Ruano, Eloy. "Algunas rentas de Jorge Manrique." *Hispania* (Madrid) 25 (1965): 113-19.

———. "Autógrafos de Jorge Manrique." *Archivum* 18 (1968): 107-16.

———. "Un episodio bélico (y un autógrafo de Jorge Manrique)." In *Estudios dedicados al profesor D. Angel Ferrari Núñez* [*En la España medieval*, 4] 2 vols. Edited by Miguel Ladero Quesada. Madrid, 1984. 1: 139-46.

Bergara, E.P. *Jorge Manrique. Fuentes bíblicas de sus Coplas.* Montevideo, 1945.

Blanco White, Joseph. *Variedades, o mensagero de Londres.* London, 1823/24. See "Noticia de don Jorge Manrique" 1: 148-58.

Blecua, José Manuel. "Los grandes poetas del siglo XV." In *Historia general de las literaturas hispánicas.* Edited by Guillermo Díaz Plaja. Barcelona, 1951. 2: 116-26.

Borello, Rodolfo A. "Las *Coplas* de Jorge Manrique: estructura y fuentes." *Cuadernos de filología* 1 (1967): 49-72.

———. "Para la historia del *ubi sunt.*" In *Lengua, literatura, folklore: estudios dedicados a Rodolfo Oroz.* Edited by Gastón Carrillo Herrera. Santiago de Chile, 1967. 81-92.

———. "El *ubi sunt* en la poesía española antes del siglo XV." *Cuadernos de filología* 6 (1972): 87-117.

Borghini, V. *Giorgio Manrique. La sua poesia e i suoi tempi.* Genoa, 1952. Rev. by J. de Entrambasaguas in *Revista de literatura* 2 (1952): 455.

Buceta, E. "Dos papeletas referentes a las *Coplas* de Jorge Manrique." *Bulletin hispanique* 29 (1927): 407-12.

Burkart, Rosemarie. "Leben, Tod und Jenseits bei Jorge Manrique und François Villon." In *Kölner Romanistische Arbeiten I.* Marburg, 1931.

———. "Methodisches zu Curtius' Aufsatz 'Jorge Manrique und der Kaisergedanke'." *Zeitschrift für Romanische Philologie* 55 (1935): 187-93.

Cabada Gómez, Manuel. "El personaje oyente en las *Coplas a la muerte de su padre* de Jorge Manrique." *Cuadernos hispanoamericanos* 335 (1978): 325-32.

Camacho Guisado, Eduardo. *La elegía funeral en la poesía española.* Madrid, 1969.

Cangiotti, Gualterio. *Le Coplas di Manrique tra medioevo e umanesimo.* Bologna, 1964.

Caravaca, Francisco. "Estudio de ocho coplas de Jorge Manrique en relación con la traducción inglesa de Longfellow." *Boletín de la Biblioteca Menéndez Pelayo* 51 (1975): 3-90.

———. "Estudios manriqueños. Notas sobre el título: *'Coplas' de Jorge Manrique 'a la' muerte de su padre."* *La torre* 73/74 (1971): 185-221.

———. "Foulché-Delbosc y su edición 'crítica' de las *Coplas* de Jorge Manrique." *Boletín de la Biblioteca Menéndez Pelayo* 49 (1973): 229-79.

———. "Notas sobre las llamadas 'coplas póstumas' de Jorge Manrique." *Boletín de la Biblioteca Menéndez Pelayo* 50 (1974): 89-135.

———. "El paralelo Villón-Manrique." *Neophilologus* 50 (1966): 59-76.

———. "La qasida de Abu'l Baqa, el Rondeño, y algunas coplas de Jorge Manrique." *Boletín de la Biblioteca Menéndez Pelayo* 46 (1970): 171-259.

———. "¿Quién fue el autor del retrato de Jorge Manrique?" *Papeles de son Armadans* 65, no. 193 (1972): 89-99.

Caravaggi, Iovanni. "Nota Manriquina." *Studi di litteratura spagnola* (Rome, 1966): 155-67.

Carrilla, Miguel. "Las *Coplas* de Manrique en versos americanos." *Boletín del Instituto de Cultura Latinoamericana de la facultad de filosofía y letras.* (Buenos Aires) 8, no. 48 (1944): 487-92.

Carrión Gutiéz, Manuel. *Bibliografía de Jorge Manrique 1479-1979.* Palencia, 1979.

———. "Gómez Manrique y el protonotario Lucena: Dos cartas con memoria de Jorge Manrique." *Revista de archivos, bibliotecas y museos* 81 (1978): 565-82.

Carrizo, Juan Alfonso. *Antecedentes hispanomedievales de la poesía tradicional argentina.* Buenos Aires, 1945. See pages 128 and 283 on glosses of "Siempre amar y amor seguir" and "Sin vos y sin Dios y mí."

Castañón, Jesús. "Cara y cruz de las *Coplas* de Jorge Manrique." *Publicaciones de la Institución Tello Téllez de Meneses* 35 (1975): 141-73.

Castro, Américo. "Cristianismo, Islam, poesía en Jorge Manrique." *Papeles de son Armadans* 9 (1958): 121-40. Reprinted in his *Origen y ser de los españoles.* Madrid, 1959. 70-86.

———. *Hacia Cervantes.* Madrid, 1960. See "Muerte y belleza: un recuerdo a Jorge Manrique" 83-89. Reprinted in his *Semblanzas y estudios españoles*. Princeton, 1956. 45-51.

Cepeda Calzada, Pablo. "En la coyuntura de un centenario. Nueva recordación de las *Coplas* de Jorge Manrique." *El diario Palentino*. Sept. 4, 1976.

———. "Evocación de Jorge Manrique." *Publicaciones del Instituto Tello Téllez de Meneses* 28 (1969): 25-43.

Cernuda, Luis. "Tres poetas metafísicos. Jorge Manrique, Francisco de Aldana, y el autor de la *Epístola moral*." *Bulletin of Hispanic Studies* 25 (1948): 109-18. Also printed in *Insula* 3 (1948): 1, and in his *Poesía y literatura*. Barcelona, 1965. 55-64.

Chediac, Abelardo. "La elegía de Abulbeca y las *Coplas* de Jorge Manrique." *América española* 19, no. 65 (1956): 65.

Colonnello, Pio. "Honra e honrar nelle *Coplas por la muerte de su padre* di Jorge Manrique: Loro ambito semantico." *Annali dell'Istituto Orientale*. (Naples) *Sezione romanza* 19 (1977): 417-34.

Correa, Gustavo. "Lenguaje y ritmo en las *Coplas de Jorge Manrique a la muerte de su padre*." *Hispania* 63 (1980): 184-94.

Cossío, José María. "Mensaje de Jorge Manrique." *Escorial* 1 (1940): 337-40.

———. "El mote 'sin mi, sin vos y sin Dios' glosado por Lope de Vega." *Revista de filología española* 20 (1933): 397-400.

Cummins, John G. "Pero Guillén de Segovia y el MS 4.114." *Hispanic Review* 41 (1973): 6-32.

Curtius, Ernst R. "Jorge Manrique und der Kaisergedanke." *Zeitschrift für Romanische Philologie* 52 (1932): 129-52. Reprinted in his *Gesammelte Aufsätze zur Romanischen Philologie*. Berne and Munich, 1960. 353-72.

Danker, Frederick A. "The *Coplas* of Jorge Manrique." *Boston Public Library Quarterly* 10 (1958): 164-67.

Darbord, Michel. "Sur deux allegories des *Coplas* de Jorge Manrique: Les fleuves et le chemin." *Ibérica* 1 (1977): 81-88.

Darst, David H. "Poetry and Politics in Jorge Manrique's *Coplas por la muerte de su padre*." *Medievalia et Humanistica* 13 (1985): 197-203.

Del Monte, Alberto. "Chiosa alle *Coplas* di Jorge Manrique." *Quaderni-iberoamericani* 31 (1965): 61-79.

Díaz, Ramón. "La cortesía de Jorge Manrique con la muerte." *Papeles de son Armadans* 60, no. 178 (1971): 139-48.

Díez de Revenga, Francisco. "Dos aspectos del tema de la muerte en la literatura del siglo XV." *Anales de la Universidad de Murcia* 29 (1970/71): 95-117.

Domínguez Rey, Antonio. "El otro Jorge Manrique." *La estafeta literaria* 612 (1977): 10-13.

Dornseiff, Y.F. "Das Geheimnis der Form von Manriques *Coplas* und Villons *Ballade*." *Zeitschrift für französische Sprache und Literatur* 64 (1942): 170-74.

Dunn, Peter N. "Themes and Images in the *Coplas por la muerte de su padre* of Jorge Manrique." *Medium Aevum* 33 (1964): 169-83.

Fernández Alonso, María del Rosario. *Una visión de la muerte en la lírica española: La muerte como amada*. Madrid, 1971.

Ferrer, José. "Las eternas *Coplas* de Jorge Manrique." *Asomante* 3 (1947): 76-87.

Flasche, Hans. "Die Deixis in den *Coplas q[ue] fizo don Jorge Manrique a la muerte del maestre de Santiago don Rodrigo Manrique su padre*." In *Sprache und Mensch in der Romania*. Edited by E. Ernst and A. Stefenelli. Wiesbaden, 1979. 61-79.

Foulché-Delbosc, R. "La traduction latine des *Coplas* de Jorge Manrique." *Revue hispanique* 15 (1906): 9-21.

García Alvarez, Emilio. "Del morir y de la muerte en las *Coplas* de Jorge Manrique." *Ciencia tomista* 106 (1979): 303-18.

García Berrios, A. "Una nueva lectura de las *Coplas* de Jorge Manrique." *Convivium* 33 (1965): 641-43.

García Fuentes, María Cruz. "Pervivencia horaciana en Jorge Manrique." *Cuadernos de filología clásica* 9 (1975): 201-11.

Gatti, J.F. "El *ubi sunt* en la prosa medieval española." *Filología* 8 (1962): 105-21.

Gillín y Aguirre, Tomás. *Sencillos comentarios a las Coplas de Jorge Manrique*. Bilbao, 1927.

Gilman, Stephen. "Tres retratos de la muerte en las *Coplas* de Jorge Manrique." *Nueva revista de filología hispánica* 13 (1959): 305-24.

Gimeno Casalduero, Joaquín. "Jorge Manrique y Fray Luis de León (Cicerón y San Gregorio)." *Actas del séptimo congreso de la Asociación Internacional de Hispanistas*. Rome, 1982. 1: 553-60.

———. *La creación literaria de la edad media y del renacimiento*. Madrid, 1977. See "San Jerónimo y el rechazo y la aceptación de la poesía en la Castilla de finales del siglo XV" 45-57.

Gómez Galán, Antonio. "Contribución al estudio de las *Coplas* de Jorge Manrique." *Arbor* 45, no. 170 (1960): 56-71.

Guillén Villena, Benilde. "El tiempo en la poesía española." In *Estudios literarios dedicados al profesor Mario Baquero Goyanes*. Edited by Victorino Polo García. Murcia, 1974. 157-74.

Hart, Catherine. "La circularidad del canto: En torno a dos 'coplas' de Jorge Manrique." *Hispanic Journal* 1 (1979): 17-20.

Hatzfeld, Helmut A. "Esthetic Criticism Applied to Medieval Literature." *Romance Philology* 1 (1948): 305-27. See "Villon and Manrique" 322.

Ibáñez Garrido, D. "Las *Coplas* de Jorge Manrique." *La ciudad de Dios* 119 (1919): 9-11, 134-50; 120 (1920): 440-49.

Ibérico y Rodríguez, Mariano. *Jorge Manrique, poeta de la añoranza.* Lima, 1951.

Janner, Hans. "La glosa española. Estudio histórico de su métrica y de sus temas." *Revista de filología española* 27 (1943): 181-232.

Javierre Mur, Aurea L. "Fernando el Católico y las órdenes militares españolas." In *Vida y obra de Fernando el Católico.* Edited by A. de la Torre, et al. Zaragoza, 1955. 287-300.

Kinkade, Richard P. "The Historical Date of the *Coplas* and the Death of Jorge Manrique." *Speculum* 45 (1970): 216-24.

Krause, Anna. *Jorge Manrique and the Cult of Death in the Cuatrocientos.* Berkeley: Publications of the University of California at Los Angeles in Languages and Literatures 1, 1937, 79-176. Also published as "Jorge Manrique y el culto de la muerte en el cuatrocientos." *Anales de la Universidad de Chile* 1128, no. 117 (1960): 7-60.

Labrador, J., A. Zorita, and R.A. Difranco. "Cuarenta y dos, y no cuarenta coplas en la famosa elegía manriqueña." *Boletín de la Biblioteca Menéndez Pelayo* 61 (1985): 37-95.

Lapesa, Rafael. "Poesía docta y afectividad en las *consolatorias* de Gómez Manrique." In *Estudios sobre literatura y arte dedicados al profesor Emilio Orozco Díaz.* Edited by A. Gallego Morell, Andrés Soria, and Nicolás Marín. 2 vols. Granada, 1979. 2: 231-39.

Lapidus, Nejama. "Contribución a la crítica manriqueña." *Humanidades* (La Plata) 27 (1939): 221-57.

Leal de Martínez, María Teresa. *Gómez Manrique: su tiempo y su obra.* Recife, 1959.

Lemartinel, J. "Sur trois coplas de Jorge Manrique." *Cahiers de poétique et poésie iberique et latino américaine* 1 (1976): 68-74.

Liborio, M. "Contributi alla storia dell'*ubi sunt.*" *Cultura neolatina* 20 (1960): 114-209.

Lida de Malkiel, María Rosa. "Una copla de Jorge Manrique y la tradición de Filón en la literatura española." *Revista de filología hispánica* 4 (1942): 152-71. Reprinted in *Estudios sobre la literatura del siglo XV.* Madrid, 1977. 145-78.

———. *La idea de la fama en la edad media castellana.* Mexico, 1952.

————. "Para la primera de las *Coplas de don Jorge Manrique por la muerte de su padre*." *Romance Philology* 16 (1962): 170-73. Reprinted in *La tradición clásica en España*. Barcelona, 1975. 201-06.

Linage Conde, Antonio. "Tipología de la vida religiosa en las órdenes militares." *Actas del congreso internacional hispano-portugués sobre las órdenes militares en la península durante la edad media: (29 de marzo-9 de abril de 1971)*. Madrid and Barcelona, 1981. 33-58.

Lluch Mora, Francisco. *La huella de cuatro poetas del cancionero en las Coplas de Jorge Manrique*. Yanco, Puerto Rico, 1964.

Lomax, Derek. "¿Cuándo murió don Jorge Manrique?" *Revista de filología española* 55 (1972): 61-62.

López Estrada, Francisco. *Los "primitivos" de Manuel y Antonio Machado*. Madrid, 1977. See "Manrique, poeta del tiempo" 179-206.

————. "Nueva lectura de la *Representación del nacimiento de Nuestro Señor*, de Gómez Manrique," *Atti del IV Colloquio della Société Internationale pour l'Etude du Théâtre Médiéval*. Viterbo, July 10-15, 1983. 423-44.

López González, V. "La salvación del mundo en las *Coplas* de Jorge Manrique y en la *Crónica del condestable Miguel Lucas de Iranzo*. Una generación de poética de hombres barrocos." *La ciudad de Dios* 155 (1943): 433-53.

Lorentzen, Eva. "En av verdens-litteraturens store elegier." *Kirke og Kultur* 71 (1966): 153-59.

Lucero, Dolly. "Aspecto de la lírica cortesana del siglo XV: Asedio a la poesía amorosa de Jorge Manrique." *Cuadernos de filología* 6 (1972): 137-62.

Maetzu, Ramiro de. *La brevedad de la vida en nuestra poesía lírica*. Madrid, 1935.

Mancini, Guido. "Esquema para una lectura de las *Coplas* de Jorge Manrique." *La palabra y el hombre: revista de la Universidad Veracruzana* 17 (1976): 55-63.

————. "Schema per una lettura delle *Coplas* di Jorge Manrique." *Prohemio* 1 (1970): 7-18.

Manrique, Gómez. *Cancionero*. 2 vols. In *Colección de escritores castellanos*. Edited by Antonio Paz y Melia. Vols. 36 and 39. Madrid, 1885.

————. *Regimento de príncipes y otras obras*. Edited by Augusto Cortina. Buenos Aires, 1947.

Márquez, C. Humberto. "Jorge Manrique y su contexto histórico." *Meridiano* (Pasto), no. 10/11 (1971): 37-52.

Martín de Nicolás Cabo, Juan. "La Mancha santiaguista según los libros de visitas (1480-1511)." *Actas del congreso internacional hispano-portugués sobre las órdenes militares en la península durante la edad media: (29 de marzo-9 de abril de 1971)*. Madrid and Barcelona, 1981. 469-91.

Martín Descalzo, José Luis. "La tercera vida." *ABC*, 23 Jan. 1977: 32.

Martín Jiménez, José. "Filiación de los linajes de Jorge Manrique (consideraciones sobre el lugar de su nacimiento, su fisonomía moral y su personalidad literaria)." *Boletín de la Real Academia de Córdoba de Ciencia, Bellas Letras y Nobles Artes* 38 (1969 [1972]): 183-207.

Martínez Esteruelas, Cruz. "Jorge Manrique, poeta cristiano." *Estudios de Deusto* 15 (1967): 121-34.

Martínez Ruíz, Florencio. "Manrique se llora a sí mismo." *ABC*, 23 Jan. 1977: 33.

Martínez Villada, Jorge. "Jorge Manrique." *Revista de la Universidad de Córdoba* 39 (195): 1065-90.

Matjasic, Sister Mary Appolonia. *The History of the Criticism of Las Coplas de Jorge Manrique*. Madrid, 1979.

Mendoza Negrillo, Juan de Dios. *Fortuna y providencia en la literatura castellana del siglo XV*. Madrid, 1973. 266-77.

Menéndez Pelayo, M. *Antología de poetas líricos castellanos*. 13 vols. Madrid, 1890-1908. See 6: 104-151.

———. *Antología de poetas líricos castellanos*. Part I: *La poesía en la edad media*. Santander, 1944. See 2: 379-421.

———. "Jorge Manrique." *La España moderna* 84 (1895): 16-62.

Mercado Egea, Joaquín. *Jorge Manrique y Garcilaso (Glosas Giennenses)*. Jaen, 1980.

Mesa poética de Castilla y León en honor de Jorge Manrique. Palencia, 1974.

Michaëlis de Vasconcellos, Carolina. " 'Recuerde el alma dormida.' Duas palavras ao auctor da *Antología de poetas líricos*. III, 100-16; VI CIV-CLI." *Revue hispanique* 6 (1899): 148-62.

Moglia, Paul. "Manrique en un soneto de Boscán." *Revista de filología hispánica* 7 (1945): 392-93.

Morales, Ambrosio de. "Noticias históricas sacadas del archivo de Uclés." In *Opúsculos castellanos*. Edited by Francisco Valerio Cifuentes. Madrid, 1793. 2: 24.

Morales Pino, Augusto. "Jorge Manrique y sus coplas inmortales." *Boletín cultural y bibliográfico* 16 (1979): 173-80.

Moreno Báez, Enrique. "El gótico nominalista y las *Coplas* de Jorge Manrique." *Revista de filología española* 53 (1970): 95-113.

Moreno Castillo, Enrique. "Vida y muerte en las *Coplas* de Jorge Manrique." *Papeles de son Armadans* 82 (1976): 133-61.

Morreale, Margherita. "Apuntes para el estudio de la trayectoria que desde el *¿ubi sunt?* lleva hasta el '¿Qué le fueron sino . . . ?' de Jorge Manrique." *Thesaurus* 30 (1975): 471-519.

Muñoz González, Luis. "Jorge Manrique y la memoria de su trascendencia." *Estudios filológicos* 16 (1981): 35-49.

Nader, Helen. *The Mendoza Family in the Spanish Renaissance, 1350-1550.* New Brunswick, N.J., 1979.

Navarro, Genaro. "Segura de la Sierra, lugar de nacimiento de Jorge Manrique." *Boletín del Instituto de Estudios Giennenses* (Jaén) 11 (1965): 9-18.

Navarro Tomás, Tomás. "Métrica de las *Coplas* de Jorge Manrique." *Nueva revista de filología hispánica* 15 (1961): 169-79. Reprinted in his *Los poetas en sus versos: desde Jorge Manrique a García Lorca.* Barcelona, 1973.

Nieto, J. *Estudio biográfico de Jorge Manrique e influencia de sus obras en la literatura española.* Madrid, 1902.

Orduna, Germán. "Las *Coplas* de Jorge Manrique y el triunfo sobre la muerte: Estructura e intencionalidad." *Romanische Forschungen* 79 (1968): 139-51.

Ortega, Teófilo. *La voz del paisaje.* Burgos, 1928.

Ortiz, R. " 'Recuerde el alma dormida' di Jorge Manrique, et sua analisi estetica." In *Fortuna Labilis. Storia di un motivo medieval.* Bucarest, 1927.

Palencia Flores, Clemente. *El poeta Gómez Manrique, corregidor de Toledo.* Toledo, 1943.

Palumbo, Pietro. "L'ordine delle strofe nelle *Coplas por la muerte de su padre* di Jorge Manrique." *Medioevo romanzo* 8 (1981-83): 193-215.

———. "Sull'interpretazione de alcuni luoghi delle *Coplas* di Jorge Manrique." *Medioevo romanzo* 9 (1984): 403-20.

Panceira, Julio. "Jorge Manrique y su tiempo." *Boletín del Instituto de Investigaciones Literarias de la Universidad del Plata* 1 (1937): 119-85.

Pérez Gómez, Antonio, ed. *Glosas a las Coplas de Jorge Manrique.* 6 vols. Cieza, 1961-63.

———. *Glosas a las Coplas de Jorge Manrique: Noticias bibliográficas.* Cieza, 1963.

———. "Notas para la bibliografía de Fray Iñigo de Mendoza y de Jorge Manrique." *Hispanic Review* 27 (1959): 30-41.

————. "La primera versión impresa de las *Coplas* de Jorge Manrique, Zaragoza s.a. (1482-1483)." *Gutenberg-Jahrbuch* 40 (1965): 93-95.

Petriconi, H. "Algo más sobre las *Coplas* de Jorge Manrique." *Investigación y progreso* 7 (1933): 356-58.

————. "El argumento de las *Coplas* de Jorge Manrique." *Investigación y progreso* 6 (1932): 151-53.

————. "Villons *Ballade* und Manriques *Coplas.*" *Zeitschrift für französische Sprache und Literatur* 59 (1935): 343-60.

Piccioto, Robert S. "Meditaciones rurales de una mentalidad urbana: El tiempo, Bergson y Manrique en un poema de Antonio Machado." *La torre* 12 (1964): 141-50.

Pinna, Mario. "Didattismo e poeticità nelle *Coplas para el Sr. Diego Arias* di Gómez Manrique." *Annali dell'Istituto Orientale.* (Naples) *Sezione romanza* 24 (1982): 135-42.

————. "Echi delle *Coplas* de Jorge Manrique nella poesia contemporánea." *Filología moderna* 3 (1962): 89-99.

————. "Jorge Guillén: Que van a dar en la mar. Buenos Aires, 1960." *Quaderni ibero-americani* 32 (1965/66): 443-49.

Portnoy, A. "Universalidad de los sentimientos que predominan en las *Coplas* de Jorge Manrique." *Proteo* (La Plata) 9 (1927): 26-41.

Post, Chandler Rathfon. *Medieval Spanish Allegory.* Cambridge, 1915. 273-74.

Pretel Marín, Aurelio. *Una ciudad castellana en los siglos XIV y XV (Alcaraz, 1300-1375).* Albacete, 1978.

Prieto, Adolfo. "El sentimiento de la muerte a través de la literatura española." *Revista de literatura moderna* (Mendoza) 2 (1960): 115-70.

Renedo Martín, Agustín. *Escritores palentinos.* Madrid, 1919. 2: 44-64.

Rennert, H.A. "Der Spanische Cancionero des Brit. Museums (MS. add. 10431)." *Romanische Forschungen* 10 (1899): 1-176.

Rey, Jose Mª del. *Ensayos sobre poesía.* Montevideo, 1956. See "Manrique o el tiempo" 87-110.

Rico, Francisco. "Unas coplas de Jorge Manrique y las fiestas de Valladolid en 1428." *Anuario de estudios medievales* 2 (1965): 515-24.

Rivera, M. Milagros. "Dos presupuestos de reparación de la muralla de Uclés a fines de la edad media (1494-1525)." *Actas del congreso internacional hispano-portugués sobre las órdenes militares en la península durante la edad media: (29 de marzo-9 de abril de 1971).* Madrid and Barcelona, 1981. 465-67.

Rodríguez, Conrado. "El teatro religioso de Gómez Manrique." *Religión y cultura* 27 (1934): 327-42.

Rodríguez Puértolas, Julio. "La literatura del siglo XV y *Las cortes de la muerte." Revista de literatura* 33 (1968): 103-10.

———. "Jorge Manrique y la manipulación de la historia." In *Medieval and Renaissance Studies in Honour of Robert Brian Tate.* Edited by Ian Michael and Richard A. Cardwell. Oxford, 1986. 123-33.

Rodríguez Salcedo, Severino, Ramón Revilla Vielva, and Arcadio Tous Martín. "Calabazanos a la vista. La Reina Católica y los Manrique. Nuevos datos." *Publicaciones de la Institución Tello Téllez de Meneses* 6 (1951): 347.

Round, Nicholas G. "Formal Integration in Jorge Manrique's *Coplas por la muerte de su padre."* In *Readings in Spanish and Portuguese Poetry for Geoffrey Connell.* Ed. by Nicholas G. Round. Glasgow, 1985. 205-21.

Salazar y Castro, Luis de. *Los comendadores de la Orden de Santiago.* Prólogo del marqués de Ciadoncha. 2 vols. Madrid, 1949.

———. *Historia genealógica de la Casa de Lara.* Madrid, 1697.

Salinas, Pedro. *Jorge Manrique o tradición y originalidad.* 4th ed. Buenos Aires, 1970. Rev. *Bulletin hispanique* 51 (1949): 58-63.

———. "Una metáfora en tres tiempos." In *Ensayos de literatura hispánica.* Edited by Juan Marichal. 3rd ed. Madrid, 1967. 177-92.

Sánchez Arce, Nellie E. "Las glosas a las Coplas de Jorge Manrique." *Clavileño* 7 (1956): 45-50.

———. *Las glosas a las Coplas de Jorge Manrique.* Madrid, 1956.

Sánchez Ferlosio, Rafael. *Las semanas del jardín.* Madrid, 1974. See "El caso Manrique" 211-64.

Santiago, Miguel. "Jorge Manrique o la sola frescura original. Luis Pérez, protonotario de Felipe II, natural de Portillo, glosador erudito y pedante." *Diario regional* (Valladolid), 22 Dec. 1971.

———. "La poesía burlesca, un ambiente inédito en la obra de Jorge Manrique." *Publicaciones de la Institución Tello Téllez de Meneses* 40 (1977): 207-16; 41 (1978): 217-26.

Sarrias, Cristóbal. "Jorge Manrique, quinientos años." *Razón y fé* 199 (1979): 523-24.

Scholberg, Kenneth R. *Introducción a la poesía de Gómez Manrique.* Madison, 1984.

Senabre, Ricardo. "La primera edición de las 'Coplas' de Jorge Manrique." In *Serta philologica F. Lázaro Carreter.* Edited by Emilio Alarcos, et al. Madrid, 1983. 2: 509-17.

Serrano de Haro, Antonio. "Un combite que hizo don Jorge Manrique a su madrastra." In *Libro-Homenaje a Antonio Pérez Gómez*. Cieza, 1978. 203-17.

―――. *Personalidad y destino de Jorge Manrique*. Madrid, 1966.

Sieber, Harry. "Dramatic Symmetry in Gómez Manrique's *La representación del nacimiento de Nuestro Señor*." *Hispanic Review* 33 (1965): 118-35.

―――. "Sobre la fecha de la muerte de Gómez Manrique." *Boletín de la Biblioteca Menéndez Pelayo* 59 (1983): 5-10.

Silverman, Joseph. "Concerning the *arraval de senectud* in Manrique's *Coplas por la muerte de su padre*." In *Studies in Honor of Everett W. Hesse*. Edited by William C. McCrary and José A. Madrigal. Lincoln, Neb., 1981. 135-41.

Sorrento, Luigi. *Jorge Manrique*. Palermo, 1946.

―――. *La poesia e i problemi della poesia di Jorge Manrique*. Palermo, 1941.

―――. "Nel quinto centenario di Jorge Manrique, l'essemplare del poeta e del soldato christiano della Spagna." In *Italia e Spagna. Saggi sui rapporti storice, filosofici ed artistici tra le due civiltà*. Florence, 1941. 123-54.

Spitzer, Leo. "Dos observaciones sintáctico-estilísticas a las *Coplas* de Manrique." *Nueva revista de filología hispánica* 4 (1950): 12-24.

―――. "Etude ahistorique d'un texte." *Modern Language Quarterly* 1 (1940): 7-22.

Swietlicki, Catherine. "Life as a Game: The Tablero Image in Jorge Manrique's *Coplas por la muerte de su padre*." *Kentucky Romance Quarterly* 26 (1979): 433-44.

Teresa León, Tomas, and Alejandro Nájera. "Fichero de nuestra historia a través de los archivos: Cartas de don Rodrigo Manrique a la villa de Paredes de Nava." *El diario Palentino*. 18 August 1944: 3.

―――. "Paredes rinde pleito homenaje al conde don Rodrigo Manrique." *El diario Palentino*. 11 August 1944: 3.

Tomé, Eustaquio. *Comentarios a las Coplas*. n.p., 1930.

Trend, J.B. "Musical settings of famous poets." *Revue hispanique* 71 (1927): 547-54.

Uriarte Rebauldi, Lía. "Sentido de la vida y de la muerte en las *Coplas* de Manrique." *Comunicaciones de literatura española* no. 1-3 (1972): 19-27.

Villena, Luis Antonio de. *Dados, amor y clérigos. El mundo de los goliardos en la edad media europea*. Madrid, 1978. 144-62.

Villoslada, Ricardo G., S.I. "El tema del *ubi sunt*: Nuevas aportaciones." *Miscelánea Comillas* 45 (1966): 5-114.

Viñas de San Luis, P. Tomás. "*Coplas* de Jorge Manrique en latín y castellano." *Revista de archivos, bibliotecas y museos* 47 (1926): 125-39 and 405.

Vinci, Joseph. "The Petrarchan Source of Jorge Manrique's *Las Coplas*." *Itálica* 45 (1969): 413-28.

Ward, Robert S. "An interpretation of *A Psalm of Life* with reference to Manrique's *Coplas*." In *South Atlantic Studies for Sturgis E. Leavitt.* Edited by Thomas B. Stroup and Sterling Stoudemire. Washington, D.C., 1953. 191-98.

Whyte, Florence. *The Dance of Death in Spain and in Catalonia*. Baltimore, 1931.

Yndurain, Domingo. "Los poetas mayores del XV (Mena, Santillana, Manrique)." In *Historia de la literatura española*. Edited by José María Díez Borque. Madrid, 1974. 450-61.

Zambrano, María. *Pensamiento y poesía en la vida española*. Mexico City, 1939. "See Jorge Manrique" 115-24.

Zimic, Stanislav. "El teatro religioso de Gómez Manrique (1412-1491)." *Boletín de la Real Academia Española* 57 (1977): 353-400.

INDEX

Jorge Manrique was the greatest poet of fifteenth-century Castile and one of the three or four greatest in Spanish literature. Frank A. Domínguez offers here an introduction to Manrique's poetry and the first book-length study of him in English in fifty years.

After presenting the biographical and historical context of Manrique's poetry, Domínguez examines the poet's love lyrics, describing the large fund of commonplaces and forms that Manrique's verses share with those of other poets of his age. Manrique's highly stylized language and parallel verse structures express the obsession of the lover with the beloved. Morever, his attention to parallel constructions, to language patterning, and to the expressive quality of his lyric verse, Domínguez shows, prepared the poet for the creation of the *Coplas* on the death of his father, his major work and a poem that has come to be recognized as one of the world's greatest.

In treating the *Coplas*, Domínguez not only offers a sensitive reading of the elegy but also examines questions of text, structure, and style. Like the love lyrics, the *Coplas* presents a high incidence of parallel structures that make for clarity and symmetry. Domínguez also finds that the complex stylistic relationships of the verses provide the *Coplas* with a unity that is deeper and more fundamental than has generally been perceived.

This study, eclectic in its critical approaches, will be the standard English work on Manrique for years to come.